THE COMPLETE
BOOK OF
SPIRITUAL
ASTROLOGY

About the Author

Per Henrik Gullfoss (Norway) is an internationally known astrologer who has run the first astrological school in Norway for the last 15 years. He has been a professional astrologer for 25 years and is also a lecturer and published author. His critically acclaimed book, *Your Starsign*, was a bestseller in Norway. In addition, he has published several other books on astrology, tarot and other spiritual development topics in Scandinavia.

With his extensive knowledge of astrology, mythology, spirituality and religion, Gullfoss has inspired listeners and readers throughout the world. *The Complete Book of Spiritual Astrology* is his first book to be widely available in the U.S. and English-speaking countries.

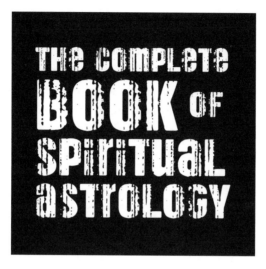

THE COMPLETE BOOK OF SPIRITUAL ASTROLOGY

PER HENRIK GULLFOSS

Llewellyn Publications
Woodbury, Minnesota

First Edition
First Printing, 2008

Book design by Donna Burch
Cover art: leaf background © Brand X Pictures, celestial image © Visual Language
Cover design by Kevin R. Brown
Llewellyn is a registered trademark of Llewellyn Worldwide, Ltd.

Library of Congress Cataloging-in-Publication Data for *The Complete Book of Spiritual Astrology* is on file at the Library of Congress.
ISBN: 978-0-7387-1258-1

Llewellyn Publications
A Division of Llewellyn Worldwide, Ltd.
2143 Wooddale Drive, Dept. 978-0-7387-1258-1
Woodbury, MN 55125-2989, U.S.A.
www.llewellyn.com

Printed in the United States of America

Contents

A Personal Note from the Author . . . *vii*
Introduction . . . *1*
Astrology and Enlightenment . . . *7*
The Times They Are A-Changing . . . *11*
In the Beginning . . . *17*

1: The Signs . . . 21
Enlightenment through the Elements . . . 21
The Movement of Light . . . 25
Enlightenment Through the Qualities . . . 27
Signs . . . 31
Elementary Combinations . . . 41
Houses . . . 44
As Above, So Below: MC and IC . . . 56
As Within, So Without: Ascendant and Descendant . . . 71
Signs in Houses . . . 85

2: The Planets . . . 93
The Sun . . . 95
The Moon . . . 97
Integration of Sun and Moon Principles . . . 106
Mercury and the Union of Sun and Moon . . . 107
Venus and Attraction and Repulsion . . . 120
Mars and the Path to Enlightenment . . . 130
Venus and Mars and How to Get Some Satisfaction . . . 139
The Play of the Inner Orchestra . . . 142
Jupiter, Saturn, and Our Spiritual Playpen . . . 145
The Outer Planets and the Endless Sea of
    Inner and Outer Space . . . 157
Uranus and the Free Spirit . . . 158
Neptune and the World of the Soul . . . 169
Pluto and the Law of Eternal Change . . . 178

Involution and Evolution . . . 187

The Planets in Houses . . . 189

Rulerships . . . 190

3: Aspects . . . 201

Individual Aspects . . . 206

Planetary Groups . . . 212

Aspect Combinations . . . 213

Retrograde Planets . . . 229

4: Astrology and Time . . . 245

A PERSONAL NOTE
FROM THE AUTHOR

Dear Reader,

I hope you will have as much joy and insight while reading this book as I had while writing it. I hope you will discover that we are living in a marvelous world and at an amazing and fantastic time. When we get caught up in the outer world and our ego's little games, this planet can seem like a very harsh and difficult place to be, and these times can seem to be strange, threatening, and full of stupidity and ignorance. But as we go to the inner world and begin to listen to the voice behind the scenes and to see all the new revelations and perceptions that are becoming available, we truly discover that to be here—on this planet at this moment—is a great gift, one that gives us the ability to take part in a unique and exciting adventure.

There are three beings to which I will especially give my thanks and love for making this book possible. The first one is the great spirit of All That Is. I feel so blessed by this spirit to have been allowed to write this book and to have received the insights and understanding you will find here. I am so grateful for having done this work, and I cannot say anything but hooray and thank you.

The second and third are people living on Earth at this moment. I am very happy that they have chosen to be here at the same time as I, and I feel blessed by their presence. The first is my wife and eternal friend and companion, Tone Isis Briana Holberg. We have been working and teaching astrology together for two decades. Besides being a personal joy and inspiration to me, she has also helped me to become clearer and more precise in everything I do. She is five-times Virgo, so this comes naturally to her, and I am so happy to share so much of my life and work with her.

And third, but not least, I want to thank Diana Brownstone, a beautiful artist and astrologer from New York. Without her outstanding work with this book, it would never have reached your hands. As my agent, she presented it to Llewellyn Worldwide in a way that was so professionally and delicately done that I am thoroughly impressed. She has also taken my somewhat crude, rudimentary, and grammatically inconsistent English and changed it into the product you hold in your hands at this moment. Again, I can just say thank you and bless the fate that through strange ways led to our meeting and friendship.

And I will also say thank you to Lisa Finander from Llewellyn, whom I have never seen or talked with, but who has taken this project of mine and helped us in such a caring and enthusiastic way to create the product that it has become.

Joy, love, beauty, and wisdom from me to you,

Per Henrik Gullfoss

INTRODUCTION

You are about to embark on an adventurous journey into the world of spiritual astrology.

This book will show you how to understand astrology as the language of the universe. It will give experienced astrologers a completely new and amazingly simple yet precise way of using astrology. And it will give new astrologers a wonderful and fantastic introduction to the real essence of astrology as humanity's tool on its voyage toward awareness and awakening.

If you are an advanced astrologer, you might want to skip the next few pages, which will give a short outline of the basics of astrology from a spiritual perspective. If you are quite new to the "game," you should read this thoroughly and internalize as much of it as possible.

The twelve most basic letters in the language of astrology are the signs. The astrological signs we use in Western astrology differ from the constellations we see in the heavens. If somebody tells you that your Sun isn't really in the sign you believed it to be, he or she might be right. The reason for this is that Western astrologers do not use the stars as measurement for the sign. What a modern European astrologer does is divide Earth's orbit around the Sun into twelve equal parts. The Sun will always enter the first degree of Aries at the equinox and the first degree of Capricorn at the midwinter solstice.

In this way, the signs are like twelve stages, each carrying a special energy and quality within itself. As the year develops and changes with the changes in the relationship between night and day and heat and cold, so too do the signs develop. Aries, the first sign of spring, is of course about beginnings and fire rising through budding life. Pisces, as the last sign, is about melting and thawing—the fingers of winter letting go their grip on the land.

Most people have heard about their Sun sign. But a personal horoscope is so much more than just your Sun sign. All the planets we have in our solar system also exert their influence on us. But first let us talk about houses. If we say that the signs are like a wheel with twelve segments, we can put this wheel down on a piece of paper. And we then put another wheel over this. The basic setup of a horoscope consists of these two wheels.

The wheel of houses comes from a division of Earth's rotation around its axis (day / night) in twenty-four hours. In this time, it makes a complete 360-degree journey, just as it does around the Sun in one year. This circle created by the twenty-four-hour rotation of Earth is also divided into twelve equal segments, which we in astrology call "houses." As the signs have their rhythm, the houses also have theirs. The first house is around sunrise, the tenth begins as the Sun reaches its zenith, the seventh as it sets, and the fourth at midnight. We could say that as each period of the day has its qualities and specific energy, so do the astrological houses have their qualities and specific energies.

Signs and houses are like two alphabets that go from one to twelve: twelve signs and twelve houses. There are similarities between signs and houses that have the same number. The first house and Aries have a lot in common, but there are also several differences. We could say that while the signs show energies and qualities that come through in a person's horoscope, the houses show the inner and outer areas of life where these energies come through and manifest. Libra, the seventh sign, is about harmony, beauty, balance, justice, and longing for union. The seventh house is about the person, the object, the area, or the inner quest, where we meet and try to unite and create that harmony and balance the Libran energy seeks.

If we look at the horoscope as a kind of stage, we can see the combined wheels of houses and signs as the setting for playing out our life. How the two wheels are put together tells a lot about our basic psychology and energetic possibilities. But, as we know, a theatre without actors is dull to look at. The actors on our astrological stage are the planets. At the moment we were born, every planet in our solar system had an exact location in a sign and a house. Every planet represents a special part of our psychological and mythological being. A planet's placement in house and sign tells us about any special qualities and needs we have. To tap into our life force and keep our energy fresh and vibrant, we have to use the qualities the sign of the planet makes available for us, and we have to use them in connection with the areas shown by the house placement of the planet.

So with planets and signs and houses, we have our framework for playing out our life story. But there also have to be conflicts and alliances and challenges, and gifts and surprises and magic. And this comes through the aspects. The aspects are specific energetic connections between the planets (players), and they either force us to act to solve certain challenges or give us some great opportunities for going where we want to go.

To use another metaphor, we could see our astrological horoscope as an orchestra, in which our soul is the conductor—or like the colors available on our palette, with the soul as the painter.

In some ways, our horoscope is a given factor, and in that respect it could be said to give us a fated life. There are no possibilities for exchanging our horoscope for a better one after we have arrived at birth. But the freedom in life comes from how we use the available colors to paint our picture or how well we play with the instruments of our personality. An example of the differences that can occur through the use of free will is the fact that Adolf Hitler and Charlie Chaplin had almost identical horoscopes. One became a dictator and started a world war; the other made a hilarious film about a dictator that started a world war.

And just briefly, why does the horoscope work? As we know, the Sun and Moon have a great influence on all life on Earth, as well as its water.

Some say that the outer planets have too little effect to be counted. Well, since most of us rarely know what we have until we lose it, we could use the same technique with a planet. Let us take Saturn as an example. If it has no influence, we could move it from the solar system without causing any trouble for humans and life on Earth. But let us hope nobody really tries this, because the whole solar system would go into terrible chaos and life on Earth would probably disappear if we removed Saturn from its orbit.

And one more thing: why is the moment of birth so important? Until we are born, we are in symbiosis with the mother organism. It is the moment the umbilical cord is cut that we become an independent organism, and it is when we take our first breath that we connect with the energetic condition in the world as a unique being.

A Short Explanation of Astrological Language

As mentioned, we have twelve signs. These twelve signs are divided into four elements and three qualities, as follows:

- Aries, Leo, and Sagittarius are fire signs.
- Taurus, Virgo, and Capricorn are earth signs.
- Gemini, Libra, and Aquarius are air signs.
- Cancer, Scorpio, and Pisces are water signs.
- Aries, Cancer, Libra, and Capricorn are cardinal signs.
- Taurus, Leo, Scorpio, and Aquarius are fixed signs.
- Gemini, Virgo, Sagittarius, and Pisces are mutable signs.

We also say that we have cardinal, fixed and mutable houses. Planets in signs need to express themselves and behave in accordance with the qualities of that sign. The same goes for planets in the houses.

- The cardinal houses are the first, fourth, seventh, and tenth. Planets in these houses have a great need to express themselves in the world and to create something through their will and through cooperation with others.

- The fixed houses are the second, fifth, eighth, and eleventh. Planets in these houses have a great need to use their full potential and to create things through staying power and their own force. They also have a need to create some kind of manifestation of their energy into form.

- The mutable houses are the third, sixth, ninth and twelfth. Planets in these houses have a need to seek and understand the matrix that is behind the world. They can be organizers or communicators. They seek to understand how things work and are always looking for meaning and structure.

There are ten major planets and players in our solar system. Each of these planets, as mentioned, expresses itself through a house and sign.

When we say that Mercury is in Earth, for instance, it means that the mental and logical energy displayed through Mercury will need to express itself in an earthy and sensible manner. If it is in the eleventh house, we know that this logical and practical mental energy needs to be directed toward the future. The person with this placement needs to have ideals, plans, and aspirations to fulfill his or her needs in order to live a full and satisfying life.

In this book you will be shown step by step how these combinations work. You will get a thorough understanding of how each element, quality, and sign functions, as well as a full explanation of what the planet residing in a house and sign needs to do to fulfill itself.

In this way, this book will not be just another book about astrology. It will be a map to your true self, a map that can show you the road to fulfill your life's purpose and teach you how to live as full and fulfilling a life as possible. It will also be a map for reaching that stage of consciousness that many call "awakened" or "enlightened." For those who seek to fulfill their ego, astrology is a great tool to achieve that. For those who seek to leave their ego behind and live a life in oneness with existence and the moment, this spiritual astrology is an even better tool.

ASTROLOGY AND ENLIGHTENMENT

Many masters describe enlightenment as a state that is absolutely natural. It is also described as bliss, ecstasy, devotion, and total peace of the soul.

Sounds good to me—even better than a cup of hot chocolate.

Most of us would like to buy some of this enlightenment stuff, if we just knew where to buy it. The strange thing is that the road to enlightenment seems to be for sale in so many places these days, and still I have met so few who have really walked that road. You know, it isn't enough to buy the map or let someone guide you a few steps down the road. You have to go all the way to the end of the line—and walk a lot of it by yourself too.

Some say that enlightenment is the end of the game: we come home, dissolve into All That Is, and become lost in the sea of bliss and oneness. This is neither my belief nor my experience. While there may be an end station like this, I think it is far, far away in eternity. We humans live in a three-dimensional world, and if you think there exists maybe a 112-dimensional world with 112-dimensional beings ... whoa. That is a long way away from our little playing ground. In my experience, what we call enlightenment is just the arrival of one being in the next dimension of reality, which is the dimension of eternal now and is outside the perimeters of time and space.

So we need a map to this dimension. Of course, we have our intuition and inner knowing. We have the spiritual instincts of a salmon. The salmon was a holy animal in so many old societies. I believe this was because the salmon instinctively knew how to find the way home to its birthplace. It struggled up rivers and climbed great obstacles, only to return to the place it came from. This same longing and knowing exists in humans—not for our physical birthplace, but to find our spiritual place of birth and to reunite with All That Is.

But humans are not salmons. We have developed this strange thing that is called mind, consciousness, cleverness, awareness, and thought. In my opinion, the human mind is not an accident. We do not reach the state of natural oneness and innocence by devolving into children and savages. We move toward such a state through evolving and becoming so intelligent that we are no longer fooled by the tricky shadow plays of emotions, mind, and brain. In my opinion, to stay innocent and child-like takes a mastermind—one that is able to remain clear and focused, cut through all the bullshit, avoid all the traps, and stay in the field of naïve innocence and bliss by choice. For most of us, this is the main road on which to learn and become enlightened, to make choices—to learn to make the true choices. And since we exist in time and space, we need a map that can show us the road from time and space to the eternal now, a map that can help us to see deeper into who we are, a map that can show us the equipment we have to work with on this journey through time and space, and a map that can show us how the time-space dimension really functions. It is obvious that as long as we do not understand time and space, we will be trapped there. And ladies and gentlemen, we are so happy that there exists such a map—a map that contains all of those things and even more—and that, my dear fellow travelers on this road to enlightenment, is the astrological horoscope. It conveys the brilliant intelligence of the stars (astro-logic) to human beings.

Psychological astrology has proved through the decades that astrology is an excellent tool for seeing deeper into the human psyche. With the personal horoscope, you can go directly into the underlying blueprint of the psyche and understand what is driving a person, how complexes and fears are formed, and how to remove those complexes. But although elements and insights from psychological astrology will play a part in this book, this is not its topic.

A horoscope shows the tools an incarnated being has to work with. It is not necessarily a set of psychological complexes. Rather, it is your heavenly choir: the voices you have to use to tune in to the cosmic song of oneness. Or it is your palette: the colors you have to paint your life, the colors you use to create and become that rainbow that will be the bridge between time and space and eternity.

And then, astrology is the science of time and space—not symbolically or as a metaphor, but quite literally astrology is the science of time and space. And then of course, it is also the science that can show us the road to what is behind time and space.

To make this simple: what creates time and space? Or even clearer: what creates our notion and experience of time and space? To this there is only one answer: the movement of the celestial bodies, like planets and suns and galaxies! Day and night are created by Earth rotating around its axis, and the house system in astrology is a direct reflection of this rotation. The year is created by Earth rotating around the Sun, and the signs of the zodiac are a direct reflection of this movement.

And the Moon's dancing around Earth creates our rhythm in time and space. It creates our inner and outer tidal waters and waves. It creates the rhythm of sinking in and going out—a rhythm we easily forget when we live in electrified cities and almost never see and feel the difference of the tiny, silvery sliver of the new Moon compared with the round and shining belly of the full Moon.

THE TIMES THEY ARE A-CHANGING

Well, the truth is that it is not just the times that change. Time itself is changing. As we have seen, we have our own notion of time, even if time itself may be an illusion created by the movement of celestial bodies. And it is this notion in the human consciousness about what time is and how it functions that really is changing. In fact, we are moving from limited, linear time and space to time as the growth of an eternal now, where all dimensions of time and space exist simultaneously beside each other.

In the beginning of humankind's existence on this planet, humans experienced time as an eternal return. In a way, they lived in eternity, where the same Sun rose and set every day. The religious rituals of these humans often consisted of helping the gods to keep this eternal rhythm flowing.

And in the absolute beginning for Gaia, life on this planet changed exceptionally slowly compared to what happens today. The same amoeba came and went for millions and millions of years, until it slowly changed and started to become more complex. Every time life on Earth reached a certain level of complexity, a new evolutionary step kicked in. The biggest leaps may have been life moving from sea to land, the farewell to dinosaurs and the hegemony of warm-blooded mammals, and the emergence of humans. The change that took place when dinosaurs became extinct could be seen as a change in which life on Earth started to develop feelings instead of instinct as a ruling guide of behavior. The next great step came when things became so complex and evolution had speeded up to such a degree that intellect and self-consciousness started to develop: in other words, the entrance of humans on the stage of Mother Earth. Today the complexity of life on Earth and the speed of time seem to have reached a new point of crisis, where evolution needs to take a huge step forward to master the new conditions.

It may sound strange to you that our notion of time, as well as time itself, is changing. But look at it this way: As Einstein proved, we live in a world of relativity, and the parameter that defines this world is time and space. We can say that time and space are dependent on each other. If time is changing, our understanding of space has to change too. And if space changes, our notion of time has to be changed. Einstein proved that if we could move through space faster than light, time would start to change, and we would eventually start to move backward through time—in theory. But clearly, the speed with which we move through space is important for creating our experience of time. And today we move through space faster than at any time before. With our bodies, we can move around Earth in only a matter of hours. And through the Internet, we can be at many places around the world at the same time.

We can have a conference with people from all around the world, and all our consciousnesses will be in the same "virtual" reality. So, time is speeding up and space is shrinking down. We can look at this from another angle. If nothing happens and nothing changes in your life in a certain span of time, you feel that life is an eternal repetition and moves slowly. Our experience of time, then, is also connected to how much stuff is crammed into a certain amount of outer time (such as a day). And you know, in one day I get more input of ideas and information about the world and have to relate to more people and opinions than I might during a whole life in the Middle Ages. So time is really speeding up. For many of us, it speeds up to a velocity that makes it hard for us to keep track. Time goes too fast. So much happens and so much has to be decided with so little time to do it that we become frustrated, lost, and stressed and end up totally exhausted and unable to make those choices and cope with our lives. We get stressed because our old tools —instincts, emotions, and mind—do not know how to deal with all of this. We feel unable to find a way out of the conflicts and turmoil. There seems to be no way back to the old, but also no way ahead to the new. So we get stressed and frustrated and feel stuck in an unsolvable situation. The only solution is to really understand that the fundament of time-space on which we have based our reality is changing. We have to develop a completely new set of skills and a new tool to deal with a new time-space frame and reality. This tool is called intuition. It is called awareness. It is called the ability to live in the now, the ability to be to-tally true to who you are *now*, not who you were yesterday, and totally open for what the world is *now*, not stuck in a world that is a day or a week or a century old. Only through being here, in the now, can we learn to thrive and flourish in this new time-space dimension that is opening up for humanity.

And of course, the perfect map and tool to find your way through this maze of time and space is the astrological horoscope. It is the per-fect description of how your being is manifested into time and space and the perfect map for this being to find the magic doors into the eter-nal now.

For a long time, humanity has adored and fought with and respected God as if he or she were our father or mother. We could say that time and space has been the playpen where humanity has been able to learn and grow through its childhood. Now something is really changing. Humanity is no longer satisfied with having been created. We have started to create ourselves. We change nature and the conditions for life on Earth. We influence the weather and almost pollute ourselves to ex-tinction. We even start to plunder with genetic technology and the clon-ing of living beings and in some ways create new life. We are not satis-fied with being created and put in the playpen of time and space. We want to be creators. And as creators, we are not just children of one or many gods. We are starting to become like gods ourselves. We desire to be equal to the Creator, because we are creators, just as children start to become equals to their parents. But then first there has to be puberty, and I have a suspicion that this is where mankind is at the moment: in our difficult, rebellious, and self-contesting stage of puberty. And this is a difficult time. Again, the best map to lead us through this difficult time is the horoscope, which can describe exactly what will happen when we let our immature emotions and egoistic old ways govern our lives, and what will happen when we go with our godlike nature and follow the true essence of who we are in our souls. And this book is about going with our souls. It is not about our faults and shortcomings, but about using the horoscope as a guide to the open, true, and therefore perfect expression of who we are.

And where are we headed? Well, in the first instant we are not headed out of the playpen of time and space, but rather we have to take responsibility for it ourselves. God has fixed the playing grounds for such a long time, now we have to do it by ourselves. We have to see that we are not just created in time and space. We have to realize that we are creators of time and space, as well as all that happens within the frames of this playpen. And as we learn and understand and take responsibility for our own personal time and space, as well as our collective time and space, we start to move outside the playpen. Then we can be trusted with participating in a bigger universe—a universe that consists of an endless number of time-space realities stacked on top of each other, in the same way that different directions lie beside each other.

In physical time and space, we have 360 degrees of possible choices of directions. In the next stage of our development, we enter a reality that has a similar 360-degree total view of choices for time-space realities.

And once again, the horoscope is a guiding map through these challenges and gifts. It is what the soul has chosen to be and experience through in this incarnation into time-space. It is the tools and energies we need to flow with and create with if we want to become fully aligned with that reality that is natural for the soul: the reality of multidimensional reality.

One of the things that may need some clarification in this respect is the relationship between fate and free will. Is astrology about fate, and is the horoscope a definition of who you are that you cannot escape? Or is astrology about your freedom to use your will to be and become whatever you are capable of? In the space of eternal now, there is absolutely no difference between fate and free will. There is no conflict and no dispute. They are the same. You have totally free will to follow your current fate or to create another fate. And that which you do with your free will creates your fate. At the same time, you are what you are, and no matter what you do, in your core you will go on to be what you are. In the end, your unavoidable fate is to realize fully what you are, but at the same time, you have complete freedom in when and how you realize this. And the closer you come to the moment of eternal now, the more your only longing becomes to be what you are and to fulfill the fate of what you are meant to be and do.

IN THE BEGINNING...

There are only two ways to live your life.
One is as though nothing is a miracle.
The other is as if everything is.

—ALBERT EINSTEIN

Once upon a time, the silent universe exploded in what our scientists call the Big Bang. From that core, light started to spread throughout the universe. As time went on, the light began to slow down and started to form galaxies, solar systems, and planets. On some planets, life started to evolve, and on our particular planet, humanity evolved. So the famous line "We are the dust that stars are made of" is not just a poetic description, but also a true statement.

As is everything else, we are descendants of the explosion of light that started the universe—or even truer, we are that light.

As we know, light appears sometimes to be a particle and sometimes a wave. For a long time, we seem to have been caught in the experience of ourselves as a separated particle. In psychology, this particle identity is called the ego. We seem to have forgotten our wave nature and the fact that we emerged from and are part of the force that created the whole universe.

The Force of Light

The force of light manifests through what astrologers call the four different elements: fire, earth, air, and water.

Through the element of fire, the universe seeks to express the joy of just being. Aries, Leo, and Sagittarius are the signs of joy.

Through the element of earth, the universe seeks to express the beauty of its own creation. Taurus, Virgo, and Capricorn are the signs of beauty.

Through the element of air, the universe seeks to express the wisdom that penetrates everything. Gemini, Libra, and Aquarius are the signs of wisdom.

Through the element of water, the universe seeks to express the force of love that flows everywhere. Cancer, Scorpio, and Pisces are the signs of love.

An Example

I have Sun in Taurus. I need to experience and express the beauty of the spiritual manifested in the physical world. My Mercury is also in Taurus, and I want to express and communicate beauty in a beautiful and practical way. With Venus in the Twins, I love and am attracted to wisdom. I also want to communicate this wisdom (Gemini) in a beautiful way (Mercury in Taurus in mutual reception to Venus). With a Scorpio Ascendant I want to show the world my love, and I like to be seen as a loving person (although I would not like to be seen as a fool of love with Scorpio rising). Since my Mars is in Cancer, I want and need to express my love through actions. Jupiter in Virgo shows my need to create, step by step, a more beautiful society, world, and life. With Saturn in Sagittarius, I find it hard to accept limitations and boundaries, except when they are created and used for and with love. Uranus in blazing Leo urges me to express the joy of spontaneity, freedom, and being an individual. Neptune in Scorpio gives me a longing for merging and love and a capacity for unselfish love through the inner world. As Pluto is situated in Leo, it gives me a need to transform joy to new levels of energy. To do this, I enjoy removing the taboos that block the pure expression of joy. I also seek to learn to feel joyful around death issues, because death is just a joyful movement to another reality.

One Cannot Exist Alone

Joy, beauty, wisdom, and love are the natural and spontaneous manifestation of our inner nature. To reach this expression, we have to stop being distracted by our limited nature as a particle, and we have to let the force that moves move through us. But remember, to express one quality, you need to have an understanding of the other three. To be pure joy, you also need wisdom, love, and the ability to appreciate and create beauty.

THE SIGNS

Enlightenment through the Elements
Earth: Taurus, Virgo, and Capricorn

Earth is the element of form. It is connected to the outer experience of form manifested in time and space. This form can be your body, a mountain, or even money. Money in itself is an abstract concept, but somehow it seems to manifest in time-space reality as coins, bills, and even electronic numbers in a bank account.

The spiritual significance of the earth element is to see the beauty of life as it unfolds through the form. It is not to be ruled by the outer form, or to cling to it, or to fear losing it. Form is spirit playing its game of eternal change through what, in one way or another, is manifested in a limited sense for a certain amount of eternity (time).

To master the element of earth, we have to understand that its main essence and purpose is to show the beauty of spirit manifested. In one sense, beauty needs to have some kind of form if we are going to recognize and appreciate it. Today, mankind seems to be very much stuck in thinking of the earth element as something one needs to control—or just stuck in seeing the outer form and not the beauty that is behind it and that shines through the form. The way we need to work with the element of earth, in order to move toward a new state of being and experiencing, is to feel gratitude and gratefulness. The earth element is also connected with abundance and endless richness in the physical world. To connect with this richness, we have to appreciate and feel gratitude for the fantastic miracle and beauty that form has to offer. Through this gratitude, we will start to create a whole new experience of abundance, and we will start to find that all we could ever need is given and available. On this road, we will also arrive at a point where we deeply understand that there is no lack, and we will see clearly that this notion of lack is just an idea that fearful people, with a need to control their fellow beings, have created in our minds. In becoming more and more in contact with gratitude, we get closer and closer to a world without lack and filled with abundance. The end station for a planet in Earth in the personal horoscope is to be so filled with gratitude that nothing can draw it away from this attitude. Then Earth literally starts to shift under our feet, and we connect with an experience of inner and outer heaven. We start to understand that we already are in the land of plenty—that paradise is where we are.

Fire: Aries, Leo, and Sagittarius

In many ways, the element of fire is the first. Fire can be seen as flames in the outer world, but it can also be experienced as the inner flame. If the body is the vehicle our spirits use to drive through time and space, spirit is the driver. Spirit is also our inner fire and connection to the eternal source of life. The fruits on the tree of life are flames. Even when we exist in an outer world of time and space, spirit is that inner flame that connects us to the eternal now. Fire lives in the moment; it is burning or it is dead.

The essence of the element of fire is joy. You may wonder how so many religions lost track of what really matters and became lost in fear, guilt, and the notion that life on Earth is nothing but an experience of limitation and suffering. Most religions have this idea that earthly life is a testing ground. Western religion has divided unity into heaven and hell, and Eastern religion has depicted life as an endless suffering where the lucky ones manage to get out of the dreary circle of reincarnation. The reason for this is that they have lost the connection with the essential essence of life and God, which is freedom and joy.

Life in itself exists out of pure joy. Life experiences being as a pure miracle. What do you think makes a plant grow? It is nothing but the pure joy of life—of growing and being alive.

So the first attribute of God is joy and life. Planets in the element of fire reach their full potential by connecting with this spiritual fire and by becoming more and more tuned in with a state that is totally focused in the now, and totally focused in life and the joy of being and living. This totality of being is one of the tasks you set before yourself when you are born with planets in fire: to reach for and hold a state of eternal ecstasy and bliss. No more and no less is needed for moving the energy connected with planets in fire into the next stage of evolution than staying on the stage of nowness and eternal joy.

Air: Gemini, Libra, and Aquarius

Air is the element that reminds us of our eternal unity and connection. Humans are like fish on the bottom of an ocean of air. Our air is like one big outer lung that we share. In some ways, we are just as much breathed by the air as we are breathing it. If you try to stop breathing, you will eventually pass out and be breathed back to life again. The moment we stop breathing is the moment we leave this dimension of time and space. In truth, we all share the same breath of life; unfortunately, we seem to forget this every now and then.

In my native language (Norwegian), the words for "breath" and "spirit" are the same. So breath is spirit flowing through us as consciousness. On the outer level, air is the element that makes it possible to speak. It connects our brains through its fluid nature. Air also makes it possible for all kinds of communication signals—and even for brainwaves, as demonstrated through telepathy—to move from one destination to another. Air has made thinking and the Internet possible. Through this meeting of minds and ideas, we have developed not only language, but also our capacity for thinking. And the miracle of air, logically enough, also becomes the foundation for our development of awareness. Air is what fills the space between us and makes it possible to have distance, but also to connect with oneness over distance. And this is really what time-space is about: distance making new awareness possible, and oneness and connection through this distance. Of course, the element of air on one level is connected with the rules for human behavior: the dos and don'ts of human society. Through the element of air, we get the ability to develop awareness, and another word for awareness is *wisdom*. Many of us have been caught in the outer form of wisdom and have mistaken knowledge for wisdom. We could say that planets in the element of air search for enlightenment through becoming spirited and inspired. In Latin, *inspirare* means "to breathe in." The attitude that planets in this element strive to develop is the attitude of amazement and surrender. Awareness is to surrender to the inner knowing of All That Is. It is not to be smart and clever, but rather to remember what spirit and life are all about. And through the element of air, we all have access to each other, so we can help one another to remember. In one way, air is the element of friendship: friendship with all living beings, and through that, friendship with All That Is. Air whispers in our ears that we have never been alone, forgotten, outside, or isolated. We just have to remember that we are one with All That Is, and just like that, we start to move into that eternal dimension of always now.

Water: Cancer, Scorpio, and Pisces

Water is the element connected with our ability to sense unity through our inner worlds.

The outer manifestation of this quality is found in rivers, lakes, rain and the ocean. It is also associated with tears, sweat, and everything that is a part of that strange and wonderful fluid substance we call water. On the inner level, water is the ability to feel. It is also the ability to dissolve all impurities in the ocean of love. As on the outer level, our inner water can become polluted and contaminated. When our inner water is murky, it gives rise to what is called negative and destructive emotions. In its natural state, water is pure. It dissolves, cleans, and nurtures our physical body so it can grow and become healthy and beautiful. In the psychological aspect of understanding, water is our emotions. It is our feeling of life and how this feeling moves us or makes us move: in other words, "e-motion," or energy in motion. Experienced on spiritual levels, water is that inner feeling of connectedness to All

That Is. Just as air is our outer access (air is electric and yang) to unity through the outer world and consciousness, water is our inner access (water is magnetic and yin) to unity, through feelings and our inner ability to connect with All That Is. The access door to the kingdom within is opened by allowing oneself to sail on the river of love. As fire is the pure joy of life, love is the pure joy of experiencing a life other than your own. Love needs a meeting and a seeing. It can be something as prosaic as love for hamburgers, or it can be a deep love for God or the universe. But love requires that somebody loves and that something is loved. Even when love is the bliss of unity and love for All That Is, there has to be somebody there to love All That Is—somebody that is not absolutely one with All That Is. To explain the quality of this state of absolute love is something many enlightened beings have tried to do, but it is impossible to really understand it without experiencing it. The way to enlightenment through the element of water is devotion. Devotion creates a place of unity and sharing. It opens an inner gate, and when we walk through this gate we experience a miraculous melding between our being and what we are devoted to. A melding occurs between the personal and the impersonal feeling of love, and we reach a state of total inner peace, where there is no divergence between the inner and outer oneness. We love absolutely everything in the outer world and feel absolutely loved by everything that exists in our inner universe, and we understand that the outer and seemingly limited is but a reflection of the inner unlimited.

The Movement of Light

Aries, Cancer, Libra, and Capricorn are cardinal signs. The energy that moves them is a pulsating flow that expands and contracts in rhythmic waves.

Taurus, Leo, Scorpio, and Aquarius are fixed signs, and they stand in the doorway between the unlimited source and the limited world of time and space. They are movers of energy from one level to another.

The mutable signs Gemini, Virgo, Sagittarius, and Pisces are moving through time and space, always changing back and forth between particle and wave.

There is also another way of looking at the quality of the signs.

The cardinal signs are connected with the energy we call electric. They create something where there was nothing before. They initiate, electrify, and have the will to move into the unknown.

Aries initiates movement through the joy of moving and creating. Cancer initiates closeness, so new love can be created. Libra initiates relationships, so wisdom and sharing can be created. Capricorn initiates new forms and reality, so beauty and growth can be created.

The fixed signs are connected with the energy that we call magnetic. They have a need to hold things together, to find a synthesis and create order out of the impulse in the cardinal signs.

Taurus is the binding force that wants to create beauty in form. Leo is the focused power that wants to hold joy in a constant flow. Scorpio is the inner force that wants to create a constant field of love energy. Aquarius is the consciousness that wants to hold all of the individual consciousnesses together.

The mutable signs are in many ways the forces that want to connect the electrical impulses and the magnetic fields. These signs are very much connected with the force of gravitation. They seek to be in constant movement and at the same time have a central point of gravitation, which makes this movement coherent and focused.

Gemini is the gravitational pull toward new information, and the need to order this information so it becomes a coherent and understandable flow that can be part of the river of absolute wisdom. Virgo is the force that seeks to order reality and the physical approach so it becomes understandable and at the same time moving and changeable. It seeks to create a point of understanding of reality that all the rest can circle around. Virgo longs to walk on the road of eternal beauty. Sagittarius is the force that seeks to find the center of the gravitation, and to be oriented toward this center, so that it has a reference point that can be the point of focus for all its activities. Thus, Sagittarius seeks to be able to stay in the flow of unending joy. Pisces is the force that seeks to find the inner point of emotional gravitation, or the inner central point of loving, so life can rotate around this point. Pisces longs for the ability to stay in the never-ending flow of love.

Enlightenment through the Qualities

"Cardinal" is about will. "Fixed" is about power. "Mutable" is about choice.

In the same way that the distribution of planets in elements in a horoscope gives your total being and each of the planets a specific challenge and gift, the distribution of planets into the three categories mentioned above offers specific challenges and gifts for the owner of the horoscope.

Mastering the Cardinal Quality

As mentioned, Aries, Cancer, Libra, and Capricorn are cardinal signs. They are all connected to the right use of will and force. On the physical level, this can be seen as learning to use the right amount of will and power to achieve something in the physical world and learning to use the right pressure to make something move. On the psychological level, the cardinal signs are known to be pushy. Even the gentle Libra and the sensitive Cancer have their ways of pushing—or holding. To cling or to hold one's energy back is also a subtle way of pushing others to do as one wants. Those signs have the challenge of possessing a strong will and mastering this will in the relationship with the world. In the same way as they must in the physical world, they have to learn to use the right amount of pressure, to know when to push, and to know when to withdraw the pressure. On the other end, they have to learn when to hold and when to let go. They even have the challenge of learning when and how to retreat and when to come out of hiding.

To move through the physical world as effortlessly as possible, they have to learn to use the exact right level of energy at the exact right moment. In the psychological world, this effortlessness is shown by knowing when to go into a battle of wills and when to withdraw. You must learn respect for others, so you don't use your willpower to overwhelm somebody, and at the same time don't let yourself be overwhelmed by the willpower of others. You also have to learn to stand still and not use your will, and you have to know when to come out of the neutral zone and apply your willpower. The same goes for using your will when it is seen as pure energy. As a cardinal sign, you do not really understand what it means to go with the flow. In some sense, you *are* the flow, and you have to learn to regulate it so it becomes smooth and effortless. The old saying of "doing without doing" goes for the cardinal signs. In the time-space dimension, this challenge is very much connected with knowing exactly when to use your willpower and knowing exactly where to direct your force, and then directing it with the exact level of willpower that is required in the situation. To become enlightened, for the cardinal signs, is to achieve the mastery of using the will in time and space. Into this mastery goes the deep understanding of respect for other beings and their freedom to make their own choices and follow their own wills, as well as the deep respect for your own freedom to be in contact with and express your own inner nature. When you get a thorough understanding of this, you will no longer see the world as a place for battles of wills. You will see it as a place where wills create a beautiful dance of rainbows together.

Mastering the Fixed Quality

While cardinal energy works through the will, fixed energy, as shown by the signs Taurus, Leo, Scorpio, and Aquarius, works through the steadfast use of power. We could say that cardinal energy is the power that makes the river flow, and fixed energy is the riverbank that holds the river as it flows. In many ways, fixed energy can be compared to that of a transformation station. The fixed quality is the conduit that lets energy flow through it. To make this happen, a planet in a fixed sign has the challenge of mastering power to get the right input, to hold a certain amount of energy, and to give it the right output.

If the fixed planet is blocked at the input, it will become stuck, fixated and unmoving, or it will become depleted and lack energy to maintain the power output. If the input is open and the output is blocked, it will be overloaded and will explode and lose the energy in different ways. It can be experienced as a burnout or as an unstable and volatile system (human being) that cannot control the energy it tries to hold. If the output is open and the input is blocked, it will give out more energy than it takes in, and the whole system will be depleted.

In many ways, the fixed signs need to have a stability and balance within themselves to master this task. One of the risks is to be stuck in one specific level of energy and be unable to follow the needs of the moment. Think about it as energy: if it only operates on three hundred volts, it will burn something that doesn't need more than five volts, and it won't be effective on something that needs three thousand volts. The fixed signs have the challenge of mastering the use of the right amount of power in any given situation and being able to stand the pressure of the energy it builds up within itself. On the psychological level, this is like being able to wait and hold, letting yourself be filled when the inflow comes and using your power effectively and at the right level of intensity. To do this, the fixed signs need to be very aware of what kind of psychological input energy is available and what kind of output will be most effective. Efficiency and focus on getting the desired result through your actions are very important for anything in a fixed sign. On the spiritual level, the fixed signs work with transforming energy from one level to another. Either they take very high vibrating frequencies and make them available for time-space manifestation or they work with energy manifested in one frequency in time and space and change it to a higher frequency. In other words, they create manifestations in time and space out of dreams, ideas, feelings, and possibilities, or they refine what is already created. To reach for enlightenment for such a planetary energy is to be the impersonal conductor who uses him or herself as the vehicle for reaching higher and higher levels of frequency, or consciousness. The drive to create more and more beauty, joy, love, and wisdom is what makes these planets tick. As they transform themselves through transforming the outer world, they reach higher and higher states of consciousness, and in the end they become enlightened as a consequence of the work they do.

Mastering the Mutable Quality

The mutable quality has a totally different story than fixed or cardinal. The mutable signs seem to work with quite a different aspect of reality. Planets in the mutable signs—Gemini, Virgo, Sagittarius and Pisces—dance to a different drummer. They are not about will and power, but about understanding, change, and mutability.

As mentioned, these planets are about making choices. Of course, cardinal and fixed planets also have to make choices, but not at the same fundamental level as mutable planets. The spiritual concept of going with the flow seems to be made for these planets. They do not want or have the force to hold and struggle and fight like the kind of warriors we find among cardinal and fixed signs. It is quite understandable that most of the humans that go out in the world and fight for profane power and prestige are connected with fixed and cardinal energy. Most of the time, art, science, and spirituality are the areas in which mutable beings have an energy that allows them to reach positions of great influence and acknowledgment.

On the physical level, they are challenged to find the right paths for them to survive and find a meaningful place in the world. In some ways, they are very occupied with right and wrong. The fixed is more like, "If it works, it is right, and if it doesn't, it is 'wrong.'" And for the cardinal, right and wrong depend on whether they get their will and then come to where they want to go ... or not. The mutable wants to know what is right and what is wrong on the philosophical level, so they can be sure of getting it right when they make their choices. Because of this need to be right, they can become very occupied with condemning those others who are wrong and pushing out their own truth at all costs. Even if they do not have the disposition for becoming tyrants as do fixed and cardinal, they do have a disposition for being fanatics.

On the psychological level, mutables weigh one possibility up against another or they become stuck with one unchanging truth. But it goes deeper. They are not just challenged to find the right path in the outer world, but also challenged to find the right answer to who they are. All stimuli has to be processed, weighed, and taken into consideration before they reach a conclusion. On the level of spirituality, they have to learn to choose and change between two different states. We know that on a sub-atomic level the universe is in flux between order and chaos. This same flux applies to the mutable signs. We know that light sometimes is a wave and sometimes is a particle. This goes for the mutable signs as well, which can be very confusing until you get the hang of it. They have to choose when to be a particle and bump into reality and take a stand and when to be a wave and just go with the flow, and they are challenged to make the shifts on an aware and conscious level. If mutable planets get stuck in the wave, they become chaotic, lacking a core and always taking the easiest way out. The end result of this would be a wave with no place to float. If mutable planets get stuck in the particle form, they become very limited and judging and will feel great pain because of loneliness and isolation. So, making the choices of where to flow and how to flow is the main challenge of the mutable: to learn when to become solid and fixed and take a stand and when to just let go, when to accept fate and create no re-sistance and when to be that one single point that raises its voice and shares its understanding and wisdom. To make these choices, and to learn from inside what choices are the correct ones for oneself in any given sit-uation, is the challenge and the golden road to enlightenment for persons and planets in mutable signs.

Signs

Humanity has advanced not because it has been sober,
responsible, and cautious, but because it has
been playful, rebellious, and immature.

—TOM ROBBINS

The signs are waves of energy, like bands of colors from the rainbow that we move along. The sign is the shade we have on our palette for this lifetime. It is not the canvas, nor a description of the painter, but each tells a story about what we have to use when we are applying colors and texture to our lives. The signs of the zodiac are steps in the Sun-dancing ritual; they are stages in this beautiful little planet's yearly dance around the yellow star that is our Sun. The houses, or mansions, as they were formerly named, are the expression of the rhythm of our planet. The planet is spinning joyfully around its central axis, bathing one side of its face in light as the other lies in the soft and mysterious darkness. As the signs connect us to the solar system, the houses connect us to the planet. They show how we are earthed and where the forces of gravitation are strongest. In short, we are gravitating toward the house where the planets, which are the real dancers in our ballet of light, are holding their little show.

In the following text, you may think mainly about the descriptions of the signs as Sun signs. But each is just as much a valid description of how any planet in that sign needs to express itself.

The first division of the signs is the traditional division between masculine and feminine signs. This can also be seen as a division between yin and yang signs. The air and fire signs are described as active, masculine, outgoing, and extroverted; the earth and water signs are seen as passive, feminine, reflective, and introverted.

Many of these words are loaded with connotations that evoke feelings and judgments. Most of us find it more attractive to be active than to be passive, and so on. The truth is that the earth and water signs are just as active as the air and fire signs, but they need something to be active in relation to. A better word to use than *passive* is *reactive*.

Described on an energetic level, we could say that fire and air, the yang signs, are connected to the force of electricity, or the moving electrifying current. We could also say that the yin signs, which are earth and water, are connected to the force of magnetism, or the force that creates order and holds universes and families together.

It is no contradiction to say that both fire and earth and the cardinal quality are connected to electricity, and that the fixed quality is connected to magnetism, together with water and earth energy. A living human being is a mixture of those energies, and you could say that on the energetic level, our life mission is to create a balance between those two forces.

In Taoism, this balance is called Tao. *Tao* means "the road," and it is connected with gravitation. The word *planet* means a "wanderer." The wandering of the planets around the Sun is held in its path through the force of gravity. To stay on this path is to be in balance and harmony, and this force of gravity is associated with finding the right balance between the electric and magnetic forces. Science seems not to have a complete understanding of gravity, but it will probably do better when it sees gravity as a combination of the electric and magnetic forces.

I'm not just talking about the outer and measurable forces of magnetism and electricity. They also have to be understood as forces that operate on the inner level, on the psychic planes, and essentially as spiritual forces. The way the forces operate within the created world of time and space only gives us a glimpse of their essential quality and possibilities. They are in essence, as mentioned, inner forces of spiritual nature or the nature of that force and what many refer to as God.

Aries: Power of Joy

Aries is like a pulsing generator of light. Not unlike the power of the expanding and contracting universe, this is energy potent enough to create something new where there was nothing before. An Aries who follows this natural impulse will expand and contract in a rhythmic way. When this beautiful, rhythmic wave has been distorted, the person moving on Aries energy starts to lose the joy. If the energy is never or is only partly allowed to expand and explore the unknown regions, the feeling of inhibition occurs. To follow such a flow is only natural for the Aries impulse, but the contraction is just as necessary. When the Aries energy gets stuck in full speed at its outer borders, it rapidly becomes depleted and will eventually crush in on itself in what might be called psychological breakdown or depression.

As the first of the cardinal and fire signs, Aries is the archetype of joy expressed through pure being. With all this inner fire exploding out, Aries can't be expected to take the peaceful middle road of no extremes. Quite the contrary: Aries has to learn to find balance in extremity, to let its natural impulses and exuberant joy be guided by the wisdom of balancing its own expression with the rest of the world.

Oneness through the Joy of Being

Taurus: Transformation through Beauty

Taurus stands in the doorway between form and formlessness, between the manifested world and the world of possibility. By bringing energy from the uncreated land of plenty, Taurus can bring beauty into the world. Taurus can also take something that already exists in the world of time and space and raise its vibrations so that it becomes more in tune with the spiritual and eternal. Standing in the doorway between eternity and the world of time and space, Taurus needs to be able to trust its inner strength of love, in order to not become crushed under the pressure. A Taurus that gets caught in the solely material world loses the deeper understanding of beauty. To be freely giving is one of the first commandments for a Taurus. A Taurus that resides only in the spiritual dimensions loses its joy and love for the external world. As Aries can create where there was not, Taurus can create beauty where there was not.

Oneness through the Beauty of Doing

Gemini: Understanding of Wisdom

As with all the mutable signs, Gemini is attuned to both time and space but has to learn to harmonize them. Gemini energy moves in a straight line as well as in circles, approximately in the same way the solar system moves in one direction while the planets go in circles. If a Gemini only moves along the time line, it comes to a goal, but it hasn't experienced anything on the road. In a way, it has arrived at an empty shell of knowledge. If a Gemini gets stuck in the circular movement, it repeats itself endlessly, something that becomes very boring. It's like talking about where you want to go but never going there. In Gemini there is a great need to explore and to understand what is around. In fact Geminis, as are all the mutable signs, are more interested in the essence of an experience than in the actual result in the outer world. In a way, they have to see that life is a journey. The wisdom and understanding they seek has to be experienced in their being, not only in the brain. Life has to be processed so that knowledge and understanding can become wisdom.

Oneness through Ever-changing Eternal Wisdom

Cancer: Power of Love

This water sign is truly a carrier of love expressed in action. As the other cardinal signs do, it has a pulsating energy. But Cancer is like the ocean caressing the shore with an endless row of waves. Cancer is this feeling of love, rising from the depths of the inner ocean and, as a consequence of its nature, moving to the shore. Cancerian energy will be depleted if the feeling of love tries to stay on dry land all the time. Cancer love has to move inward and center itself, before it moves outward in a new wave. If the love feeling is trapped inside, there will be great inner turmoil, which probably will result in a breakdown, or a terrible wave of rage and discontent that will hit dry land with great force. Like the Moon's waxing and waning, the love of Cancer has to wax and wane: sometimes poured out freely and sometimes held back. Cancer energy has an equal need for withdrawing and outpouring. The most important thing for Cancer is to learn to focus the power of love through oneself and the inner world into the outer world. Cancers need to go in and love themselves. If not, they will be depleted and feel guilty for not loving enough. They need the land to be fertile, someone to love. But Cancer itself is the sea and loses energy if it tries to hold on to the land. One of the lessons is that it is the rhythm, movement, and quality of the love that is important, not whom the waves are fertilizing or how they are received. Cancer energy is giving of personal love with impersonal expectations.

Oneness through Loving

Leo: Transformation through Joy

Leos roaring are the inferno of the blazing sunrays reaching the world. To be a Leo is to be caught in the pressure between the force of your personal energy source and the collective energy source. You have access to the unlimited source of power, but how much of this power are you as a person able to handle? The size of the ego decides how much light, warmth, inspiration, and joy comes through. The energetic learning process of Leo is to become as clear and transparent as possible, so that the personal can become a vehicle for the transpersonal. The joy, love, and warmth that is experienced and expressed on the individual level can be a vehicle for the eternal and boundless. If you allow more energy to pass than your emotional and physical body can handle, you will experience some kind of burnout. If you are blocked and don't allow the higher frequencies to be channeled through you, you will be depressed and tired and will feel the weight of darkness inside. Your job is to channel as much light, love, and warmth as you and the receiver can handle, and to remember that you, on the individual level, are the vessel the force moves through, not the force itself. Your job is often to spread warmth and enthusiasm where there is lack of it, not to stand in the light so others can see how much you blaze. The "I" shall be a vessel for the unlimited creative source. To believe that the power of the unlimited source is the same as your personal energy will lead to great energetic trouble. It is important to see that the reward for sharing energy, warmth, enthusiasm, and joy with others is being able to give even more of the same. In time, the more you give, the more you have. This is true for all signs, but it is overwhelmingly important to understand for Leo on the spiritual path.

Oneness through Self-expression

Virgo: Understanding of Beauty

This little seeker of the purest of the pure is also attached to the movement through time and space. Virgos seek to find the perfect path and the perfect way to move through time and space. The way of moving is often much more important than where to move. If they lose the path, as they easily can, they seek perfection as a static thing and become very stuck. If they only see the path, they don't really see the landscape they move through, and even if they reach the goal, they haven't really been here at all. The Virgo world can be seen as an elongated sphere, much like a beehive. Virgos move through this sphere one compartment at a time. If they move too fast, they become lost and will try to fill too many compartments with honey at the same time. This can be a very frustrating task, which feels like endless labor with no result. If they get caught in one compartment, it becomes too cramped, and they become very stuck. The Virgo energy has to fill one room at a time and then move out of the room when it is full and start on the next room. In other words, finish the job, and let go when it's finished. Virgo energy is supposed to be fulfilled by the *process* of creating beauty, not by the result. They shall learn to be happy by seeking perfection that is only experienced in small moments, and then letting go and moving toward the next moment. The honey created by movement and search is to be shared with the world. When perfection and beauty are seen as something that already exists, all you have to do is to use it and make it clearer the Virgos can quite effortlessly create more and more of it. And when Virgos reach the deep essence of their soul, they experience themselves as the honey, and therefore are in no need of the constraining walls of the beehive to take care of the honey.

Oneness through Acceptance of Their Own Perfection

Libra: Power of Wisdom

Libra's pulsating rhythm goes from the inner world to the outer and then back. Libra has a need to experience oneself through a reflection. The personal energy moves out like a wave, meets the other person, and is reflected inward. If Librans are caught in the need to express themselves to the world, they become exhausted and do not find any path through life. If they are caught in the reflection, they lose themselves in the outer—the need to be loved and liked—and wander around without seeing who they are or what they are doing. Libra energy has to learn about the exchange between inner and outer and the exchange between you and me. In a way, for me, you are the outer. Through this exchange, a Libra starts to gain consciousness of the exchange of energy between inner and outer. It learns that the inner and outer in many ways are the same, only reversed. And slowly there is a deep experience of the inner and outer as different ways to experience the same energy. A master of Libra energy is able to stand in the doorway between inner and outer, between you and me, and let the energy float both ways at the same time, without either destroying or disturbing the other. This person will be the silent point of balance that others can move around. To be a spiritually evolved Libra is to be the watcher who sees everything and judges nothing.

Oneness through Watching Movement and Stillness

Scorpio: Transformation through Love

Scorpio as a sign is primarily connected with the inner world of the person. It resides at the point where your individual inner world connects with the collective inner world. As with the rest of the fixed signs, Scorpio is fixed in a spot where the personal power meets the collective. In Scorpio's case, this spot is the great ocean of feelings, images, and longings that connects each individual to the inner space of humanity. Scorpios have to find a balance between their own inner world and need, and their "need" to be a channel for the collective. If they become too attuned to the collective and lose their individual perspective, they become literally possessed with whatever goes on in the collective strata and then have to live out these collective longings and feelings. If they disconnect with the collective stream of images, they will be overwhelmed by feelings of separation, loneliness, and lack of meaning. In a way, the energetic purpose of Scorpio is to become aware of what lies hidden in the collective unconscious and to bring this collective energy into the light by personalizing it and becoming an individual expression of the collective. A Scorpio takes itself, and the rest of us, to a place of greater unity and understanding. The challenge is to not be overwhelmed and to not close down, but to choose in which way you as a person want to manifest your part of the collective energies. The main challenge for Scorpio is to change what is connected to fear and prejudice and shame through the force of love.

Oneness through Oneness

Sagittarius: Understanding of Joy

The energy in Sagittarius can be seen as a moving ball of fire. It has to move in a direction, and at the same time it has to expand and fill the area it moves through. The energetic law of Sagittarius is a need to send energy with high quality out into the world, without discriminating to whom it goes—in short, to spread enthusiasm, warmth, and joy to whoever might be in the vicinity. It's important to not let the smallness of others diminish the gifts you have. You are supposed to radiate because you have the energy, not because somebody else has deserved it.

At the same time as you radiate, you need movement—to be on a quest for a better and even more meaningful and glorious future. You need a vision of the future in order to radiate fully in the present, and you need to be fully present in the now in order to get enough energy to move toward the future. Without a vision, your energy will be depleted, and without awareness of the now, you will have nowhere to go with your vision. As stated earlier, Sagittarian energy is like a ball of light, rolling ahead while shining out in all directions.

Oneness through Growth

Capricorn: Power of Beauty

The Capricorn version of the pulsating energy is the understanding that you have to go as deep down as you go high up. Think of Capricorn energy as always striving to reach a higher and more refined state, like a singer always striving to reach a clearer and higher note. A singer knows that you have to have a solid foundation to reach the wanted heights, just as a rocket needs a solid foundation to be able to launch. If the Capricorn energy only strives upward, it becomes hollow and will eventually collapse into itself. It can also be forever dissatisfied with the foundation and therefore never dare to launch itself into the world or the upper regions. This Capricorn energy will then be caught in the inner darkness and lead-filled chambers of the personality. The Capricorn can't be only light or only heavy. To function, it must be as light as it is heavy and as deep and strong as it can be, playing and dancing. Capricorn energy needs to move in both directions at the same time. As branches stretch toward the sky, roots go deeper into the ground. There is a need to learn that satisfaction lies in the experience of having this great inner span, not in the solely outer experience of reaching the top. It's the ability to stay at the energetic top at the same time as one goes deep down in the valley that gives the rich understanding and satisfaction that Capricorn strives for.

Oneness through Embracing the Totality of Existence

Aquarius: Transformation through Wisdom

Again, this is like standing in between two rooms. In one of the rooms is the collective truth—or truth as an absolute condition. The personal truth is in the other room. These two truths have to be handled, separated, and merged. If Aquarians think their personal truth is the absolute truth, they are asking for trouble. But they must also understand that the absolute truth is different from their personal truth, because they as people live in a relative and physical world, not in a theoretical or ideal world. Their individual and personal lives and energy vibrate on a slow frequency compared to the energy of the absolute. Because they are caught in this energy, their consciousness must learn to handle the pressure from many different frequencies at one time, and if it is not able to do this, to be more or less torn apart. The ego has to learn to take the energy from higher frequencies and slow it down so that it can be used in our world of time and space. It also has to learn to harmonize the mental frequencies with the actual frequencies of what is manifested. This is necessary if there is going to be a meeting between what is and what may be. Aquarius has the need to create a meeting point between theory and practice and to take the thought energy in our world and speed it up so that the vibrations can be heightened and come more into tune with the eternal truth. Aquarius has to be the personal point of power that makes this transformation possible.

Oneness through Merging of Individual and Collective Consciousness

Pisces: Understanding of Love

This is the last of the signs in the zodiac, and the energy of Pisces always seeks a kind of conclusion. It is the mutable energy moving in the inner world. The love energy seeks to encompass and radiate in all directions. This is often seen as the compassion of Pisces. On the other hand, the inner energy of love and longing need to have a goal. Without a goal, Pisces, figuratively speaking, drowns in the inner world of compassion. If the compassion is forgotten, Pisceans can move very determinately toward a goal, but they will never really arrive because they haven't really experienced the movement necessary to reach the inner destination. They are also moving between the timeless inner world and the outer world of time and space. The nature of Pisces energy is to dream the world into reality and to change reality by dreaming up another reality—to embrace fantasy and have the creativity to see with the inner eye that a totally different world can be created. If Pisceans get stuck in the timeless inner space, they lose contact with outer time and space and become "lost" to the world. If they get stuck in the world, they lose contact with their inner self and become machinelike and unhappy. To be able to see love as both personal and impersonal at the same time is a must for a happy fish.

Oneness through Lack of Distance

Elementary Combinations

Don't ask yourself what the world needs;
ask yourself what makes you come alive.
And then go and do that.
Because what the world needs
is people who have come alive.

—HAROLD WHITMAN

In most horoscopes, there is a domination of two and sometimes three elements. Often, planets or important axes in elements make those given elements dominate. Those elements are like cotton threads, weaving a pattern of light that we are dancing in and with. They say something about the colors that are accessible to us for making the tapestry that is called our earthly life.

Lack of an Element

When one element is totally or almost lacking, this element becomes very important. You have not incarnated on Earth to work through that element, but you have to learn to handle it in order to make the other elements work. If you lack fire, your primary concern is not the expression of joy. But without joy, your ability to express true wisdom, love, and beauty will be very small. So you have to incorporate joy into the rest of your life.

A lacking element, or especially an element with one single planet in it, will sometimes take over and dominate. You will have a problem with handling this element. With love/water as the underrepresented element, you will have a tendency to avoid love and deeper feelings, and you will be so overwhelmed by them when they come that you feel helpless and drowning. As mentioned earlier, you need to learn to handle this area adequately so that it doesn't disturb your work and you can focus on the areas that are more dominating in your horoscope and life.

The following combinations are guidelines for what our soul or spirit seeks to experience and express on its earthly journey. The section will show what your main focus is when you have two dominating elements in your horoscope.

Earth and Fire

When beauty and joy are woven together, life becomes a search to embody grace. This combination is expressed through enthusiasm. The joy is giving the fire and light, and there is always the great joy of manifesting this through a form. Grace is the feeling of being blessed with the capability to appreciate and to create what is beautiful.

Grace, Enthusiasm

Earth and Air

This is the great combination of wisdom and beauty: the wisdom to see the beauty in the world as it is, and through this inner feeling of contentment, the ability to create and experience deep inner peace. With wisdom and beauty, one can always reach a place of innocence. In many ways, you can become the fool with your eyes open, so aware of the beauty that you can never be fooled—not because you have a clever mind, but because you see through confusion and can reach into the simple core of everything.

Peace, Trust

Earth and Water

With this combination, you can behold the abundance of the world in your heart. You can see that there is plenty of everything for everybody, everywhere. There is a deep understanding of the richness and texture of the tapestry of light that constitutes our physical and spiritual world. When you allow it, a deep-seated feeling of delight rises from your inner sanctuary and overflows into the world.

Abundance, Delight

Fire and Air

Oh, what a flying and dancing magical carpet life is, so full of possibilities, so much a dance and a play with sparkling energy everywhere. This combination is given the deepest understanding of freedom: to be and express whatever you want to. This is the inspiration to search the unknown, and to experience life as a wonderful adventure. This is the gift of inspiration and the freedom to create yourself anew from moment to moment.

Freedom, Inspiration

Fire and Water

Just being is the gift of this combination—just being full of bliss. This is to let everything pass through you, to accept everything, and to understand from the deepest part of your inner being that life is a ride of bliss. This is to let spontaneity fill you, to love whatever you love whenever you love it, and to be able to express it freely. What else could bliss be?

Bliss, Spontaneity

Air and Water

This combination represents the clarity of mind and the innocence of heart walking together and seeing everything, and not with a critical eye. Everything is woven into this beautiful synthesis of life. This gives one a deep understanding of compassion. Compassion is experienced as a flow of love and understanding born from the experience of belonging to the same oneness. This is the innocence that comes from the knowledge that we all are the same light, only woven and dancing in different ways.

Compassion, Innocence

Houses

Just as a human is one with many shades and sides within the one, the horoscope is one. The horoscope is primarily a description of an integrated unity. Psychology has divided our inner world into layers and compartments. We have subconsciousness, consciousness, superconsciousness, shadow, anima, animus, libido, and so forth. The truth, however, is that the inner space of a human is one. It's convenient to use these divisions to understand what composes a human being and his or her inner world, but as soon as we reach a deeper understanding, we see that a being is an undivided whole. There are areas of the psyche that will lie in darkness, because we don't want, don't know how, or maybe just aren't interested in seeing in that direction. Think of your inner space as a big space, like the universe, and your individual consciousness like a sun on a flashlight. You can direct the flashlight wherever you want, or wherever others have told you to direct it. If you don't have an extremely strong flashlight, like the illuminated masters, you can't flood this enormous space with light. Instead, you have to decide where to focus and direct this flashlight.

At the same time as our eternal spirit is manifested within time and space, the soul lives within the house of the body, yet it also lives within the mansions of time and space. But there are limits. We cannot do everything at the same time. We have to choose different aspects of our unlimited spirit and express them in sequence, as demanded by time and space.

These inner dimensions and mansions of the spirit are symbolized by the houses. The houses are a division of day and night, of Earth's rotation around itself, into twelve areas. And since Earth is where we live, the houses become symbols of the inner and outer areas of our lives as they are here on Earth. As there is a time for sleep, a time for work, a time for housework, and a time for waiting on the bus, there is a house for work, a house for deep feelings, a house for dreams, and several houses for sharing. The sign is the wave of the solar and stellar energy as it beams down to Earth, and the houses are the areas the energy fills up with its light.

The Road Less Taken

The Ascendant is the meeting point of body and soul. The body is strongly connected to the first house, and the soul to the eleventh. The Ascendant is also the gate for the expression of the personal ego. This ego is created by the meeting of soul and body. In this respect, the ego is just a temporary state. It cannot survive without the body, and it is a tool for expressing our soul and for balancing soul and body on this trip called life. Some people adore the ego, and the ego is their master. Others look down on the ego and think it is a selfish and stupid thing, something to get rid of if you want to realize your spiritual potential. The ego is the focusing point that allows the soul to express itself through the body. It should be obvious that both body and ego have opportunities to express themselves through life. After all, this is the only chance they have. But it is equally valid to think that the soul is the part of the triad that has the most access to wisdom, love, joy, and beauty. To live a rich life, there needs to be cooperation and democracy among these three parts of our selves.

The development of ego and body most often is seen as moving through the houses in a counterclockwise direction, from the first house to the second and so forth. The soul, on the other hand, develops the other way through the houses. The twelfth house contains our soul's purpose for incarnating and the deepest longing of the soul. As it moves through the houses, these intentions of the soul are tested out toward the reality of time and space. The soul and the ego meet halfway through their journey, on the Descendant, and experience the deeper understanding of relationships. As they move through the full circle, the soul is completely manifested through the ego (first house) and the ego is completely an expression of the soul intention (twelfth house). In our world, this journey of the soul, clockwise from the twelfth to the first house, is the road less taken.

First House

The soul is an individualized part of our spiritual self. When manifested in earthly form, the soul expresses itself through the vehicle of our body, our earthly identity. The first house is the area the soul identifies with, and this is where it expresses itself through the ego. The sign and planets associated with the first house tell us about the special quality and vehicle the soul has to express itself through. A sign in a house says that we have to work through that energy in order to express the content of the house. When you have a red car, you have to drive a red car. You can dream about and wish to have a blue car, but for you the universe has only red cars. If you have a Virgo Ascendant, you have to work through a Virgo Ascendant. You can dream about having a Leo or Sagittarius, but your soul has chosen to work through the Virgo screen this time. If you have a fire Ascendant, you will have a need to express your soul by showing and embodying joy. If you have a water Ascendant, you will need to express your ego and your soul through love. With air, you need to be the vehicle of wisdom, and with earth, you need to express and create beauty through your person. As far as the first house goes, it is important to remember that what your soul wants is to express love, joy, beauty, and wisdom. Your ego, on the other hand, has a tendency to want others to see you as loving, beautiful, wise, or entertaining. This is one of the major causes of leaking. As long as you put the point of focus outside yourself, your energy will leak and be depleted. There can be a great conflict between the ego and the soul that goes on in all the houses, where the ego primarily wants to *be* acknowledged, loved, and so forth, while the soul wants to acknowledge, love, and so forth.

Twelfth House

The real movement of the planets through the houses goes from first to twelfth to eleventh. In this section, I will honor the Sun's and the planets' rhythm through day and night, as they are experienced from Earth. The Ascendant is where night breaks into day, and the day starts in our twelfth house. This is also a description of the soul's journey through the houses.

There is an archetypal connection between signs and houses. If the Earth had no rotation around its own axis, the planets would move counterclockwise through the horoscope. This provides one reason for the connection between signs and houses. The fourth sign and house are connected. But at the same time, they are quite different. Cancer is the lightest time of the year in the Northern Hemisphere. The fourth house is the darkest hour. The tenth house is the daily Sun on its highest peak. Capricorn is the sign in which the day is shortest and the Sun spends the least time above the horizon. Seen from this perspective, the houses and signs balance each other. Combined, they give a perfect balance of light and darkness. Yin and yang are in perfect equilibrium, two mirroring wheels dancing together.

As stated, there are different ways to picture human development through the houses. Some see the cusp of the ninth house as the place of conception, pregnancy from ninth through twelfth, birth on the cusp of the first, and life in the body stretched from first through eighth. As mentioned earlier, it's very common to think of the development of the ego as starting in the first house and moving counterclockwise through the houses. You could say that the ego starts from scratch and has to be built from the fundament of the soul. The soul, on the other hand, exists prior to birth and comes with intentions and dreams already included. I like to think that the development of the soul follows the true movement of the planets clockwise through the houses, starting in the twelfth and then moving into the eleventh and so on. The beauty of a symbolic language and understanding is that you can see the same phenomena from many angles, even totally opposite ones, and they all make sense.

Whereas the first house holds the soul's need to express itself through the ego, the twelfth house shows the ego's need to experience itself through the soul. For the ego, the twelfth house is a door to a greater reality, a door where the ego opens up for the soul, and the soul for the spirit. Through the soul, the ego experiences a deeper purpose for being an ego—or it feels lost and dissolves. Through the quality of the twelfth house, the "I" finds a road to connecting with its origin and source, a road to experiencing itself as one with the rest of creation. And the soul seeks to connect with the "I," to get a vehicle to work through and with on its earthly journey. In the first house, the soul needs the ego to express itself; in the twelfth, the ego needs the soul to experience its real inner and eternal nature. If this cooperation works out, the soul and the ego will mutually benefit from each other and will have all available possibilities for a great time throughout their visit on planet Earth.

Eleventh House

The twelfth house was a door to the inner world, to the unending possibilities and qualities in the soul. The eleventh house is the longing to express all those qualities into the world, taking them from the inner sanctums of the soul to the outer dreams and reflections of the "I." In the eleventh, the soul and the ego seek to cooperate. There is a desire to create these fantastic images and feelings that exist in the inner world as something visible and touchable in the outer world.

In the eleventh, you yearn to share the dreams of your soul and your ego. In the twelfth, it was okay to share with the ultimate oneness, but in the eleventh, you want something other than yourself to share with. This is a house of great visions, and those visions are expressed and take shape according to the quality of the signs and planets connected with the eleventh house.

Tenth House

The tenth house is the place for testing out the dreams and visions from the twelfth and eleventh in actual reality. It's the need to create something that is visible and tangible. It's the peak of the Sun's journey, where the Sun is highest. In the tenth, the soul needs to make itself as visible as possible, and it does this through the actions of the ego. Through this visibility, the soul can share what it has arrived here on Earth to share with the rest of humanity. And through this visibility, the ego becomes very aware of how it works, what it can manage, and what it can't manage. In the tenth house, the ego always becomes the *one*, shining out to the many. In the tenth house, equality is of no interest. This is the point where each and every one of us can shine out as a singular being. And our rays and energy are sent not to someone in particular, but to the collective of beings that surround us, much like a singer who sings for the audience, not for any particular member of the audience. In the first house, the soul needs the ego to express itself in a personal manner. In the tenth, the soul needs the ego to express itself in an impersonal manner. Or the expression may be personal, but it cannot be directed toward a person. This is why people can say, "You are lousy at your job, but don't take it personally." The description of your performance (tenth house) doesn't necessarily tell anything about the quality of your personal expression (first house). The tenth house is the combined performance of your soul and your ego.

Ninth House

The ninth house shows the soul's and the ego's need to understand their experiences: to evaluate what they have done, to find a deeper meaning in it, to see the essence, and to see where to go next. In the tenth, the soul made its performance. It reached the peak, and where does it go after the top? You—the Sun—cannot go higher in your orbit. So you have to find meaning in something other than getting higher. You have to find a new road, one you haven't traveled before. In the ninth, the soul needs to reconnect with a deeper understanding, so it can see how consciousness creates the experience of life, and change what kind of experience it wants to happen next, by changing the awareness. And the "I" needs to relax and try to understand what this journey through life can mean to the ego. Where does the ego want to go? And how can it cooperate with the soul to get there? The real wisdom in the ninth house comes in seeing how the soul and the ego can travel together and have great fun and exciting experiences on this adventurous journey called life. Many conflicts involving the ninth house or planets connected with the ninth house, reveal that the soul and the "I" need to learn to cooperate and find a common interest and meaning in this incarnation. This is important. True wisdom, love, beauty, and joy come from being both spiritual and focused in the material world. The ninth house gives information about where and how the person finds the road to deeper meaning and wisdom: where to go to grow and learn more and to become greater and more than he or she was before. Much pressure on the ninth house tells us to *grow* and to *expand*, and that we need to include more and more of everything in our conception of reality. The ego is on a search for wisdom, and the soul wants to share the wisdom it has. You could say it is a hunt for widening and exploring the deep inner fundament of life.

Eighth House

The ego is a manifestation of the nature of our soul, created for a limited time and under unique circumstances. In the eighth house, both ego and soul have to face the deepest inner truths about themselves. If you avoid the soul's journey, you will try to avoid the truth about your eighth-house planets. For the soul, the eighth house may be the loneliest. It's connected with what the mystics call the "dark night of the soul." But this is the process of all transformation. You have to let go of what you have and stay for some time in an empty state before the new pours in. In the eighth house, both the "I" and the soul want to change, and through the deep inner experiences of the outer doings of the "I" the soul will be changed. One of the reasons we incarnate on this lovely little planet is that it gives our soul ample opportunities to develop and grow. In the eighth house, the "I" can connect with the deep longings in the soul, and sometimes with the pain of not having expressed itself as it had planned or wished. To feel guilty is a stupid thing. Most of the time we feel guilt because we haven't lived up to others' expectations and standards. But the deep pain that we sometimes give the name "guilt" is the painful feeling of experiencing the gap between our soul's intentions and plans for our earthly journey and what the ego has really been up to. In the eighth house, the gap between ego and soul, between our deepest dreams and our actual performance, needs to be bridged, and to do that we have to be scrupulously honest. We need to see as clearly as possible what the real longings and intentions of our soul are and what the deepest yearning of our ego is. And when we can do this without feeling pity for ourselves, and when we dare to be ruthlessly honest, we will see that the reasons for our longing and for our pain are the same. And when we really start to express our soul and our ego with total honesty, we find a deep feeling of belonging, togetherness, and total peace. The loneliness has ended, because we have stopped alienating ourselves.

Seventh House

The seventh house is an area where both the soul and the ego experience the world by meeting the other. As I have said, the meeting can be between the soul and the ego or between the soul and another soul. While the eighth house seeks the deeper merging that is necessary for the death of the old and the birth of the new, the seventh house is concerned with the meeting. To create a new life, male and female have to merge, at least on the energetic level.

To have a marriage or a meeting, it is necessary for there to be two different people or souls. God took the consequence of his being only one, and the impossibility of one having a relationship, and created the many. In the seventh house, you seek to learn and experience and understand something that is different from you. In many ways, the seventh house is the house for really deep and personal friendship. In the seventh house, the soul wants to see its own beauty and being reflected in another soul's beauty and being. The only way for the soul and the ego to recognize themselves and to see and understand their own unique qualities is by meeting with someone who is different. The seventh house is the area where we meet and have the possibility to really see and be seen, to experience our differences as a confirmation of our uniqueness. It has been said that God created the physical universe to make it possible for God to have an experience of God. For this to happen, there had to be something that was experienced as not God. On this level, the seventh house is where both "I" and God experience themselves through meeting the not "I" or not God. There is a tremendous joy in this: to experience a "new" side of the spirit by meeting it outside yourself, and to love this other side of the spirit, and through loving this outer manifestation of the spirit, to experience a greater love for your inner spirit being.

Sixth House

The sixth house is a nice house for karma, yoga, and experiencing the freedom of accepting circumstances you can't change. Through the sixth house, the soul learns to be occupied in the physical world of time and space. No other house is so connected to the sequential experience of time and space. It pinpoints the here and now to the exact time-space here and now. And as mystics say, there is no other way to liberate the soul from its illusions than being totally aware in the here and now, so the sixth house is a tricky one for the soul. It gives a deeper understanding through accepting what can't be understood. The Zen saying that before you were enlightened you carried water and chopped wood, and that after you were enlightened you carried water and chopped wood, is a sixth-house saying.

The ego learns the law of time and space through the sixth house. Having many planets in this area reveals that your soul has a very great need to learn about—and to learn to accept—the circumstances of being incarnated on Earth, and the quality of the sign on the cusp says a lot about the quality of your life in time and space. You may ask what your soul's purpose is for being incarnated. And the answer might very well be that you are incarnated so you can learn to understand the reason for soul to incarnate in flesh. This is like a dog chasing its own tail, and it evokes the sixth-house feeling that you are a mouse caught in a wheel going around and around. You eat and you shit and you buy food, and then you make food and you wash the dishes, and then you eat and you shit and you buy food.

Then suddenly you get a glimpse of the old symbolic picture of the universe, the great Oroborus, or serpent biting its own tail. And suddenly you get the idea. The meaning of life is life. The meaning of being is being. And being in time and space in the limited here and now is just as meaningful as being anywhere else or anything else. The meaning is the same whatever you do. So just do what you do and be what you are, and you will miss nothing.

Fifth House

In this house, you learn the major lesson that a human being isn't useful. We have often learned that to be useful is to have a meaning and that a useless being is a meaningless being. Of course, "useful" is in this respect related to practical and economic usefulness. In fact, everything that is really important in life, such as art, spirituality, love, and joy, isn't "useful." The qualities of expressing what you are and just being are connected with the fifth house. In many ways, your lesson, with emphasis in this area, is to learn to be yourself. You were created by the universe to be yourself; if the universe had wanted somebody else, I can assure you the universe would have created somebody else. Through this expression, both the soul and the ego discover who they really are. Many people who go to an astrologer or otherwise seek to find themselves often want to know who they are and what to do before they do it. This isn't possible. We have arrived here to experience what we do not know, and the discovery of my soul and who I am begins with expressing something and then seeing what kind of person I am who might have done that. Planets in the fifth house are in training for being themselves. One feature about being yourself is that it's unpredictable. It's always changing, and it is in a constant state of growth and motion. At the same time, a sort of unseen signature runs through all the actions of a soul. This signature can be seen in the child as well as the grownup, in the evil sorcerer you were ten lifetimes ago, in the stubborn fisherman you were three lifetimes ago, and in the rich lady you were in your last lifetime. The fifth house is the pure and simple expression of who we are in the moment. The fifth house is very much about letting the ego be a channel for expressing the soul. We could say that here the soul plays through the ego. The ego in turn experiences the joy of being an ego and the joy of channeling the inner world of the soul through the ego. There is a great naivety in the fifth house: the naivety of not expecting, the naivety of just wanting to be, the naivety of not wanting to go anywhere special. Through the fifth house, the universe gives us a chance to discover what is really meant by the saying that you have to become a child again to enter heaven.

Fourth House

The fourth house is the fundament for both our ego and the soul. For the ego, it's the personal history that starts with birth, and it is connected with the influence from your family, your culture, your race, and so forth. The fourth house is also your inner fundament, in other words, your soul. But for the soul, the fourth house is the history of many lifetimes—the soul's history from the day it was created. It can be seen as the point of connection to the earth, to our common spiritual history, and in the end to the history of the universe.

To experience and understand some of these connections is the purpose of being in the fourth house. Wise historians claim that we are bound to repeat what is forgotten.

The fourth house is one of the main gates that connect our individual self with the collective. To understand your own history—to understand what kind of flower you are by learning about the earth you grew up in and your growing conditions—is one way of learning the fourth-house lessons. The fourth house is a gate to that place where our individuality merges with that of the country, the tribe, the family, and so on. Put differently, what matters in the fourth house is not our individuality, but our individuality as an expression and manifestation of the collective. The fourth house is there so that we can always know that we are never alone, but rather that we belong and are a part of a bigger whole. If we have problems with our fourth house, we are here to learn that we belong and that we are part of some kind of family.

When the Indians worship the ancestors and the Aborigines honor the creators from the Dreamtime, it's a worship of the spiritual through the fourth-house gate. The sign on the fourth-house cusp gives information about what you need to cultivate to have a proper fundament and connection with your past. Since there is so little written about the IC (*Imum Coeli*), I will give a description of how all the signs work on the IC. In extreme latitudes, the IC can be seen as differing from the fourth-house cusp; the information given in the IC section will be valid for both IC and the fourth-house cusp.

Third House

The prime lesson and challenge in the third house is to make choices. When the soul is limited by time and space in the physical world, it has to do things very sequentially. It has to choose what it wants to express and learn and where it wants to go. These choices make other choices impossible, at least in the short run. The third house is associated with communication and the art of speaking a language. One of the challenges in the third house is to learn a language that makes it possible to express both your "I" and your soul. The third house says that it doesn't matter how much you have understood if you are unable to share this with the rest of the world. In the third house, the soul has to express itself through the mind. The soul seeks to find a way to express the timeless and eternal through a mind that operates in linear time. On the ego level, the "I" has to learn to express its wishes and ideas to others in an understandable way. An emphasis on this house shows that one of the reasons you are visiting the planet is to learn the noble art of expressing yourself in a clear and distinct way. To do this, you have to know what you want to say (that is, to know your own will and wishes) and then make choices.

The sign on the cusp will show what kind of energy you have to use to be able to make the right choices and to communicate your choices. With air, you have to use wisdom and communicate with clarity. With water, you have to listen to your feelings and communicate your decisions with love. With fire, you have to connect to your real desire and express your choices openly, spontaneously, and joyfully. With earth, you have to use your common sense to understand what you really want to do and then act it out in a sensible and concrete manner. You are learning to say exactly what you want in a simple and nice way.

Second House

The second house is very much connected to the experience of reality through touching it, as well as what kind of reality we like and what kind we want to avoid. It's very much about experiencing the ego and the soul through manifesting values and creative force into material form. In the second house, there is a necessity to experience the product. The inner value given to an act or an idea is only an abstraction until the idea is manifested. The second house is associated with the soul and the ego learning about material reality by being a part of it and by feeling and sensing it through the body. This experience of the outer reality gives rise to inner preferences and values, and these values are very important for how we choose to manifest ourselves in the outer world. If you go on instinct and follow the lead of the ego, you will go on forever manifesting the values that your first impressions of the world gave you. But as you manifest these inner values in action and form, you get the ability to see what kind of results you have created, and you can reevaluate and change direction. Are the values you have really in accordance with the needs and wishes of your ego and soul? One of the great joys of the second house is precisely to manifest oneself into tangible form. A planet in this house has a need to do this. In fact, it is the only way it can learn to understand what it really wants. This process of trial and error will, as time goes on, clarify what its real values and preferences are. And as one matures, one can see that the values of the ego may be very different from the values of the soul. Through trial and error in the second house, one can learn to change values and in the long run, how to harmonize the values and needs of the soul with the values and needs of the ego. In this instance, the ego will be the willing instrument for expressing the needs of the soul. At the same time, the ego will be able to feel great joy in the physical world and experience itself in a very pleasurable way through the five senses. The body becomes the outer expression of the soul, and the soul becomes the inner reality of the body.

As Above, So Below: MC and IC

Be as the Sun and Stars, that emanate the life-giving essence;
give life without asking for anything in return;
to be a sun, breathe rhythmically and deeply;
then as RA shall you be.

—GAMMEL EGYPTISK INSKRIPSJON

In most horoscopes and house systems, MC (Midheaven) and IC (*Imum Coeli*) are the cusp of the tenth and the fourth house, respectively. When a person is born at a certain distance from the equator and at a certain time so that the house systems collapse, the astrologer may use a system with Equal Houses and disconnect the MC and the IC from the tenth and fourth houses. In those cases, one needs to take a look both at the cusp of the fourth house and at the IC to understand one's roots.

The house system is a division of the diurnal rhythm in twelve sectors. The actual fact is that this diurnal rhythm collapses in those latitudes where you have light twenty-four hours a day in some parts of the year and no light at all in other parts (north or south of the polar circles).

As an astrologer, you have (at least) two choices. You can say that people born at those places and times of the year have a different structure of their interior psyche than people born in more normal (that is, ordinary) latitudes: you could say that their psyches have fewer walls and compartments and are more like one big open space. Or you could say that since it's impossible to use a house system, we can put these cases into the most structured and organized form of house division there is: the Equal House system. As stated earlier, in symbolic systems things may seem to be in opposition but at the same time will not contradict each other. I have used both systems, and they both work on their own premises, just as it has made sense for a client to work with a tenth-house cusp and an MC that can be in the twelfth house at the same time.

One thing is sure, though: if you have an MC, you will have an IC, and they will be directly opposite each other.

One way to see the MC is as the point of authority expressed in the world. And the IC is the real foundation for this authority. To have a real and inner authority, you have to satisfy the needs as shown by the sign and planets connected with the IC. If your authority is based on the ability to scare or to use power or punishment, you have what is called a fake authority. You will be afraid of opposition and feel threatened by other authorities. You may seem very powerful and strong, but this outer strength is a protection against your inner insecurity.

We have all met teachers who didn't have inner or outer authority, poor bastards. There were also those teachers that ruled by terror and fear. They survived, but you didn't enjoy them, and they didn't enjoy themselves either. No sane person would envy them, their lives, or the power they had achieved. Fear and guilt are the energies that make this kind of authority.

Then again, most of us have been lucky enough to meet the extraordinary kind of teacher, who achieved respect not through threats, promises, or manipulation but through his or her own presence. These were the ones who had the power of the MC rooted in the foundation of the IC.

We could also be so daring to say that IC represents the goddess or god within, while the MC represents the heavenly or outer god or goddess. The IC is the point between our feet aiming toward the core of Earth, and in many ways connected with the planet itself as a sacral being. The MC, on the other hand, points outward and is connected with solar deities.

Personally, I find it natural to connect the IC with the womb, the mother, the night, and the earth.

IC in Aries

The Fear
With this IC, you fear conflict and being alone in the world. You fear that you are egotistical and selfish and that you will become unable to act.

The Repressed
A repressed Aries IC is seen when you always seek harmony and balance. You make allies with others, because you don't trust yourself. You won't stand up and fight for your real needs and feelings.

The Reason
With IC in Aries, you learn to trust your deep impulse. When moving in or handling the outer world, you have to trust an inner feeling of direction, a joy connected with the action taken. With this IC, there is no

way you can know where to move or what you really want before you start the action. You have to take care of your own needs in order to trust yourself. It's obvious that if you can't trust yourself, you have no hope of trusting others. You have to make the decision to move by your own inner force and joy, but you must be very ready to share your achievements with others.

Soul Level

You have arrived here to learn to trust your own inner feelings of joy, and to see that you are free to act and do what you want. On this level, you are on Earth to experience the joy of being an individual and using your will to explore the unknown regions of life.

The Joy of Being an Individual

IC in Taurus

The Fear

Starvation and poverty. You fear not being able to take care of your own needs. There is also a fear of having to live a life that is ugly and filled with disharmony.

The Repressed

The denial of Taurus on the IC is seen by an intense and powerful outer personality who seeks security by controlling others. This personality is afraid of having because it might lose, clings to everything it acquires, and tries to be very clever and interesting because it fears to be seen as all too normal and simple.

The Reason

You arrive with a Taurus IC so you really can connect with the world. You need to learn that all life is sacred and holy and that you are on Earth to live an earthly life. You will learn to appreciate stability, physical security, harmony, and the simple joys of life. Your inner fundament is built on simplicity and a deep understanding of what really constitutes a good life.

Soul Level

Experiencing the beauty of Earth and physical life is having an experience of God moving so slowly that you can touch, smell, and feel the being of God manifested in form. This connection with the outer God gives your soul a deeper understanding of the inner God.

The Beauty of Being on This Beautiful Planet

IC in Gemini

The Fear

Fear of being unable to communicate, and fear of loneliness and isolation. This IC will often give a sort of fear of being stuck—an inner restlessness that is rooted in the fear of being trapped in one place and one time.

The Repressed

A repressed Gemini IC is shown by too much enthusiasm. You have a desperate need to be occupied by something meaningful, so you can avoid feeling real possibilities and facing the prospect of no meaning. Instead of really choosing, you always take the easiest way out.

The Reason

This IC is given to you so you can test the depth of your thoughts. By questioning your own motives and beliefs, you can reach a place where your action is based on real choices, not just stereotypical choices. You are here to learn to have a foot in all camps, to be able to see reality from many angles, and to switch the angle when time and circumstances ask you to do so. Your belief and enthusiasm should have a basis in wisdom.

Soul Level

To understand that we are many, and still "one." This IC is something you have chosen so that you can learn to communicate with all aspects of creation, from humans to trees and stones. And by this sharing of consciousness, you can realize the truth that the many are one and the one are many.

The Sharing of Wisdom with All Beings

IC in Cancer

The Fear

This is the deep fear of emotional isolation, of not belonging to any greater organism or whole. There can also be a fear of every form of addiction or need, because the need to belong is so strong.

The Repressed

Denial of these deep Cancer roots is shown by an outer display of not needing anybody, an "I can take care of myself" attitude, and clinging to outer security, position, and control.

The Reason

You have chosen this IC so you can learn to share; learn to understand that you belong to something bigger than the ego, both emotionally and practically; learn to experience the great joy and sometimes pain of tight bonds and very strong and deep feelings; and learn to understand on a deep level that we need each other and that the man who stands alone is the weakest or most afraid of all men.

Soul Level

This IC is chosen so you can learn to love and be loved: to open your heart and give of yourself unconditionally and to receive love in the same manner. Your understanding of the spiritual grows as the circle you share and receive love from grows.

The Love of Sharing Love

IC in Leo

The Fear

This is the fear of being nobody, an anonymous person with no purpose in life. It is the fear of being just a leaf blowing in the wind, the fear of being powerless, weak, and without influence on your own or others' lives and destinies.

The Repressed

Out of fear of not being enough, you run to ideals and theories that are unrealistic. The world ought to change first, and then you can prove your worth. You can become so afraid of being nobody that you have to demonstrate your uniqueness and originality all the time.

The Reason

You have chosen this IC so you can learn to see and respect the very foundation of your own and others' individuality. You seek to understand how togetherness can be built on the free choices of individuals rather than forcing a herd of cows together. Through learning to love yourself, you learn to love all people and life. When you can trust yourself and your own integrity, you are ready to trust and share with the rest of the world.

Soul Level

This is very much about the joy of being an individual, about finding the deep joy in experiencing and expressing your own uniqueness. Through this experience of love for your own freedom and joy, you learn to love the freedom and joy of all beings.

The Joy of Sharing My Joy with the World

IC in Virgo

The Fear

This gives you a deep fear of never being ready for the next move. You just want a little more time for preparation (but a whole lifetime is never enough preparation). You always look for the fatal flaw that will make life a tragic ride in the back of the garbage truck on its way to the dump.

The Repressed

You are always doing something: going with the flow, being of service, trying to be good so nobody will see how "bad and imperfect" you really are. You never stop long enough to connect with your own fear. You are always living your life on others' premises and you never really stand up for yourself.

The Reason

You are here to learn to choose between what has value and what does not, which causes are worthy and which aren't. IC in Virgo needs a foundation of deep personal integration. It is like carrying your own luggage. As you move on, you have to throw out the old and get a new wardrobe. To learn to let go, and to know what to take in, is a lesson for Virgo IC. Your home is what you have chosen as your best alternative for now. This placement makes for a practical idealist.

Soul Level

On this level you have arrived to merge the mind with the heart, to be clear and precise, and at the same time to be led by purity and innocence. When this purity is your base, you will be safe wherever you go. If fear of imperfection is your base, you will always walk in fear. To trust, even though imperfection exists, is a lesson for your soul.

The Beauty and Wisdom of Innocence

IC in Libra

The Fear

As some others do, this IC has a fear of loneliness. Here, it is not the fear of not belonging to a group, but rather the fear of not having what it takes to form those personal relationships and of not finding a person that is special to you and only to you. There is also a fear of being the victim of injustice, a fear of being exploited, and a fear of having enemies that work against you.

The Repressed

Whoa, you take on all the challenges. You fight for the weak and the meek. Or you are the strong, lonely rider fighting your own way through a world populated with warriors. No one shall be allowed to see you have fear. It's like a display of bravado that hides your longing to be loved and liked. Sometimes your fear is so great that you can hide your vulnerability so well that you yourself will have forgotten its existence.

The Reason

You have a deep need to live a life in harmony, beauty, and balance. You are here to share, and to do that you have to take responsibility for yourself. You need to make your life, your home, and your inner garden a beautiful place that you can share with others. To be alone would make your life meaningless. But you can't count on others to share their beauty with you. This is justice: you get as you give, not as you think you deserve.

Soul Level

The deep sharing with and respect for all beings is a lesson sought for with this IC: to be equal with all but superior to none. There is a deep need for the meeting of souls. What you have come to learn is that this meeting can happen if you can open your soul and others can open theirs. So a meeting happens when both parties are connected, aware, and able to share their inner soul energy. And when you have opened your soul, you are a soul mate with every other being that can open its soul (and all the rest, though they don't know it yet).

The Wisdom of Sharing in Love, Joy and Beauty.

IC in Scorpio

The Fear

Here we find the fear of losing what you already have. This can also create a fear of having anything, on the emotional level, because what you don't have, you can't lose. You might try to compensate by having a lot on the material level. This IC gives you an inner experience of the ruthlessness of life. This can create a fear of everything that is unknown.

The Repressed

When you repress your deep Scorpionic fundament, you start to value outer comfort and security more than being alive, and you renounce your need for passion and the strong emotional forces that are the foundation of your being. You stop risking the dangerous and unknown, and you become more and more unhappily caught in a peaceful and safe existence devoid of meaning.

The Reason

This is the right incarnation to learn to love your enemies, to trust your own instincts, and to accept your own passion and feelings. You need to do what you do one hundred percent. The most important thing here is to live your life in accordance with your deeper feelings and truths and not to be overly concerned with the results. The experience of meaning comes from being passionate and investing totally in what you do, not in the outcome.

Soul Level

Your soul is seeking the pure essence of love and desires to reach an experience of love, connectedness, and compassion that can never be lost. When you have met all the temptations and survived all the pitfalls, you will have a love that is based on experience and inner knowledge—a love that is a part of your being, not a part of your meaning or thinking.

The Joy of Love that Never Can Be Lost

IC in Sagittarius

The Fear

You often fear you are too much for the world. The world isn't ready to receive your energy, nor your visions and ideas. You easily fear that you are too naive and gullible and will be exploited. You also fear that there is no way to live without making compromises and betraying pure ideals, and you fear being part of a masquerade in which the masks are on all the time.

The Repressed

When you repress the deep Sagittarius need, you turn off the fountain of fire and live solely through the head. Ideas and theories and intelligence replace enthusiasm and idealism. You can become a dry little theoretician who believes in nothing but your own clever ideas. You want to be friends with those who have success and position, not with the people you really like.

The Reason

You have a Sagittarian IC so you can understand the true meaning of the saying that you have to become a child again to enter the inner kingdom of heaven. You are here to trust and to let yourself be filled with enthusiasm and great expectations. Then you can use your mind and social circumstances to manifest these ideals in the outer world. To throw yourself with great gusto into the unknown river of life is important. Your heart knows where to go, so use your mind when you want to find out how to get there.

Soul Level

As mentioned, this is an IC you have chosen in order to learn about total trust. The word *enthusiasm* means "to be filled with a god." To trust this inner natural flow of hope, trust, faith, and meaning that fills you up from within is your challenge—to be what you are and see the great simplicity at the core of every miracle.

The Joy of Being in an Adventure Called Life

IC in Capricorn

The Fear

Buried in this IC is a fear of not being needed: that you are meant to take care of yourself and nobody else really cares about you. There is a fear of being caught in a meaningless form and experiencing life as a dull repetition of the same automatic responses over and over again. You also have a fear of losing control and showing the world how vulnerable you really are and how much you need the world.

The Repressed

You listen deeply to the feelings of others, but not to your own. You want to help people and make them like you and *need* you. You take care of yourself and as much as you can possibly manage of the world. You allow yourself to be burdened and overwhelmed by the needs and opinions of everybody. What they need is always more important than what you need.

The Reason

This IC is there so you can learn to go slowly and see clearly, to discern between what are real needs and what are just wants and ways to "get it cheap." You have to find the deep and lasting values in yourself and your attitudes toward whatever you get involved in. You need to take responsibility primarily for yourself. When you have learned this, you can help others in a constructive way. If you cannot trust yourself, how can others trust you and how can you trust others?

Soul Level

The soul has arrived to learn how truth, integrity, and honesty can be created and used as a basis for life in the physical. How can the ego and the body be a vehicle for the energy of the pure spirit? Through personal responsibility and absolute integrity, the physical vehicle becomes a conductor for the spiritual. To be in the world is to express the bliss and the beauty of manifesting pure spirit in form.

The Beauty and Bliss of Absolute Truth

IC in Aquarius

The Fear

The fear here is of not being free: of being caught and stuck and not being able to do what you want. You also have a fear of being an ordinary nobody. Normality isn't something you think of as an attractive quality. You fear being caught in routines and boring repetitions, living the past again and again. The thought that you have done it all and nothing new and exciting will ever happen can really make you depressed.

The Repressed

The world has to see how unique and special you are. This is the placement for people who think that the solution for those who don't get famous is to become notorious. You are more concerned with your reputation and the respect you can get from others than with your inner feelings and how much you respect yourself. You become an egoist. Sometimes you fight for a lost cause. You're not really for the cause, but because you need to see yourself in the role of a hero, what is better than the misunderstood hero for the lost cause? In one scenario, you feel free, because others around you are less free than you.

The Reason

You have chosen this IC to seek, find, and understand the implications of a togetherness and collective based on free individuals. You are supposed to find your own way through life, to follow your ideas and ideals and see where they lead. There is a great opportunity to explore different ideas and possibilities from those who are mainstream. You have chosen a deep connection with freedom and the possibility of creating different futures by choosing different paths through life. You will learn that real freedom comes when both you and those around you are autonomous and free individuals.

Soul Level

You have chosen this IC to explore how you have total freedom and at the same time are an integrated part of the whole. That freedom isn't the freedom to do everything you want, but rather the freedom to be what you are. By becoming yourself as an individual, you become an archetype and align yourself with the collective. In the deepest sense, you are here to experience how being an individual can merge with being an expression of the collective. This is a bit like understanding that every spark contains the total fire.

To Be a Joyful Expression of Wisdom

IC in Pisces

The Fear

You have a deep fear of annihilation or a deep feeling of not being here at all, like being invisible. In fact, everything can be scary if you aren't friends with your own emotions. You have to feel secure *in* the flow.

The Repressed

You repress this deep need for going with the flow by trying to control, understand, and master every little aspect of your life. You make all of your decisions based on what seems to be sensibility and logic. In fact, you try to avoid the feelings of helplessness and losing yourself by separating yourself from everything. The consequence of this repression is a bottomless feeling of loneliness and not belonging.

The Reason

You have arrived with IC in Pisces so you can always remember that on an inner level you are not separated. Part of your earthly training is learning how to be a distinct and individual wave of energy, while at the same time being aware of and connected to the oceanic togetherness. Your job is *not* to be solely responsible for correcting all of the faults and relieving all of the suffering in this world; it is to let your inner world of dreams and images manifest in the outer world as concrete expressions. You explore and discover your individuality and your deeper reason for being here by manifesting in distinct and individual form what is born in your inner world—in other words, to be an example of your own dream.

Soul Level

Remember you are both the dreamer and what is dreamt, both the creator and the created.

Your soul is standing on a fundament of unity. With this I.C. you need to feel at one with your surroundings and feel at home with all emotions and feelings that are present. You have the challenge of letting the whole river flow though you, without identifying with a special stone or piece of wood floating in that river. You are blessed with a deep feeling of connection with all that is, and at the same time a great longing for harmony, togetherness and love without limits. This I.C. is chosen so you can really learn that separation and unity are not opposites, but two sides of the same coin. On one side you are at one with existence, at the other you are a very unique and special individual.

The Love of Loving and Being Loved

As Within, So Without: Ascendant and Descendant

One of the first things newcomers to astrology learn about is the significance of the Ascendant. The Ascendant is also called the rising sign. If you were born at sunrise, your Sun would be at the Ascendant. This point could be said to be the point of sunrise in your horoscope: the place where you come out of darkness (your inner world) and become visible to the outer world.

Directly opposite the Ascendant we find the Descendant, which is the sunset point in your horoscope. This is where your consciousness goes into the darkness and you have to trust your intuition or become lost in your insecurity and projections onto others.

The Ascendant is often described as your image, or like a colored filter you use to express yourself through. In older books, the Ascendant is used to describe how you look. Certain Ascendants are said to have heavy eyebrows and sharp noses, others to have reddish complexions and bright eyes. There is a certain connection between your Ascendant and your physical image, but there are also a lot of other components in the horoscope that create a background for your physical appearance. The Ascendant is more connected to the way you express yourself in

the world. As a child, you will have learned that certain ways of expressing yourself are favorable and get a better reaction than others.

The Virgo Ascendant has learned that a neat, and clean, and perfect
image gets the best response. Aries rising, on the other hand, has experienced that a direct, no-nonsense, self-reliant, and unsophisticated manner of expression gets a better result.

So the Ascendant gives an astrologer much information about how
a person prefers to be seen and the way that person expresses him or
herself to the world. One of the questions surrounding the Ascendant
is, how much of the real personality does it allow to pass through?

Just as we have learned that certain ways of expressing ourselves are
preferable, we have also learned that certain ways of expressing ourselves are not acceptable.

The Descendant is very often the filter through which we perceive
others. If there is a lot of suppression surrounding how we can express
ourselves to the world (Ascendant), this suppressed energy will be projected onto the other (Descendant). Simply put, what we will not acknowledge and see in ourselves will be projected and seen in some sort
of twisted form in others. On the psychological level, the Ascendant/
Descendant axis is the axis of projections and unclear images of others
and ourselves. In astrology, there have been enormous amounts of liter-
ature written around the Ascendant; in this book, we will mainly look
at the Descendant and how it really works.

Since the Descendant is how we perceive others, it can easily be
filled with both fear and longings. Through the filter of the Descendant, we might, as noted, see distorted versions of ourselves in others.
We might see wonderful and beautiful sides of our inner being that we
have suppressed or not acknowledged, or we might see and meet sides
of ourselves that our normal consciousness does not accept as parts of
our being.

In previous times, the seventh house (the cusp of the seventh house
is always the same as the Descendant) was called the house of marriage
and open enemies. It is in close relationships and marriages that we become most strongly confronted with our shadows and everything we
want to hide from the rest of the world. But it is also the attraction and

longing for union and togetherness that makes us see the best and most fair and beautiful qualities in others.

On the spiritual level, the Ascendant/Descendant axis is connected with the union of personality and soul. It is associated with our longing to become one, total and whole in ourselves. When it is connected to the Ascendant, it is the longing to be able to fully and absolutely express our total being to others. When it is connected to the Descendant, it is our longing to discover ourselves through a complete and total meeting with the other. We could say that the highest expression of energy of any Ascendant is to express oneself as a total instrument for love and joy without any fear or withholding. Similarly, the highest expression of energy of any Descendant is to express our joy and love for another without any limitation or withholding. On the spiritual level, the Descendant becomes a place where we can meet and integrate new sides of our soul and spiritual energy through meeting, playing, merging, and opening up to our ability to love and enjoy and our ability to be loved and enjoyed. The Descendant can be seen as a place in the horoscope where we project our shadows, longings, and dreams toward the outer world. It can also be a place where we always feel disappointed with the outer world, because it doesn't meet the expectations and longings we have inside. Somehow, this is most easily seen in romantic love. Either we never find the perfect love we long for, or we find the prince or princess and kiss this heavenly creature only to discover that it turns into a frog. The real magic along this axis begins when we start the process of integration—the process of learning unconditional love for both others and ourselves. It can be seen as starting to kiss the frog, and through this kissing and the joy of being allowed to have such a fantastic relationship with such an amazing creature, transforming the inner and outer frog to a prince or princess.

Descendant in Aries

The Shadow

You are the neat, just, and balanced Libra Ascendant. The "other" has to carry your projections of being the rude, harsh, insensitive, greedy, aggressive, and unjust Aries archetype.

The Dream

You are the careful, balanced, bound, and oversensitive Libra Ascendant. The "other" has to carry your projections of being the self-reliant, decisive, brave, unhesitating, free-spirited, and strong-minded Aries archetype.

The Integration

As you start to allow yourself to express more and more of the self-reliant, rude, aggressive, brave, decisive, and free-spirited qualities that exist inside your being, your need to project them onto others will become less. Then you can start to appreciate and be attracted to people and circumstances that are more balanced, harmonious, and agreeable.

The Soul Integration

You start to see the wholeness and divinity in yourself and others by accepting the total need for freedom that is inside yourself and others. With this, you become able to balance the soul's understanding that we are fantastic mirrors of one another (Libra) and at the same time totally independent of one another (Aries). As this inner and outer merging happens, you learn to be separate (Aries) and at the same time in union (Libra).

Descendant in Taurus

The Shadow

The "other" has to carry your projections of being stubborn, stuck, and too materialistically occupied. They want to have things and are trapped in the world of money, achievements, and possessions.

The Dream

The "other" has to carry your projections of being happy, unconcerned, and satisfied. It is like you are overly sensitive and always in inner turmoil while others are calm and without problems and have this easy and simple life you should be able to have. To them, life is just a stroll in the field of flowers, while it is a struggle for you. You also have an admiration for people who can do things easily and in an unaffected manner.

The Integration

You start to see the wholeness and divinity in yourself and others by accepting your own need for security, comfort, and safety. As you start to see yourself as quite simple and just a member of the same race and humanity as the rest of the gang, the integration begins. As you accept your own earthly side and its needs and fears, the integration is well on its way.

The Soul Integration

As you see that Earth is a paradise and that your soul will be just as happy being here as anywhere else, the melding of being and soul begins. There is no need to search for something truer, more real, or better than where you are. As Earth becomes for you just as soulful and spiritual as the unfathomable depths, you begin the process of learning how to be totally present in the here and now.

Descendant in Gemini

The Shadow

The "other" has to carry your projections of being the insensitive talker who always has to give their opinion and show others how much they know. There is also a projection of others taking the easy way out, as well as forming opinions and feeling secure without having seen the whole picture. You can become very irritated with others who know all the answers and don't want to ask the questions.

The Dream

The "other" has to carry your projections of being the one who can make choices. You admire those who can devote themselves to a goal and really go for it. You will also be attracted to those who seem to have an easygoing, no-cares attitude. And you like the innocent, flamboyant free spirit, and you wish you could be just as free and unhampered by doubt and all the thoughts in your mind.

The Integration

As you learn to listen to others and to see that their point of view is just as viable as yours, the integration begins. There are many ways to get to Rome, and you have just one. As you start to understand what it is like to walk in the shoes of others and on the road of others, the integration process begins. The trick is really very simple. To really become interested in others and the words, thoughts, and experiences of others, instead of seeing them as receptors for your meaning and activities, is the key.

The Soul Integration

You start to see the wholeness and divinity in yourself and others by accepting that we are one and many at the same time. You learn to see the truth as one, even if it can be looked at and expressed in a multitude of ways. You learn to trust the universe at the same time as you use your mind and consciousness to read the road maps of life. You take your soul and your soul's longing for freedom and joy seriously, and you guide the inner child and the soul through the world with a clear and alert consciousness.

Descendant in Cancer

The Shadow

The "other" has to carry your projections of being whiny and sensitive. You can feel very annoyed by those who never stand up straight, who are whining and complaining, and who never know how to take responsibility for themselves. They are the soft and vulnerable ones who never grow up to understand the realities of life.

The Dream

The "other" takes on your projections of being the loving and caring ones who really are able to show their love. You see them as having rich, imaginative, and colorful inner lives. You see them as giving and nurturing, carrying with them a bag with all those goodies you long for but cannot find in yourself.

The Integration

As you start to open up to the world and let the world see your true inner feelings, longings, and vulnerability, the integration process begins. As you learn to trust others, and also to let go of control and accept the flow of feelings and life as it is, the integration goes on. And as you really get a hold on the ability to show others that you need them and are attached to them, you begin to feel more and more relaxed and complete.

The Soul Integration

You start to see the wholeness and divinity in yourself and others by accepting that the most important thing in the world is love and your ability to handle love properly. As you begin to understand that your body and the physical world at large is a vessel for love, and at the same time see that to love and respect the vessel is just as important as all other forms of love, the soul and your being begin to become integrated.

Descendant in Leo

The Shadow

The "other" has to bear your projections of being the egoistic, self-possessed braggart who wants to have all the attention. You can become furious when people only talk about themselves, when they try to be better and "more" than others, and when they are unable to see the bigger picture and can only see the world from the viewpoint of their own subjective interests.

The Dream

The "other" has to carry your projections of being the one you admire and look up to: the geniuses who stand out from the crowd and have the courage to state their opinions, the ones who dare to follow their own road and find their own answers. You admire others for their personal qualities of courage, bravery, honesty, and independence.

The Integration

As you stop hiding under the cloak of always thinking about what is right and just and how things should be, you start to become more honest. This integration happens when you are honest with yourself and others. And this is not just being honest about opinions and how things should be, but being honest about your own feelings, ambitions, needs, and lust.

The Soul Integration

You start to see the wholeness and divinity in yourself and others when you accept that your individuality is worth no less and no more than that of any other, and when you teach yourself to be free and play out your heart and joy and excitement with others. As you learn to let your soul flower amidst those who seem to be less or more than you, without comparing or judging yourself or others, your soul and your being start to sparkle—and you experience the sweet taste of real freedom.

Descendant in Virgo

The Shadow

The "other" has to carry your projections of being nitpickers, critics, and fun-spoilers. You can be extremely bored by those who you consider boring people, and you really feel bothered by the pack of sensitive, judging and small-minded people who always want to teach you a lesson or two about right and wrong and the ethics of life.

The Dream

The "other" has to shoulder your projections of being the clear-minded one who has the ability to see consequences before they act, as well as those who seem to have order, structure, and clarity in their life while you feel you are just floating around as a victim of your own feelings. You wish you could learn to be as clever, focused, and self-reliant as those you admire.

The Integration

This integration starts as you begin to combine sense and sensibility: when you learn to use your mind and heart at the same time. As you begin to get an idea of the consequences of doing and not doing, you can begin to choose what you shall act on and what you shall not act on, and so start to become clear in the ways you meet the world, on both the emotional and the mental level.

The Soul Integration

You start to see the wholeness and divinity in yourself and others by accepting that you in some way can experience unity with All That Is and in some other ways can experience being just the smallest speck of dust in a vast universe. As you stop being afraid of being alone, being small, or becoming immersed in the river of life and love, you can allow yourself to float with the tide of your soul's being and longing, and at the same time manage to handle the outer world in a rational and organized way.

Descendant in Libra

The Shadow

The "other" has to take on your projections of being independent and unreliable. You can see falseness in others, and you are irritated beyond words at people who never tell what they really mean or say what they really want. The false mask of fake friendliness is not something you like, and meaningless small talk seems to be the worst thing anyone can inflict upon you.

The Dream

The "other" has to carry your projections of being the beauty. You can be so attracted to the smell and the harmonious, pleasurable softness of others. You often see them as the gifted, beautiful, creative, and lovely people that you yourself long to be. You find perfection in others, and you experience being hopelessly attracted to them and feel that they have all that you really need to become whole.

The Integration

As you start to see your own inner beauty and create balance between independence and dependence, the integration starts. You learn that you do not always need to go first and be strong and independent. You can be the leader, but you can also allow others to lead. As you start to understand that you really need and long to be with others, and start to show your affection and communicate how important they are in your life, the inner split begins to heal.

The Soul Integration

You start to see the wholeness and divinity in yourself and others by accepting the meeting and the melding. As you see the divinity in others, it will begin to emerge in yourself. As you start to love and become devoted and amazed by those around you and become willing to give away what is near and dear to you (such as freedom), because your love for others doesn't make it a sacrifice but a gift you give gladly, your soul and your being begins to merge and you start to experience true togetherness of souls.

Descendant in Scorpio

The Shadow

You are the calm, trustworthy, and down-to-earth Taurus Ascendant. The "other" has to carry your projections of being the emotionally unstable, out-of-control, sex-monster, and greedy Scorpio archetype possessed by their feelings.

The Dream

You are solid, boring, and practical. The "other" has to carry your projections of intense passion, deep love, and the vibrant feeling of being fully alive and risking everything for what you feel in your heart and soul.

The Integration

This process starts as you allow yourself to get more and more in touch with your feelings and also to express them, to let the intensity and depth of your inner life shine through and become visible in the outer world. It is a process of becoming comfortable with the depth, passion, and intensity that is within you.

The Soul Integration

You start to see the wholeness and divinity in yourself and others by accepting both the inner world and the outer. You not only do the practical and sensible things, but you also allow your soul's experiences and longings to find a place both in your life and in your expression. You see and know that the intensity and depth of your soul is just as important as mastering the outer world. In short, you start to take the chances and challenges that your soul needs to become integrated in your life.

Descendant in Sagittarius

The Shadow

The "other" has to bear your projections of being the one who thinks they know it all. Oh, what a nuisance are those blind, self-secure chumps who are so easily fooled—the naïve idiots who believe anything and at the same time pester everybody else with their beliefs. The planet should be spared from those loud-mouthed fools who think they know something but always act without thinking and so get themselves into all kinds of trouble.

The Dream

The "other" has to carry your projections of being free and spontaneous. While you are thinking, they are living and enjoying life without a care in their minds. They are happy, lucky, and free, and gee … how much you wish you were like them.

The Integration

Here you start to find a deeper trust in yourself. You make choices and dare to throw yourself into the unknown every now and then. You learn to take a stand and to act on your beliefs, without having to know everything first, and you learn to give your undivided attention to other people. You do not stop to question, but you do start to believe in meaning and truth.

The Soul Integration

You start to see the wholeness and divinity in yourself and others through accepting that we are one and many at the same time. You learn to see the truth as one, even if you can look at it and express it in a multitude of ways. You learn to trust the universe, and to accept that different souls have different ways of seeing and expressing their deep values and meaning. You take your soul and your soul's longing for freedom and joy seriously, and guide the inner child and the soul through the world with a clear and alert consciousness. You have no more fear or shame for following your impulses and dedicate yourself to that deep inner knowing of your truth.

Descendant in Capricorn

The Shadow

The "other" has to shoulder your projections of being the hard, unfeeling, and uncaring materialist of the world. You can be really disappointed by people who seem to lack empathy and who think only about outer goals and consequences. You can feel that the "other" is a withdrawn, emotional, unavailable and ambitious egomaniac.

The Dream

The "other" has to carry your projections of being the one who knows how to handle life in a sensible and structured way. You see them as having inner discipline, clarity of ambition, and a great sense of responsibility. You can even envy his or her ability to maintain focus and not be distracted by everyone else.

The Integration

This integration comes as you learn to find the correct balance between the inner and the outer. You see that feelings have to have a container, and you learn to take responsibility for your own life and feelings instead of feeling responsible for everyone around. You also learn to find a working balance between your dreams and aspirations, as well as the action that is necessary to take to make them come true.

The Soul Integration

You start to see the wholeness and divinity in yourself and others by accepting that love sometimes is letting the other take responsibility for him or herself. You learn that you have to hold and stay with your feelings. You also start to go deeper as you become friends with the outer world and understand that life is neither harsh nor hard, but just a container you need to use and understand so your true love and soul dreams can come through and be manifested in actions.

Descendant in Aquarius

The Shadow

The "other" has to carry your projections of being the one who always has to take the opposite point of view. They are jealous, have to spoil the fun, and seem to have an obsession with their own ideas and minds. They have "big words," but not so much *action*, and they always have to be something special and different. They do not know how to just enjoy life and themselves.

The Dream

The "other" has to take on your projections of being the original and creative genius. You find them refreshing, interesting, and special. You admire their ability to stand out for themselves and to have and form their own understanding. The irony, humor, and freedom from caring about what others might think about them is very attractive to you, and you just love their independence and unpredictability.

The Integration

To understand how you can be yourself with others is a clue. To see yourself as clearly as possible, but also to see the others, is essential. To be able to be one of the crowd and to share the time in the limelight is important. This is a lesson in letting go of your subjectivity and the ego's need for attention and learning how to give your attention to others. To be special and at the same time to be completely normal and part of a group is a good way to integrate this Descendant.

The Soul Integration

You start to see the wholeness and divinity in yourself and others by accepting that you have an ego but knowing that you are not possessed by it. As you move on, the togetherness of souls and the recognition of your divinity through seeing the divinity in others will be a great step on the way to integrate soul and being. And when you really understand that you are the "other" and the "other" is you, the soul just throws a party in your body.

Descendant in Pisces

The Shadow

The "other" has to carry your projections of being unpractical, irresponsible dreamers who are just floating around and cannot be trusted for one minute. Their lack of ability to act as grownups and see the consequences of their behavior can drive you nuts. Worst of all are those who float around in their own illusions and don't even want to listen to your sensibility and good advice.

The Dream

The "other" has to carry your projections of being the ones who know how to float with life. You admire their ability to forgive and forget: their ability to be friendly and lovable and to move on to whatever life has to offer. You wish you could let go of the controls and stop being the skeptical analyst and just accept life and love as it is.

The Integration

As you learn to respect your feelings and your intuition, life becomes lighter. As you learn to love without being caught in the need to control and master, it becomes even easier. And when you learn to accept yourself as you are and stop trying to be more and better and nicer than you want to be, it brightens up your life. To learn to let go, love chaos, and accept that life and love is a risky adventure that always flows on and on is a very good way to go for a Pisces Descendant.

The Soul Integration

You start to see the wholeness and divinity in yourself and others by accepting that you are not alone. You and the "other" seem to merge, and you can finally allow yourself to trust the world, your feelings, your dreams, and the love of others. To be able to love without being caught in the pain of having to be perfect or make everything perfect for the other opens the gates of your soul. As you let go of guilt, shame, and the fear of becoming lost, you can ride the inner waves of your soul and still be totally clear and present in your being. There is no division between your soul and you, or your soul and the soul of others. We are divine players who enjoy playing... and that is all there is to it.

Signs in Houses

The sign is a wave of specific energy manifesting into the time-space dimension of a house. The combination of sign and house constitutes in many ways the setting and the stage, painted and ready, just waiting for the actors (planets) to draw the curtains so the show, "A Unique Incarnation on Planet Earth," can start. As the settings on the stage provide ideas about the psychology of the play, the combination of signs and houses provides the psychological and energetic background to the once-in-a-lifetime performance our life truly is.

Most of us are born with houses that are quite similar in size. The exceptions are, as mentioned earlier, people born very far to the north or the south. Those people cannot be measured by standard means anyway. If you go far enough, there are times of the year with eternal night, and other times with eternal day. My experience is that the house system, which is based on the cyclic movement from day to night and back, collapses under those circumstances. In other words, people born under those circumstances have an inner clock that ticks differently from those born under more "normal" circumstances. Their inner life is not neatly organized into the compartments we call houses. It's in a

way like having an inner house without rooms: there is an open concept, where everything more or less blends together without doors in
between. If we feel a need to have a functioning house system for these
people, an Equal House system based on the Ascendant will do. An
Equal House system is the archetypal pattern for a house system, something that makes it very usable.

That was the exception. When the houses are somewhat regular, or
when you use the Equal House system, the houses and signs follow an
interesting pattern. When we focus through the element, we have four
possibilities.

When you have a fire Ascendant, you will have fire on the cusp of
all of the fire houses (1.5.9). You will have earth on the cusp of all the
earth houses (2.4.6), air on the cusp of air houses, and water in water
houses.

But if you have an earth Ascendant, you will have earth on the cusp
of *all* of the fire houses. You will then have air on the cusp of all earth
houses, water on the cusp of air houses, and fire on the cusp of water
houses.

Since we have four possible elements for the Ascendant, we will get
four possible combinations of the element energy of signs and houses.
Which category a person falls into will say very much about how this
person connects with the different sides of life.

This very simple combination will show some basic ways to express
oneself, the basic approach to manifesting one's talents and creating in
form, one's basic needs and methods for communication and participation in social life, and one's ways to express one's deepest feelings,
needs, and inner world.

Fire Ascendant

Fire on 1.5.9

With a fire Ascendant, the need to express oneself and make an impression on the world, as shown by the first, fifth, and ninth houses, happens spontaneously and directly. There is a joy of being that will come
out as a manifestation of who one is here and now.

The Joy of Being

Earth on 2.6.10

The approach to mundane life, daily activities, manifestations, and career plans, as shown by the second, sixth, and tenth houses, is careful and purposeful. One does what has to be done. There is a great need to manifest products and to get a result from one's activities. The approach to money, career, and health is practical, reasonable, and security oriented.

The Beauty of Doing

Air on 3.7.11

The need for social contact, communication, ideas, and future plans, as shown by the third, seventh, and eleventh houses, is fulfilled through almost any kind of sharing. The importance here is on the sharing of ideas and the connection to similar or different opinions. The topics and themes are of less importance. Everything is interesting in a way, because the real need is in the sharing, not in the content of what is shared. The ideas are more interesting than reality, and one would prefer *not* to be burdened by too much reality or feelings.

The Sharing of Wisdom

Water on 4.8.12

The deep inner landscapes as shown by the fourth, eighth, and twelfth houses are experienced as a very deep and very private zone, only to be shared with those whom one trusts with the heart. These areas are connected with feelings of love and belonging, and if the person is uncomfortable with his or her inner world, these areas will lead to a strong feeling of loneliness. The fire Ascendant seems to show an extroverted person, but on the deeper layers, this person is very introverted.

The Boundless Love

Earth Ascendant

Earth on 1.5.9

The need to express oneself is connected to the need for results and reason. We could perhaps call it a controlled spontaneity. If there is a purpose or reason to be spontaneous, it can be allowed. On a spiritual level, the wish to unfold oneself with beauty controls the flow of personal expression. The experience of self-expression as a whole needs to have a foundation in meaning. There is a question about why one should express oneself, and that question needs to be answered before movement occurs.

Beautiful Self-expression

Air on 2.6.10

One enjoys planning the work and talking about what one wants to do—or to have done. There is a tendency to enjoy the planning and talking stage more than the actual doing. There is a need to understand the reason to do anything, and a great need for doing things together with others. Often, one likes to work with theories and enjoys spending a lot of the working time in meetings and discussions.

The Wisdom of Doing

Water on 3.7.11

The social sphere, as shown by the third, seventh, and eleventh houses is very connected to feelings and the inner world. One likes to talk and share personal things. Theories and ideas without emotional content are often found uninteresting. The tune of the voice and the emotional exchange is more important than the theoretical exchange of ideas. One can become vulnerable in social contexts, because communication is experienced as subjective and personal. On the spiritual level, it's a wish for sharing and experiencing love through communication.

Communication of Love

Fire on 4.8.12

The deep inner world is full of passion and sudden emotions flaring up. Both joy and despair are experienced with great intensity. This intensity can be hidden inside or expressed strongly. Everything that is connected with the deepest strata of the personal and spiritual is experienced strongly. One can be strongly self-occupied and subjective. There is a great need to express and act on one's inner feelings and experiences, whatever the result. To be true to one's inner self in outer action becomes very important. This may be a person who seems careful and introverted on the outside, but who can be surprisingly passionate and expressive as you come into his or her personal sphere and safety zone. These people show who they really are to the few who gain access to their inner sanctuaries—the fourth, eighth, and twelfth houses.

Intensity of Love

Air Ascendant

Air on 1.5.9

There is a great need here to communicate oneself to others. One sees words, ideas, and meanings as a way to express whom one really is. It's easy to defend one's opinions strongly, because a challenge to one's opinion is also experienced as a challenge to one's self. One needs company and sharing to experience oneself, and being alone can easily be experienced as a state of limbo. On a spiritual level, there is full balance between what the person says and what he or she does. In other words, they walk their talk.

The Joy of Sharing Wisdom

Water on 2.6.10

With this combination, one is very emotionally connected to one's doing. One needs to feel secure in a working situation. It's important that one's action is connected with one's emotional needs. There can be a great need for security, as well as a difficulty in letting go of material things, working places, and daily habits. On the other hand, when there are no emotional bonds, things disappear very quickly. There is also a great need to express one's inner world through tangible form. There can be a great love for and appreciation of the sensual and physical world.

The Love of Beauty

Fire on 3.7.11

The fiery elements will be shown through communication. Enthusiasm, inspiration, and the joy of exchanging ideas are one manifestation of this combination. Another might be a quarreling disposition: a need to always talk directly and tell the truth, no matter how hurtful or stupid it is, and an inability to hold one's tongue or let others finish their sentences. This person has a need for direct, spontaneous, and inspired communication and sharing.

The Joy of Wisdom

Earth on 4.8.12

This goes very deep. One appreciates the inner world, or feels a great deal of weight inside. There is a need to feel safe before one opens up the doors to the inner temple. One protects oneself through reason and distance. To be shown the incredible riches of these inner worlds, you have to earn it. It takes time to forge deep connections, and one must have reasons to believe that these bonds will last for a long time. On the outer level, one has the ability to be very practical around the inner worlds of feeling. There is a need to create beautiful and secure surroundings, if one is able to let the deep flow of love rise to the surface and flow out into the world. Again, there is brightness on the outside, as shown through air on the fire houses and fire on the air houses. But on the inside, there is much weight and depth, which will surprise an unaware visitor.

The Beauty of Love

Water Ascendant

Water on 1.5.9

One's personal expression, as it is shown by first, fifth, and ninth houses, is filtered through the emotions and the inner world. One's inner state will be expressed in action. There is a need to act or not act on emotions. This can be a very moody combination, because one's immediate inner reaction is directly expressed. The only way to avoid this is to freeze—to have no reaction at all—which is experienced very strongly by other people. So one's behavior and experience of the world can change rapidly. One is very sensitive to other people's reactions toward one's own self-expression, and the distance from pure joy to depression can be very short. On a spiritual level, this combination gives a very loving, direct, and joyful expression.

The Love of Joy

Fire on 2.6.10

With this combination, one has a tendency to avoid planning one's work. In the real world, one creates the road as one walks. There is great joy from using one's creative and expressive energy to create something that can be measured. One can expand a lot of energy to get results, but one can be somewhat lazy if one doesn't see the point. One also has a knack for avoiding work that's uninspiring and on the rather dull side. When one does something, one has a tendency to become caught up in it and lose track of time. One is very focused and lost in one's own process of expressing through form—or very bored.

The Joy of Creating

Earth on 3.7.11

One's social interests and connections to the world are very much governed by practical interests. One likes to talk to people about things that one is doing. And one tends to stick with people whom one is doing things with or has the same interests as. It is this shared interest that keeps them together, more than emotional bonding. One is easily bored if people talk too much about meaningless theories or feelings, and one has a tendency to act on one's own or others' ideas. One has a great ability to see how people can be of help to and support each other. In fact, one probably thinks that friends are there to help and use each other.

Practical Wisdom and Common Sense

Air on 4.8.12

With air on the cusp of these houses, one has a great need to understand and express one's inner world. One might be a person who talks about deep emotional things as if they mean nothing. In a way, one can talk about most things without being emotionally involved, which can make one either very superficial or very clear-headed and wise. One needs to gain a deep understanding of the areas shown by these houses so that one can be objective and calm and at the same time have empathy and warmth. One has a great need to share one's inner world with others. One must be sure to listen and have as much respect for others' feelings and needs as for one's own.

The Inner Wisdom

THE PLANETS

The universe is not required to be in perfect harmony with human ambition.

—CARL SAGAN

"All the world's a stage, And all the men and women merely players." This poetic statement, which comes from Shakespeare, is just as valid today as during Shakespeare's time, and it is a beautiful way to view a horoscope. The planets are players in our horoscope, and the houses and signs are the stage. But one question arises: Who am I? Am I the one playing with the planets on the stage, the director, or perhaps the playwright?

When a child is born, a disposition is already present. Astrologically, that means that some of your personality is present before you have a birth horoscope. You could say that every person born comes with a cosmic history and is a unique soul formed through many incarnations on Earth and/or other places. The first incarnation of an absolutely new soul is not a topic for this book. We could say that every being comes with a pattern or a history, which we will call karma. But every being also comes with a range of possibilities and probabilities. In this meeting between what has been and what may come, a personality is formed. It is very important to be aware that as a soul, you are *not* your horoscope.

I have had many horoscopes, and I will have others in the future. The horoscope is not a description of my being, but rather a description of how my present individual personality is formed and what energies it has to work with. This is the main reason you can be an extremely happy and joyful person and have the most challenging horoscope the solar system can produce—and the reason you can have the easiest chart ever and still be a rotten asshole.

Your connection with spirit and your soul energy and your consciousness on the soul plane, which connects with and infuses your "earthly" consciousness, is what decides on which level you want your little performance to be played.

We live in a solar system that recognizes nine major planets. Together with the Sun, this makes ten major objects in our solar system. Since Earth is our home, the tenth "planet" for us is the Moon. Perhaps the Moon can be seen as the outer reflection of our relationship to Mother Earth; some scientists believe that our Moon once was a part of planet Earth.

This solar system has been an important factor in forming our conception of the world: we have a counting system that goes to ten, and maybe it is no coincidence that we have ten fingers and ten toes. Who knows? This kind of speculation can be taken to absurd lengths, so correlations can be found between the most fantastic occurrences and circumstances. But I believe that our inner symbolic world—yes, that even our language would have been different—if we had lived on a planet with three suns, four moons, and twenty-seven other planets.

The planets are symbols and bearers of the contents in our inner psyche. They tell a story about how we experience inner and outer reality on this planet and what kind of road we have to take if we are to pass the limits of this solar system and its special way of manifesting time and space. They show the road we have to take to reach beyond the solar system and be a part of a bigger universe. As long as we are prisoners of our horoscope, we will be prisoners of our ego. To reach beyond the ego, we have to open up to the inner cosmic space that starts beyond Pluto. To be born as a cosmic being, we have to pass through our inner Kuiper belt, and reemerge as a stellar being instead of a solar being.

The Sun is the core of energy in our solar system. It is the generator, and in the following "reading" of the script of the planets, we will follow the rays of the Sun on its outbound journey.

The Sun

From a spiritual point of view, the Sun is what enlightens us. The Sun is the source of light and energy for the body, the psyche, and the soul. The Sun is also the symbol of our essence, the flame and the life force within us. It is no accident that the Sun was the major god in the Egyptian religion. The Sun is by its very nature the essence of spirit, so it is through the outer and inner sun that the life force comes into being.

As has already been explained, light, and the Sun in the horoscope, can be a wave or a particle. As a wave, the Sun becomes a channel for the spiritual force. As a particle, it becomes our little part of the spiritual force, as it is manifested here and now—in other words, our sense of identity and our inner point of focus. If the Sun is free and flowing in a horoscope, there is a lot of energy and warmth. If the Sun is blocked, there is lack of energy, low vitality, and constant tiredness. The sign of the Sun tells a story about what kind of energy we have to work with and through to manifest as much as possible of the flow of light from our inner core. The descriptions of the signs can, with small modifications, be seen as descriptions of the Sun in the signs.

Astrology is a great art of synthesis. One of the first problems the up-and-coming learner of astrology meets is the confusion that arises when they find that they have the Sun in one sign and, for most of them, the Moon in another, and Venus and Mars and Mercury and the rest of the gang in different signs. How can they be daring and direct and shy and careful at the same time? To understand how these energies float into each other and weave a beautiful pattern of all of the colors in our lives is the art of the astrologer. And no computer program can see and understand this. If we see the Sun as our fireplace, the warmth of the whole mansion (horoscope) comes from the sign and house where the Sun is. When the fire is blazing, we can walk freely with warmth through all areas of life. When the Sun is burning low, we have to stay in the house where the Sun is situated in order to get any warmth at all.

The element and quality of the Sun in our horoscope tells us where we have to go and what wave of energy we have to stay on to be in contact with life and to become filled with this light. The Sun is our access point to spirit. Our solar challenge is to master this energy as it unfolds through the palette and complexity of all our planetary energies. To become master of the Sun is to become the hero in your own life and to face the fear and the inner and outer monsters that threaten to darken the spiritual light inside and outside. To be the Sun is to create oneself again and again in an eternal flow of life. This is the steady and unchanging part of our being, in the same way that the Sun is the steady and unchanging source of light, warmth, and life-giving force in the solar system. To understand the Sun, we just have to read about the different elements and qualities as they have been explained in the earlier chapters. Since the Sun is where these energies come from, this will be valid for understanding the Sun in the horoscope. Simply put, all of the other planets are concerned with special qualities and facets of our being as it unfolds in time and space. The Sun is our source and our access point to that energy that flows from the timeless and eternal into the dimensions of time and space. The Sun is our spirit, and if we are well connected with our Sun, we are high on energy on the physical level, high on self-confidence and well-being in our psyche, and high on joy and connectedness to the spiritual center. If we have lost the spiritual experience of this energy, we might be high on energy, but at the same time we will feel loneliness in the world.

We do not connect to the source through annihilation of our center, but rather by connecting this center to the spiritual source of its origin.

The Moon

The Moon is something totally different. The Moon has three main functions. Two of them are reflection and digestion. On the physical and psychological levels, the Moon is our digestion system, our way of processing food, emotions, thoughts, and energy. Since the Moon becomes visible through reflecting the light of the Sun, the Moon shows our ability to reflect another person and to be reflected by others. When we talk about mirroring each other or about projections in psychology, we talk about the Moon. It is the light of our Sun that is projected, but it is the Moon that makes it possible to reflect a projection of another being in our inner psyche. On the most basic level, the Moon is about instincts, or our automated responses to influences from the outside world. Many would call these feelings, because these instinctual responses generate what we call feelings. We can feel safe or threatened, nurtured or dissatisfied. We could say that it always shows our response to outside stimuli, and if we are not aware, this response will generate an automatic behavior.

Since the Moon also is concerned with the digestion process, it often takes some time before we really know what we feel about a given stimulus. Remember that the Moon in itself always is round and full. It is the way it reflects light from the Sun that gives us the impression of it being new, half, or full. It takes a bit of time and processing to become aware of that part of the Moon (our reactions) that is not immediately visible in the reflected sunlight.

The Moon is also what gives us the ability to be nurtured by what we take in from the outside. We eat, digest, and take into our bodies some of the stuff from food, and then we remove the rest from our systems as waste. If we are going to grow, the same process must happen on the emotional, mental, and energetic levels. Without the Moon, we would be incapable of growth and change.

Since the Moon also is about getting the nourishment we need, it is connected with survival and the fear of not surviving. On the spiritual level, the Sun is the constant force of spirit that shines through us and out into the world. The Moon is our ability to receive spiritual energy from the outside and to be nurtured and grow through the process of assimilating the spiritual force that radiates from anything in the outside. If we take a look at healing, we can see two main pathways. The first is healing by Sun energy: to radiate out an energy or a spiritual awareness from yourself that is reflected in others and helps them to become clear and nourished. The other, in which we use our Moon, works by drawing out of the "patient" what makes him or her sick. Both of them are valid ways of working with the energetic systems of others. The danger of using the Moon way is that we become contaminated because we draw into ourselves what we remove from the other person's system. The danger of the Sun method of energy healing is that we send out our own energy without really knowing if that is what the other person needs.

The Moon is our inner flow that makes it possible for us to adjust to and nurture ourselves from the environment we live in. We could call it our inner rhythm. On the biological level, it is the rhythm of our inner clock. This is the rhythm that makes us aware of hunger, the need for sleep, the need for sex, and even the need to procreate and become parents. On the ego level it is the ebb and flow of our need to express ourselves, the need to be fed from interchange with other individuals, and the need to give from ourselves and nurture other individuals. We could also say that on one level it is the body's need to adjust to the rhythms of nature. On the social level, it is the mechanism that makes it possible for us to adjust to the rhythm of the society we live in, and on the spiritual level, it is the need to adjust to the flow of spiritual energy as it flows through everything that is. Many of our emotional troubles in modern society arise from the fact that these rhythms are out of sync with each other. Human society has created an artificial rhythm that has brought the rhythm of nature out of balance. And our individual rhythm often seems to collide with both nature's and society's. In fact, the only way to realign these rhythms is to go for the "template," or the underlying and highest-vibrating rhythm of them all. This is the rhythm of energy as it floats from the spiritual dimension into the physical world. All of the other rhythms are created by this mother-father rhythm, and when we are aligned with this, it will allow us to be in the world and at the same time be in tune with nature, ourselves, and even society.

The Moon's placement in sign and quality gives us information about what we need from the outer world to feel nurtured and grow physically, emotionally, mentally, and spiritually. And since the Moon is how others are reflected in us, it shows how we reflect back to others the light they send us. Remember, it is a lot different from the light we send out from the Sun, which is coming from our core, and the light we send out from the Moon, which is a response and reflection of the light others send from their cores (or a reflection of their reflection of somebody else's energy). The light from the Sun becomes dimmed if we lose contact with ourselves. The Moon becomes dimmed if we do not receive impulses from the world around us.

One of the most important games in life is to learn what kind of energy nurtures us and what kind of energy harms us or is without "nutritional" value. In other words, we need to know what kind of energy to take into our system and digest and what kind of energy to deflect by avoiding it or by saying "no thanks" to it.

The element of the Moon tells us quite a lot about what we need to be nurtured in ourselves and our way of nurturing others.

Moon in Earth: Taurus, Virgo, and Capricorn

As we remember, earth is about beauty and how the beauty shines through the physical. With an earth Moon, we are nurtured by being in beautiful environments and being around beautiful and physically demonstrated feelings. In other words, we need to touch and be touched. We need to eat beautifully prepared food and hang out with graceful and natural people. We nurture others by showing them our gratitude and letting them know how beautiful we find them to be. When this Moon gets sour, it feeds negative energy to people by reflecting their ugliness and faults back to them, and then we get caught in nurturing ourselves on things like criticism and negativity from others.

On the spiritual level, we get nurtured by seeing the beauty in all that is created, by being grateful for the physical world, our bodies, and a God that has taken the trouble of manifesting itself as form in time and space. To be immensely grateful for being in this physical world is the road to enlightenment and satisfaction for an earth Moon.

Moon in Fire: Aries, Leo, and Sagittarius

Moon in fire is about feeling the joy and ecstasy in creation. A fire Moon becomes weak and depleted if there is too little joy and laughter around. We need to enjoy eating, and to feel the warmth and energy from the food; we also need to feel the warmth and energy from other people's emotion, and feel the fire in their minds. As a reflection, we nourish other people through our enthusiasm, giving hope and encouragement and supporting them with joy and our belief in them. If this Moon goes sour, it becomes either empty of energy and loses the hope or it becomes filled with negative fiery emotions. Examples can be hate, aggression, and intense belief in negative thinking. For this Moon, the enjoyment of eating and the fun in life is more important than proper nutrition, common sense, and safety. The freedom to choose when you want to eat is far more important than to have regular and healthy meals. This goes just as much for emotional, mental, and spiritual "meals" as for physical eating. If this Moon enjoys its own freedom, the message it reflects back to others is that they are also free to be and do whatever they want whenever they want.

On the spiritual level, growth is increased just by feeling the life force and the joy of all living beings. Laughter is medicine for the soul, play for the body, and intensity for the emotions. Indifference and cold is a bit like poison for these Moons. This Moon reflects others' joy by sending its own feeling of joy back to them. To feel that life is joyful and that the universe is a big amusement park where we act out our different roles in an immensely exciting play is gold for the fire Moon.

Moon in Air: Gemini, Libra, and Aquarius

Air is about wisdom, being inspired, and feelings of togetherness. It needs inspiration from and connection to other minds and ideas. This Moon enjoys having company when eating. It needs stimulation and humor. It gets bored from eating the same food, receiving the same feelings, or listening to the same ideas and opinions for any length of time.

It needs new and inspiring food on the physical, emotional, mental, and spiritual levels. It becomes nurtured by new and exciting ideas and light. It does not like the heavy stuff very much, but rather likes to float around in a world of possibilities. Openness and space are important. It really needs to feel the space in between to avoid the feeling of being caught between a rock and a hard place. There is a vital need for emptiness in the form of pauses and periods of emotional silence. Also, it is a very fast Moon; it reflects and "eats" the energy that comes along in almost no time. The empty space is necessary for the digestion process. That goes for food, emotional input, thought, and spiritual energy. So it needs to feel connected to the web of life, but not too intensely or closely, because then it feels caught in the web of life instead. It nurtures others by telling them that they are seen. It reflects others' emotions, ideas, and thoughts back to them in an almost instant flow. Of course, one of the things this Moon needs is clarity: clear and fresh air, clear and fresh emotions, clear and fresh thought, and clear and fresh energy. If it does not get this input of new stimuli, it loses its inspiration and becomes dull and lifeless. If it takes in and digests stupid thoughts, uninspired food, dull and negative emotions, and meaningless spirituality, it can become very clouded and contaminated itself. Then what it nurtures others with is contaminated, unclear, and stupid.

It gets going on the spiritual road by surrendering itself to the play of life. It must aim to be a part of society and the scene without being caught in the web. It does need to find wise and clear people to nurture it. When it starts to see and understand the force that lies under All That Is and lets itself float in the infinite sea of truth, it starts to find the true wisdom. The Moon in air needs to learn that even if truth can be expressed in thousands and thousands of ways, it is one force and there is one unchanging truth that lies beneath the endless sea of opportunities and choices that makes up the outer world. In fact, when this Moon starts to become inspired by that being and truth, which is the breath of life and the awareness that runs through everything, it starts to become one with the awareness. As it reflects the mind and thought of "God," it starts to become filled by the thought of "God" and it starts to speak and express itself with the tongue of "God" (life/truth).

Moon in Water: Cancer, Scorpio, and Pisces

This is the love Moon. Simply put, it nurtures itself on the love, or lack thereof, that is available in its surroundings. And as with all other Moons, it starts life by reflecting back exactly what is fed into it. As it grows, it needs to learn to discern between good and bad love—between love that is pure, unselfish, and without conditions and love that is filled with unhealthy demands, assumptions, condemnation, and, last but not least, guilt. It needs to eat food prepared by loving hands and loving thoughts. It needs to be around people with open hearts, and it needs words and communication to be based on a foundation of love and respect for both the one giving and the one receiving. The way it nurtures others is by sending them love and making them feel that it really does care and really does want the best for them. If it tries to nurture others without getting any "food" itself, the love it gives out will get spiced with bitterness, remorse, and ungratefulness. If it is around too many emotionally unhealthy people, it will start to become contaminated and will feel a lot of dark, negative, and murky feelings. To love is to experience the joy of meeting somebody in the heart. This joy of meeting is the road to true spirituality for this Moon. When it really does become a master in the game of love, it deflects the impure emotions emanating from the environment and nurtures itself only on the true and pure love. In the same manner, it does not respond to what is without love in the outer world, but only reflects back what is loving and caring. In other words, it never criticizes or feels rejected by the lack of love in others.

The feeling behind the watery Moon's way to spiritual mastery is devotion: to be devoted to the love of life and to give oneself totally to what one loves (which on a personal level is to be devoted to what one loves in another person, not to be totally devoted to everything in that person). It is to accept the love and devotion from others without judging or putting up defenses or making demands for how one is going to be loved. This is the true love of seeing, meeting, and dancing with God, through seeing, meeting, and dancing with all the multiple forms of God that are manifested in the visible and invisible universe.

Moon in Cardinal: Aries, Cancer, Libra, and Capricorn

The quality of the Moon shows how energy is reflected and digested. It also shows the natural rhythm of the person with this Moon. While the Sun is our steady stream of being and our permanent personality, the Moon is the part of us that is always changing and moving. With a cardinal Moon, we reflect the rhythm of others by sending back an immediate response. It becomes like a springboard, where what hits us immediately is bounced back. And the cardinal Moon acts. We manifest this reflection through our actions. The digestion process happens much the same way. What comes in is exactly what comes out. Bad food gives us a bad reaction. If we digest bad feelings, we express those same feelings with our next heartbeat.

One of the things a cardinal Moon does is to reflect the environment's use of will. If you try to force a cardinal Moon into anything, it will defend itself by using exactly the same force of pushing you to do something. This Moon can easily be caught in a battle of wills. When it operates on a higher frequency, it does not experience others' wills as a threat, nor does it feel any need to push others by its own will. Instead, it starts to see the meeting of wills as a beautiful (earth), joyful (fire), harmonious (air), or loving (water) dance. It lets itself be nurtured and carried by the will of others, and in the same way it nurtures and carries others through the use of its own will. In the end, it is nurtured and carried by the spiritual force of the absolute being. And in the same way, it nurtures and carries others by being a channel for this spiritual will that flows through its system.

Moon in Mutable: Gemini, Virgo, Sagittarius, and Pisces

These Moons are about making choices. They have the capacity to let things flow through them. In some sense, they can let the input from others go through without becoming personally touched by it. They can see emotions, thoughts, and energy as just a stream. But to become nurtured, they have to make a choice about what to take in and digest and what to let pass by. They have to choose when to become individual and take it personally. If everything becomes personal, they will become confused and overstimulated by the input, because the mutable Moons can soak up everything in the flow. When things become personal, they have to learn not to go with the flow, but to choose what to deflect and what to take in. In the same manner, they will have to choose what to reflect back to the sender and what to deflect aside. On a personal level, they will reflect back everything that is personal, and if they are caught up in their own personal shortcomings, guilt, and fear, this is what will be reflected back to the sender.

For these Moons, the road to enlightenment is to reflect what has the highest energy. In the same manner, it is also to take in and digest what is purest of the emotions, thought, and spiritual energy in the big stream of life. If they stay too long in the stream without becoming personal, they will lose themselves there and become unable to choose. If they stay too long in the personal form, they will be caught by whatever comes their way, lose control over the situation, and end up feeling like a ping-pong ball that others are playing with. They do not only thrive by learning to discern the good stuff from the bad stuff; they also need to learn timing. What is good stuff at one time will become bad at another, and vice versa.

When they walk the true road of spiritual understanding, they will start to see the whole flow as a spiritual river and will know that everything is okay. It is just a game, and since they are just players but are not caught in the game, they are free to choose. When they reach mastery, they learn to go with the flow and be personal at the same time. They let the river flow, but they choose the appropriate response and nourishment at any given time. They reflect what helps others to become more joyful, loving, wise, and beautiful, and they nurture others by sending out the appropriate amount of joy (Sagittarius), love (Pisces), wisdom (Gemini), and beauty (Virgo) at the exact right moment. Truly mastering choice, they can wait or they can reflect. And by playing the game they reach a level of awareness that gives them information about what is needed for their own and others' spiritual growth. By developing this awareness about their own and others' reactions and mirroring games, they develop more and more contact with the absolute truth of the moment and do not become distracted from that.

Moon in Fixed: Taurus, Leo, Scorpio, and Aquarius

The fixed Moon could also be called the delayed Moon. When it deflects, it seems like it holds up a shield. What is sent to it is simply not taken in and falls dead to the ground. Its way of reflection when this happens is by not giving any response at all, which can drive others quite crazy. When it does take in the energy, it needs time to digest—time to digest its food, emotions, thoughts, and spiritual experiences. In this process, it separates the waste from the useful. An undeveloped fixed Moon will take the waste and reflect it back to the deliverer and keep the good stuff for itself. A developed fixed Moon will send the waste for recycling and reflect back the good stuff.

Through its inner processing, the fixed Moon has the ability to change the quality of what it receives. This even goes for food, as it can take "bad" food and recycle it in the body so it becomes nutritious. If Leo enjoys bad food it becomes healthy. If Scorpio loves bad food, it becomes healthy. If Aquarius really has a good time eating bad food, it becomes healthy. And if Taurus finds bad food delicious and beautiful, it becomes full of nutritional value. The same goes for emotions, thoughts, and spirituality. Also, this process can happen the other way around: it can remove the real nutrition from the good stuff and make it into something unhealthy for its body, emotions, and mind.

So the fixed Moon is about changing what it takes in to another frequency. The spiritual path is, of course, to always seek the highest frequency: to find the right situation for being nurtured and the right situation for nurturing and to always strive to eliminate waste and to send back the good stuff at as high and clear a frequency as available. The destructive fixed Moon, however, will always lower the frequency. Most fixed Moons will shift between lowering the energy or raising it, depending on the mood and situation. If the fixed Moon goes on to raise its reflection and digestion to higher and higher levels of frequency, it will inevitably end up as enlightened.

Integration of Sun and Moon Principles

The Sun and the Moon are, in many ways, our inner core. They are the basic forces of yin and yang, the electric and magnetic energies that make up our fundamental nature. The Sun is the energy radiating from our core, and the Moon our inner magnetic wiring that makes us attract and become attached. It's the magnetic energy of the Moon that binds and holds people and societies together. The Sun has a gravitational pull, so it can hold the solar system (itself) in balance. But it is the Moon that gives us the ability to connect and belong on a deep level with another being. We could also say that the Sun represents our ego as a particle, while the Moon represents our ego as a wave.

Since men have been thought of as primarily solar and women as primarily lunar, men have been seen as the force wanting to shoot out into new and unknown regions, and women as the force that holds society and families together. As we develop our consciousness, we start to see that every individual is as much a lunar being as a solar one. So this integration of the lunar and solar energies is the first step, and an absolutely necessary one, on the road to becoming centered in our souls.

With a weak Sun, we have a weak feeling of identity, often low energy, and a lack of contact with the central purpose of our lives. With a weak Moon, we feel a lack of belonging. We often feel alienated from our surroundings, harbor a great loneliness, and have a hard time understanding what goes on inside others.

The Moon represents our first and deepest experience of becoming a life on this planet. It's our body's remembrance of being a part of the rhythm and pulse of our mother through the umbilical cord. It's also a connection to our collective remembrance of being a part of life in the collective sea. It's our souls' remembrance of unity. The Sun is the rhythm of our heart, but the Moon is the feeling of the flow of blood and all of the other fluids in our body. The Moon is our inner rhythm, and the Sun our need to express ourselves to the outer world. When the Sun dominates the Moon, we destroy and distort our natural rhythm. When the Moon dominates the Sun, we are locked in by our magnetic energy, held in a rhythm that gives too little opportunity for beaming out and being a singular entity with an energy that is different from the collective rhythm. So one of our biggest tasks here on Earth is to harmonize these two energies.

For centuries, many of us have been born as men when we wanted to learn about power and authority and to make our way in the world, and born as women when we wanted to learn about love, holding together, serving, and forgiving. Of course, there are lots and lots of exceptions, but these are the general tendencies. Today, most of us have had enough of these lopsided experiences, and so we have the merging of magnetic yin and electric yang forces on our agenda. To do this, we have to accept the rhythm of the sign where our Moon is situated as our inner rhythm, and our Sun sign energy as our way to express ourselves in the world. You will be attracted to and feel a need to belong to something that has the flavor and flow of your Moon sign. It's important to remember that the real reason for stress is that you are moving in a way that conflicts with your natural rhythm. To try to flow with an Aries rhythm that goes from one extreme to the other would be very stressful and anxiety-provoking for a Taurus Moon. On the other hand, for the Aries Moon, the slow and steady rhythm of the Taurus Moon would feel either like a dull day in nothing-happens land or like the unbearable pressure of being fixed to one spot.

Mercury and the Union of Sun and Moon

The Sun, Moon, Mercury, Venus, and Mars are the personal planets; they constitute our personality. But there is a big difference between the Sun and Moon and the rest of the lot.

The Sun and Moon represent the core of our being. When we seek illumination, it is this core that is our essence. Mercury, Venus, and Mars are the tools and helpers of the Sun and Moon. As we become more and more illuminated, it is the very core of our being—the Sun and Moon—that changes. Of course, the way we use our tools will also change. On the outer level, Mercury, Venus, and Mars are the tools we have to express ourselves, the tools for handling the outer world and functioning effectively in it. In our search for insight, wisdom, and illumination, they will also be our tools for working on ourselves. Their power can be directed inward for change and improvement or outward for reaching goals and connecting with the outer world.

Mercury is our capacity for using language, thinking, and expressing our thoughts and conceptions. In fact, we can be illuminated without having a Mercury that is very effective in expressing itself. There are stories about enlightened masters who are more or less unable to express what enlightenment is, even unable to use language at all. To become illuminated doesn't make you a great talker or thinker.

One of the most used sayings about how to get enlightened is that you have to stop the chatterbox (Mercury) from its perpetual occupation with running around in the hamster wheel of repetition, worrying, and unproductive thinking. But Mercury has a great function: it gives us the ability to work with combining and melding the forces of the Sun and the Moon on a conscious level. Of course, it is also about cleverness and having a fast and good mind. In many ways, Mercury is like a computer: what comes out of it is what we put in.

On its own, Mercury is curious. It can find meaning in connecting things, in collecting things, and in seeing what is different in one thing from something else. In other words, it can be heavily occupied with totally meaningless information. Knowledge without any wisdom is just this: a meaningless collection of data. Imagine a computer with feelings. It would maybe hate to be turned off, and it would probably find whatever data it was processing interesting.

This is one face of Mercury running wild when it is disconnected from its spiritual source. Another face can be the messenger of dry sarcasm, bitterness, and despair. Mercury might have fooled the individual into believing that there is no spiritual source. In other words, it made the individual see himself as a closed and alienated ego. As long as Mercury accepts the Moon, one can find a meaning in togetherness and belonging to the land and family, even if one is disconnected from the spiritual source. If the connection to the soul energy of the Moon is also broken, the loneliness becomes very severe, and life a sad experience. One can become a brain and try to suppress everything else, or one can become this bitter and negative nonbeliever who only sees the cold and hard, separate from every phenomenon.

When one regains the deep understanding of Mercury's function, however, things change. One strives once again to make Mercury the messenger for the Sun, bringing the aid that makes it possible both to express oneself in a clear and precise manner and, just as importantly, to really listen to others' communication so one can understand their words through one's own spirit and soul. There is a great difference between a communication that only goes from brain to brain and a communication that goes through the brain from heart to heart and soul to soul.

In alchemy, the metal mercury was the substance needed to make the sacred marriage between the king (Sun) and the queen (Moon). This marriage was called *Hieros Gamos* and was the endpoint in the work of the alchemist, also described as creating the Philosopher's Stone or making the elixir of eternal life. On the outer level, alchemists sought to create gold out of raw material (*prima materia*), but on the inner level, they sought illumination—the gold of the soul. The metal mercury has the capacity to bind itself to gold. We could say that it was a necessary instrument for extracting the gold from the *prima materia*. In the same way, the qualities of Mercury, as it appears in the horoscope, are necessary for extracting the gold of our souls from the personality. We need to use our mind and consciousness to form the union of our Sun and Moon, which is necessary for illumination. Even if the mind and knowledge aren't necessary for enlightenment, it is necessary to use Mercury to understand how this process can happen. Mercury can find the way and point us in the right direction, and we can use our mind and logic to look for insight and understanding. It is no coincidence that the only one of the Greek gods who could travel to Hades and return was Hermes. We can use the power of this planet to see beyond time and space and the mortality of body and ego. We can understand where the real gold is hidden and then use logic, clarity of mind, and awareness to transport ourselves to this place, even if it is not our mind but our being that is enlightened.

On the instinctual level, Mercury is a prolonging of our nervous system, just as the brain is a prolonging of our spinal cord. It transports our nerve reflexes into a world of thoughts and words. So Mercury is the consciousness created through the electric and magnetic impulses of the brain. A beautiful description of this is given in Nordic mythology. The squirrel Ratatosk runs up and down the trunk of the world tree Yggdrasil, which is like nerve impulses running up and down the spine. Ratatosk tells the animals and birds in the crown of the tree what goes on farther down and brings messages from these animals to the snake lying by the roots of the tree.

Like Virgil in Dante's *Divine Comedy*, Mercury is our guide through hell, purgatory, and heaven. Mercury is the observer that can tell us what really goes on, and that can help us to not become attached. Without Mercury, we would have two choices: either to stay away from the experience or to be totally immersed in it.

Through this ability to observe what is going on, we can learn, and through this learning, we can choose to change the experience the next time a similar situation pops up. One of the problems with Mercury is that this tool easily becomes the master instead of the servant. When we lose our spiritual understanding and our inner contact with our soul, we often start to feel like just a body with a brain and a bunch of emotions. The body is not well equipped to be a leader. Many have tried to be led by their flow of changing and unstable emotions, but they have found that it leads nowhere, so they then try to govern their life through the mind function of Mercury. This is a bit like asking your private driver to tell you where you are going. By itself, Mercury is curious and interested in everything. But it has no goal outside of satisfying this curiosity. No wonder most people are driving around without knowing where they want to go with their lives. Mercury has absolutely no business in choosing our directions and goals in life, but it can be of immense help as soon as we have decided where we want to go. On the spiritual level, we can use Mercury's ability to change nerve impulses and electric impulses in the brain into thoughts, words, and ideas as a device for becoming aware of where we want to go and how we want to get there. It gives us insight that can lead the queen to the king's bed, so we can celebrate the eternal inner marriage and become whole, united, and illuminated. The quality of Mercury tells us a lot about how this messenger and computer inside us works, and the element of Mercury's sign gives us an idea about what kind of input it needs to be most effective. Will Mercury express through beauty, joy, love, or wisdom? Will it be strong and forceful and search for new territories to discover, as in Aries, or will it be methodical and build sentences like steps on a ladder, as in Capricorn? It seldom works to abuse a part of yourself (or others) to get where you want to be; at least, this does not work if your long-term goal is to become illuminated. So we have to cooperate with our mental computer to understand how we do work and how we can rearrange our inner self so that it is in accordance with the highest and best in us.

Mercury in a Cardinal Sign

On the spiritual level, Mercury is not occupied with finding the right answer. It doesn't cling to opinions or think that it has the only correct data program. It has moved out of right or wrong and seeks a deeper understanding. In the spiritual, it follows an idea or an understanding. It uses the will and its power to probe into the matter. When a cardinal Mercury reaches the crest of its capability, it lets go and returns to the center for digesting (through the Moon) what it has understood and experienced. If it never reaches out and tries for the unknown, it will be stuck in the starting position and never find out how things really work. If it goes on pushing after it has reached its limit, it will start to weaken and lose its energy. The quality of cardinal finds the road through testing various directions. Then it learns and tries a different approach the next time. Through this mental rhythm of trying and experiencing (not failing, mind you, because it no longer thinks about not getting all the way in one jump as a failure), it slowly finds out where to take the king and where to take the queen so they can meet and have this internal union.

It also shows the Sun and Moon where they need to go to be tested and find clarity. In many ways, Mercury can be seen both as the advisor and the jester of the king and queen. The cardinal Mercury provokes them with its thoughts in order to have them question and probe deeper into themselves. And it does this in the rhythm of going into an experience and then extracting the wisdom… again and again. In this process, self-irony and the ability to laugh about one's own stupidity is just as important a gift from Mercury as the advice from the clever counselor. We could also call Mercury the breath of life and spirit as it flows through our bodies and nervous system (mind). Mercury inspires and challenges the seeker.

For a person using the breath as a way of gaining clarity and peace, the best exercise for a cardinal Mercury is to breathe in and breathe out in a calm and centered way, spending just as much time on breathing in as on breathing out.

Mercury in a Fixed Sign

With this Mercury, one needs to understand how things work at different levels of reality. A truth or understanding is not a truth if it isn't understood on many levels. Take an idea about love. A fixed Mercury needs to understand love as the ultimate principle, but also to understand how this principle can work in the everyday environment of time and space. It works by holding an idea inside the mind and then expanding that idea into all different situations and circumstances.

A fixed Mercury needs to choose one tool to work with and become a master of that tool. Sometimes it is said that some people know nothing about everything, while others know everything about nothing. The fixed Mercury starts out by getting a thorough understanding of one system or one aspect of life. As it works through this one aspect, it acquires understanding and wisdom that can be used on all possible fields of wisdom and understanding. Then, it does not really need to probe deeper into all these fields, because it already understands what is behind them and how they work. The danger of this Mercury is that it gets stuck in one level of understanding and stops probing deeper or stretching higher. When it becomes clear and not blocked, it will be able to see clearly how wisdom or love or beauty or joy can be explained and obtained on all levels of human life. Hopefully, it will be self-evident not only that Mercury can see and understand all this, but also that you need other parts of your personality, like Venus and Mars, to move and act on this insight. The gift of this Mercury is the ability to stay focused and concentrated for a very long time. It can hold and follow a thought to the bitter or joyful end, not stopping until it has gotten whatever you sent it there to obtain. If it has no orders for its mission from headquarters (king and queen or Sun and Moon), it has a tendency to get stuck and become unable to change perspective.

As a breathing exercise, this Mercury benefits from holding the breath between inward and outward breaths and stretching both periods of breathing as well as the period of holding the breath.

Mercury in a Mutable Sign

This is the most curious of all. A mutable Mercury is often caught by what passes by in the moment. It can get interested in everything, and it can just as easily lose that interest. In many ways, this Mercury sifts through an endless landscape of possibilities and opportunities. And this ability to get caught by whatever catches the eye is one of its great advantages as well as dangers. It stays open and alert and easily follows the impulses and intuition that come through the mind, but it can also be easily distracted and lose sight of where it was headed and what it was doing. On the other hand, this Mercury can become particular and fixed on one single point of reality. In this case, it can end up more stuck and even more limited in its perspective than the fixed Mercury.

As mutable Mercury evolves and starts to travel on the spiritual path, it learns to change between going with the flow and keeping the single point of focus. When it is going with the flow, this Mercury becomes an explorer of unknown territory. It lets the flow of impulses and possibilities take it out into the open landscape and allows fate and the universe to decide the direction. But the moment it catches a glimpse of deeper truth or the glimmer of gold, it changes and becomes single-minded. Then all the rest of the world disappears as it moves in on this piece of truth, like a hunter stalking its prey. Nothing can stop or divert it until it has gotten the clarity and understanding it seeks. One of the dangers for mutable Mercury is that it can get stuck in holding this little piece and think it has it all. Then the person with this Mercury becomes inflexible, even fanatic, and unable to let the mind float into the sea of possibilities and the unknown. Another danger is that it never picks up the pieces of truth and makes them its own. Then the person with the mutable Mercury seems open to everything but hasn't really taken a stand on anything. On the true spiritual path, this Mercury has no standpoint on anything, but it has a deep knowledge of the inner truth it has found and dug out of its own heart and soul.

As a breathing exercise, this Mercury profits by alternating between focusing totally on the breath, without forcing it, and letting the breath flow so naturally that it just forgets about breathing.

Mercury in the Element of Earth

The element of Mercury tells us which energy Mercury needs to work through and what sort of input gives it inspiration and makes it tick.

Mercury in earth is about common sense. To think about common sense as an attribute of enlightenment is not the most preferred free-time activity, but if our mind is going to grasp the concept of enlightenment, the "hook" we have to grasp it with is Mercury. And Mercury in earth is about the practical application of thoughts and ideas. It does not get a kick out of fleeting emotion, exuberant and wild ideas, or words with no connection to reality. What gives the earthbound Mercury a kick is the practical understanding and application of ideas and thoughts.

On a basic level, Mercury in earth needs to understand how this enlightenment thing works; it needs to understand energy. If it were a Mars or Sun in earth, it would be satisfied with what works. But Mercury in earth needs to know *why* it works. It has to understand the basic workings of the stuff, and it has to see and understand the beauty of it. Mercury in earth needs a purpose. Why the hell should it want to get enlightened just to get enlightened? Why not rather occupy ourselves with what is understandable and productive for a life in the world? Mercury in earth wants to understand how things work on Earth and within the world of time and space and form. So the first thing it needs to get a grasp on is that enlightenment is a natural and reachable goal for a human being. Then it needs to understand how it will work to be enlightened and still be a part of life on Earth.

As Mercury starts to work on these concepts, it starts to understand what a beautiful thing it is to be enlightened. The mind starts to see how enlightenment creates a fantastic opportunity for beauty to fill one's life and thoughts and how it helps to create a more beautiful world within form. A Mercury in earth does not find it interesting to seek enlightenment to avoid time and space. It does not want to be left behind as the rest of the being becomes a mindless light being. It wants to be part of the fun, and as soon as it understands that enlightenment creates beauty and still allows room for common sense and understanding in this world, it becomes fascinated by the thought. And then it begins to see that the key for really understanding the universe is to see the beauty of the universe. The mind then becomes so grateful for its ability to think, observe, and create thoughts and concepts that it hardly knows which half of the brain to think with, and when this deep appreciation of All That Is starts to flow through the mind, the doors between the brain's halves start to slide away. A large part of enlightenment consists in connecting the Sun and Moon parts of our brain so that they can sleep (and stay awake) together and create a baby consciousness that grows and expands with a totally new and whole perception of reality.

This striving to see beauty, to think beautiful thoughts, to speak with beauty and gratitude, and to let the mind flood with gratitude for life and the ability to have awareness is the road that Mercury in earth can use to lead the whole system farther down the road to enlightenment. Then it really starts to know what it means when enlightened beings say that thought creates reality. For this Mercury, it is not an idea or an abstract example; it is the simple and pure truth about how thoughts work on a practical, day-to-day level. To just sit silently and observe the beauty of nature or a piece of art is an excellent meditation for Mercury in earth.

Mercury in the Element of Fire

This Mercury loves to have a bit of fire in the head. It really loves to feel the blood rush through the veins in the brain and fill the head with a wild burst of ideas and possibilities. If Mercury had been a sexual organ, it would become aroused by its own excitement. (By the way, Mercury in fire might be a kind of sexual organ. When the mind is aroused and on fire, the whole body becomes exhilarated and full of energy.)

This Mercury does not like old and dull games. It can get very bored and lose interest. We could say it simply either is interested in whatever goes on, or it is not. The lukewarm attitude is nothing for these brain cells. On all levels of life, this Mercury needs to feel the rush of excitement if it is going to use energy on something. So the trick on the road to enlightenment is to get the brain excited about the project. Sometimes the brain gets excited by itself and takes the rest of the being into new areas. And then the question arises of what makes a Mercury in fire excited. One thing is clear: it does not become excited by dull words, boring mental practices, or being silent and inactive. To tell your Mercury in fire that it has to shut down and stop getting impulses or ideas, just because you want it to be silent, is asking for trouble. Then the mind goes: spirituality ... no more fun and dullness ... let us fight it!

For a fiery Mercury, spirituality must be an adventure, a voyage into unknown and uncharted territory. It can take great strides in understanding and growth, as long as the fire of the mind directs it there. This can be either the fire of longing to experience something new or just the fire from enjoying exploring the spiritual realms of existence. In fact, it can enjoy stillness and no thought as long as you don't try to extinguish its flame. It can be like the flame of an unflickering candle, just having the joy of being a single point of fire in the mind of the universe.

But what gets Mercury to lead the rest of the being on the road to enlightenment is enjoying the process of talking and thinking—to feel the joy of ideas and communication flow through the nervous system. In many ways, Mercury in fire is not interested in the truth of yesterday or the truth of tomorrow. It loves just to be in the moment, and to be occupied totally with what is important here and now. This Mercury is not turned on by long-term plans and common sense. It is turned on and becomes enlightened by being totally present, totally aware, and totally filled with the joy of being in the moment. An enlightened Mercury walks away from dull conversations. It keeps the mouth shut and dwells in the inner joy of the mind unless it really feels the impulse to talk. It lets thoughts go unless it feels true joy and excitement in the thinking. When there is passion and love and joy, there will be words and song and laughter. When those things are not present, the mind enjoys the silence of just looking at the steady fire and feeling the peace of it. In fact, things like singing and looking into a flame are good meditations for this Mercury.

Mercury in the Element of Air

With Mercury in air, the brain just loves ideas, thoughts, and bits and pieces of information. It loves to imagine things and to express itself. Most Mercuries in air like sounds and the flow of words floating from the mouth. They need inspiration and input from other minds and ideas, more than what they generate by themselves. The exchange of ideas and thoughts is by itself an entertaining occupation for them. And they can become worried and feel dull if the flow stops and the mind becomes empty. Always on the run, they easily will be caught in a web of thoughts and ideas. Sometimes they even forget where they were going, as just to be thinking often seems to be entertaining enough. On the other hand, they can become great worriers, making up ideas and scenarios just to have something to be bothered by. Persons with Mercury in air can easily be caught in the world of information and knowledge. One of their great gifts to humanity is to spread information and knowledge, but this can easily become a goal in itself.

The spiritual path for those with this Mercury begins when they start the quest for wisdom instead of continuing to search for information, knowledge, and cleverness. In this process of seeking wisdom, they have to seek within, questioning and pondering the way their own minds work. They can even be trapped in the quest for wisdom and believe their ideas about wisdom are the real thing. These minds are very clever, and they are masters of tricking themselves with their cleverness. To reveal their own games and to stop running around in circles of thought is one of the most important steps on their way to spiritual wisdom.

To manage this, they have to create emptiness in their own head. To achieve moments of stillness and no thought is necessary for these Mercuries if they want to move on to the next level, because it is only in these moments of stillness and non-thought that new wisdom and understanding really can rise. There has to be an empty space available before something new can enter. There needs to be a balance between stillness and thought, a gap where inspiration can rise. As strange as it may seem, Mercury in air needs to surrender to the flow of inspiration and trust the mind of the universe in order to find the way to enlightenment. If it tries to always think and understand, it becomes caught in the outer web of life. It has to allow itself to open to the greater mind of the universe and to immerse itself in the collective mind of being. Wisdom is not necessarily to think, but to let the flow of understanding and wisdom move through you. This Mercury needs to see that it is a thought in the universe, not just the thinker, and that the universe is thinking through it. When it learns to surrender to the stream of wisdom and acknowledgment that floats through the mind of the universe as an eternal current of truth, it really begins to allow itself to follow the path to true spiritual wisdom and becomes filled with an enormous feeling of oneness with and inspiration from the breath of life. Then it will understand the true significance of the words "Be light and it became light." It will start to understand that true wisdom comes from understanding that the whole universe is created and upheld by awareness and that the destiny of everything in the universe is to reunite with that source of awareness that it once upon a time sprang out of.

Mercury in the Element of Water

This mind is governed by inner pictures and states that arise from the emotional body. In many ways, it is the most personal mind, and it is very connected to the state of the being having the mind. On the other hand, this mind tries to understand how the owner experiences his or her own being by probing into the inner lives of other beings. On an instinctual level, it will be caught in the endless flow of feelings that rise from the inner. On the personal level it will be caught in the endless sifting of the same feelings and will try to choose and understand what direction to take based on this emotional input. Ideas as ideas are not of interest. The ideas have to have an emotional content and be important for the feelings to hold any interest.

As easily as this Mercury is caught in the web of everyday life, feelings, and the personal, it can learn to soar high above the little world and connect itself with a greater purpose. This happens as it probes deeper and deeper into the understanding of the nature of love. On a basic level, it will try to find ways to satisfy its own personal needs and feelings. On the individual level, it will try to find a way to make those feelings and emotions work on the level of interaction with the world at large and other humans in particular. To feel inspired and to bother to work really hard, it needs to feel that the system it is a part of really has a great need to understand the topic at hand.

The clue for this Mercury is, of course, to start to seek an understanding of love. Not just love as a personal satisfaction and experience, but love as a state of being. As it reflects the nature of love, this Mercury will slowly become filled with the nature of love. We could say that the flow of emotions does not go just one way. As it advances in its understanding and depth, it suddenly realizes that it is not just feelings that create thought. It sees that it is just as true that thoughts and words create feelings. At this point, the Mercury starts to become the master of the feelings instead of the puppet of feelings. As this Mercury starts to think about the highest love, to speak about the highest love, and to form images about love, it starts to generate these feelings into the whole system. Slowly, the flow of the tide starts to change, and the mind becomes the generator of the states in the body and emotional system. As it learns to love the body, love the emotions, and think about love, this floods into the system. In the end, the thoughts of love are so strong that the queen and king just have to embrace each other and create that union. In this stage, the thought of love is not just thought. It has become a devotion and a conscious decision to choose love no matter what happens. Even if the feeling in the body is jealousy, regret, or remorse, the mind chooses to react as if the feeling were love. And when the body, the emotions, and the rest of the system have given up what resistance they might have against true, pure, and unconditional love, the enlightenment arrives as a great wave of love overtaking the whole system.

Venus and Attraction and Repulsion

Venus is about values, creativity, social participation, and love. At the bottom lies the function of magnetic energy. Venus can be attracted and repulsed by what exists in the surroundings, and it can even be attracted or repulsed by the being that has Venus in the horoscope. One can like oneself and find oneself a person of great value, or one can dislike oneself and find oneself a person of little value.

Venus is not necessarily a passive planet, waiting to attract something. But it does have to feel the pull of attraction, so its active side is more like letting oneself be pulled in by this magnetic attraction and then handling the situations as they arise. Another way of working for Venus is to turn up the magnetic force and use all its charm and beauty to reel in what it wants from the surroundings.

Of course, the level of Venus is shown by what it is attracted to and repulsed by. Venus must not be confused with love; it is more about lust, cravings, and desire.

In Venus's nature is a tendency to long for what is beautiful and harmonious and to avoid what is ugly, unkind, and unpleasant. On the level of the body, Venus can desire certain foods and despise the taste of other foods. On the social level, it can feel attracted to certain humans and social settings and be repulsed by others. In many ways, Venus can open the road to spirituality by being attracted to what is truly beautiful. This can be an appreciation for the beauty of humans or nature or the beauty of creating and experiencing art. But as mentioned, Venus is just as much about repulsion and dislike.

When understood on an energetic level, we are just as much connected with what we despise as what we adore. Venus creates opportunities and circumstances in our lives by using this magnetic force, and on the energetic level our attraction to what we really want to avoid is just as strong as our attraction to what we desire. We are just as attracted to the shadow as we are to the visible. An old spiritual proverb says that what you resist persists. Used on Venus, this wisdom tells us that all of the things Venus fears and hates and feels disgusted by will pop up in our lives from time to time. If you hate spiders, the fear and disgust you feel for spiders will lie like a shadow in your psyche and block your access to the positive magnetic force that Venus can supply, and at regular intervals the theme of spiders will come up in your life. To start to work with Venus on a spiritual level is not to start the work of attracting what you want; it is to neutralize your fears and dislikes. This work consists of removing your disgust and dislikes. You do not have to learn to love spiders, at least not in the beginning, but you do have to remove your antipathy for them. As you release the fear and negative emotions, you release more and more energy that can be used to attract what you really do want to have in your life. This work can also be done without spiritual intention, because everybody would rather attract what they deem good and beautiful than be caught in a repulsion-attraction wrestling match with their own shadow and projections. If you have done this work, you will start to attract all of the good things you really want in your life, and as mentioned, you will move closer to a spiritual point of view. You will start to see that life is a beautiful place full of gifts and that the monsters are nothing but shadows of your own fear. In connection with Venus, this fear is of *not* getting what you do desire and of getting what you *don't* desire.

When Venus moves into a spiritual understanding, you do not despise anything in creation. You love all animals and humans and feel good about those you are with. You accept and see the beauty of everybody and everything. But at the same time, you will still prefer the company of some people to others. You enjoy sharing and desire to share your love, time, and space more with some animals, humans, and landscapes than others. On this level, Venus is your personal preferences and likings. As long as you are not aware and aligned with love, joy, and beauty as a force lying behind everything in the universe, there will be a conflict between the personal and the impersonal. But once you have removed your resistance and accepted the beauty of it all, your personal preferences will not be in conflict with love as such. Personal love and impersonal love will become two sides of the same coin. You will love all dogs or trees, but you will also have a special relationship with the tree outside your house or the dog that lives inside your house. You will learn that being in time and space gives you an opportunity to learn and love through the personal as well as the universal. The spiritual mastery of Venus is to be fully aligned with your own magnetic energies and preferences, and at the same time be fully aligned with the deep flow of love that unites all that exists.

The sign and quality of your Venus tells you the road you have chosen in this life for removing your dislikes and repulsions and creating a balance between the personal and the impersonal. As long as Venus is caught in negative emotions, the union between king and queen (Sun and Moon) cannot happen. For this to happen, there must be attraction. You must feel a great need to create unity of the Solar and the Lunar energies on the inner level. In this merging there must be full acceptance and love between the two sides of you that the Sun and Moon represent. There must be attraction and no repulsion, and the union must happen with a clear understanding that this is just a repetition of the eternal, universal, and all-encompassing union between the two forces that are the foundation for the universe as it exists in time and space. We could say that Venus on a spiritual level is an intense charging of your longing to become one with God, to become a god yourself, and to meet and connect with God in all that exists. As long as you see something as outside God, this union cannot take place. (And feel free to define *God* as you prefer. It is just a word describing what is—and at the same time what is behind All That Is.)

Venus in the Cardinal Quality

When Venus is placed in a cardinal sign, it has a strong pull toward obtaining its desire. It has two main modes of functioning here. When the magnetic energy is created, it can in one way let itself be drawn toward the desired object. The pull can be so strong that it almost seems like it is Mars going for what it wants. The other method is the more usual Venus way: to magnetize oneself and then try to draw the object of desire toward oneself. Venus in Aries especially seems to be in favor of the first method. To find the right amount of magnetism is important for these Venuses. If they magnetize too much, they might "come on too strong" and get the opposite result of what they want. They also have to learn the art of stopping. When they have spent their energy and charm, they need to stop and withdraw so that what they seek can feel the pull and have time to react. On the other hand, they (especially air, water, and earth) can have a problem with showing their real intention. With Venus in cardinal, it becomes very important to show your intention without pushing too hard.

There is a strong will combined with Venus in this quality. The rhythm of the magnetic flow is very important. If it overextends itself, it will lose the energy and not have the power to hold on to what it desires. If it holds on with too much force, the desired object will feel cramped and eventually start to strive to get free. If the desire is directed toward some other living being, it is very important for cardinal Venus to not force its own desire onto the other subject. It has to give room for the other to make its own decision. To respect the desire, liking, and disliking of others is an absolute necessity for long-term success. For Venus, especially in cardinal, to know what one really wants is of utmost importance. If not, Venus can become like a woman trying to attract all men but not knowing what man she really prefers, and therefore ending up with the man who gives the strongest answer to her pull rather than the one she enjoys the most. Or it can be like the woman repelling all men, feeling tired of them, and then also repelling the man she really could have enjoyed. The mastering of turning the magnetic force off and on by use of the will is the way to handle a cardinal Venus.

On the spiritual level, Venus in cardinal has the job of following its nature and at the same time having full respect for all other beings. If it does use force, tricks, and manipulation to obtain its desires or to hold on to what it has obtained, the beauty will soon become a beast. Operating on this level, the person with this Venus feels a strong pull and attraction to what is beautiful, loving, wise, and joyful but does not fall into the trap of the game of rejection. To spiritualize this Venus, one starts to direct one's magnetic energy toward that which has a high quality, stops fighting or trying to push away persons or things one doesn't like, and, as with all other Venuses, lets oneself be guided by the longing and love for unselfish love, true joy, pure beauty, and deep wisdom. And last but not least, having learned from Mercury that thoughts create reality, one should therefore start out with being immensely grateful (earth), joyful (fire), devoted (water), and thankful (air) for all of the blessings, beauty, love, and values one already has.

Venus in the Fixed Quality

This Venus is not so much about moving toward and away from the desired. While the cardinal always has to recreate its own flow and longing, fixed is about staying with the one desired and then changing the quality of the relationship. If Venus in fixed is caught in the negative mood of repelling, it can really avoid everything it truly desires. It can be so fixed in its disliking that nothing good comes through, and it can also take something that is beautiful and good and change it into something that is not at all pleasant. On the other hand, it really can be the magic of love that changes the beast into a beauty.

While cardinal Venuses have to learn the power of their magnetic flow and how to find the rhythm of attraction and letting go, Venus in fixed has the job of learning how to change something while being in relationship to it. If Venus in fixed wants the object of desire to fulfill its own needs, it will be sorely disappointed, and then the play of guilt, remorse, and repelling starts. Sometimes this Venus will be caught in a stalemate, where nothing seems to move. Here, it is attracted and repelled at the same time. It wants the good stuff but can't let go of the bad stuff, and so it seems to be bound with unbreakable bonds to something that doesn't work at all. Well, the truth is that it experiences this situation until it understands that it has to take charge and change the situation itself. It has to meet the fears and guilt involved, and when that job is done it finds the freedom to choose whether it wants to let go or go on.

This Venus has the job of taking something that is just a possibility and then, through its own strong desire and longing, making it manifest in the realm of time-space reality. Or it can take something that exists in the "real" world and, through its devotion and love, change it into something far better and more beautiful than it was at the outset. By holding a steady magnetic flow and at the same time using that flow as a cleanser, it moves what exists in the flow into a higher level of vibration. And as mentioned, the danger here is to become stuck in a situation in which nothing ever changes, which is a contradiction to the spiritual principle that says that everything manifested is changing all the time.

In some ways, this Venus seeks the eternal satisfaction of its needs and desires. But that can only be accomplished when the whole being is on a very high spiritual level—in fact on a level where the personal and the impersonal are absolutely aligned. By being able to be personal even when the love is impersonal—say loving and caring for a dog that is totally strange to you—this Venus starts to reach toward mastery. The other side of this work is to learn to become absolutely impersonal, like loving your man or woman without conditions and giving them absolute freedom even when you have a personal wish for them to love you the most. In fact, this blending of personal and impersonal needs and desires, and the ability to not become attached, clinging, needy, jealous, or any one of those feelings that diminishes the clarity and purity, is the road to enlightenment for Venus in a fixed sign.

Venus in the Mutable Quality

Often, this Venus is floating on the open sea of possibilities. While Venus in fixed has to learn to say yes and Venus in cardinal has to find the right rhythm between yes and no, Venus in mutable has to learn when to become a particular point and declare precisely what it wants and what it does not want. As with everything in mutable, it can become fixated on and obsessed with one particular object of desire. In this endless sea of possibilities, it has to choose which possibilities to grasp and which to just let float by. In a way, this Venus has to trust and wait for the right thing to come. It doesn't help to magnetize oneself if the moment is not right, and neither does it help to close your eyes and just see what happens. With Venus in mutable, you have to be open and alert and then make the right decision in the right moment. This Venus often does just have the one chance to make it right. There will be other opportunities, but not the same again and again.

In many ways, this Venus is always a bit turned on, and it gets more turned on when others turn their heat up. It is curious and has a hard time declining an offer; what if it should miss something? This fear of losing something important is the reason why most Venuses in mutable have to learn the art of limitation. If they say yes too much, they won't have the time or the capability to handle it, and things will fall apart because they will be unable to hold the magnetic field intact. On the other hand, they will either become bored or lost in fixation if they just stay in one place and limit themselves to one choice. This Venus has to learn to hold and then let go, to enjoy the meeting and then walk away. The only way they can keep something permanent is to make that choice over and over again. They have to let themselves float in the endless sea of possibilities, and then they might make the same choice again and again.

More than any other Venuses, they need the freedom to form the relationships and live out the desires they feel are right. On the instinctual level, they become flirters and butterflies, unable to stay in the same place or follow the same pull for any length of time. On the personal level, they let their curiosity drag them into the unknown, and they go from one experience to another, always hunting for what has not yet been experienced. And they are always willing to let go of the moment if a more interesting future arises on the horizon. The other alternative is to be stuck in a boring and seemingly never-ending repetition of the same stimuli again and again. To seek security and repetition is a kind of death for these Venuses. Security can only be found if full freedom is allowed and new choices are possible.

As they start on the spiritual journey, they learn to vacillate between the personal and impersonal. They let themselves float with the stream of opportunities and at the same time are able to appreciate and take care of what they connect with. They learn to merge the timeless love and their never-ending romantic ideals with what exists and is possible to create within time and space. In some ways, it is easy for these Venuses to let go (yes, even the Virgo ones) and much harder for them to allow themselves to be confined and stay within boundaries. It is much harder to understand how love and the creating of bonds are accompanied by responsibility and a willingness to not run away than to get rid of negative feelings like jealousy and resentment. When they start to be able to be true to themselves at the same time as they are true to others, they have advanced far on the spiritual path. When they can give their love without any condition and accept whatever response they may receive, and at the same time are willing to accept that others with whom they share love and/or life are not able to do the same, and they still don't have to run away, they come closer and closer to enlightenment. As a final mastery, Venus in mutable teaches those who have it that they can be both the flow and the point at the same time—that they can be one with the endless sea of possibilities and opportunities and at the same time be closely connected and bonded with what is chosen. To love one thing totally does not exclude the option of loving everything totally.

As Winnie the Pooh answered when he was asked to choose between two goodies.

"Yes thank you, both."

Venus Seeking Enlightenment through the Element of Earth

In earth, Venus is about appreciating all that is beautiful and seeing the inner beauty that shines through the form. On an instinctual and personal level, Venus can easily be led by desire, lust, and even greed. It can also easily be fooled into believing that the shape of the outer form is what creates beauty, and not the spirit shining through the form.

As Venus moves into a higher sphere, it is filled with gratitude for the beauty of everything created in time and space. Rather than seeing the flaws in things and trying to avoid what feels uncomfortable, it enjoys every aspect of the physical. As it starts to be attracted to inner beauty, it makes the person having it in the horoscope more and more beautiful. And as the person becomes more aligned with true beauty, it will attract and be drawn to what is truly beautiful. In this way, Venus in earth will give immense riches and beauty to its owner. Not necessarily because the person becomes very wealthy or very beautiful in the outer sense, but because the person feels blessed and sees that all he or she could ever want is available. This Venus is in the horoscope to open up the eyes of the owner to the immense beauty of nature, the body, and all that the spirit can sense and experience through the body.

Venus Seeking Enlightenment through the Element of Fire

This Venus is about the fire of joy and passion running through the veins. It is about attracting things, people, and circumstances that create fiery, passionate, and joyful situations.

Venus in fire hasn't arrived on Earth to live a dull life. It feels strongly, and on a low level the nature of desires, jealousy, and dislike can be very strong. On the instinctual level, it has no patience: it wants its desires and longings satisfied immediately. On the spiritual level, it follows a deeper passion: the inner fire for what is pure (cleansed by fire) and joyful. It seeks situations of ecstasy, and it attracts the same. The person with this horoscope likes to play with fire and literally learn to extract the pure passion through this play. In the end, it becomes possessed by the joy of life and the joy of being drawn to the spiritual flame within and without. One is not born with such a Venus to be lukewarm; one is born with it to learn the art of burning with desire for what is truest, purest, and most filled with the power of life and joy. And through this desire, this Venus brings the owner of the horoscope closer and closer to the fire and essence of life: true spirit.

Venus Seeking Enlightenment through the Element of Air

This Venus is filled with the love of wisdom, togetherness, and humanity. In many ways, it wants to not be alone. It wants to share and experience the miracle of everything with fellow travelers. It is drawn toward understanding. It can be repulsed by stupidity and ugly humans and does not like to be tied down. It needs the freedom to experience new concepts, new thoughts, new relationships, and new human beings.

On the personal level, it can become superficial, and it can get stuck in something it thinks is wisdom but is really only cleverness and knowledge. Although it does like cleverness and knowledge, it has to move beyond that to find the true spiritual path. And when it starts to understand that all living beings are brothers and sisters and starts to really feel the depth of our togetherness and the beauty of sharing our breaths and lives, it attracts those filled with the same understanding and appreciation. Then it will surrender to life and the flow of coming and going that happens on Earth. It will learn to love those it is with and to share wisdom and the joy of togetherness with all. Then the owner of the horoscope will start to feel and experience the deep unity of the consciousness that binds and holds together All That Is. As time goes by, this Venus starts to experience on a deeper and deeper level this unity among All That Is. In the end, the saying that we are "one in the many and the many in the one" becomes not words or understanding but a living truth.

Venus Seeking Enlightenment through the Element of Water

Deep in this Venus lies a longing for unity and oneness. It is full of dreams and desires, and it can easily project those dreams onto the outer world. In some ways, it is very romantic and lives in a world of images and feelings. In other ways, it is doomed to become disappointed, because the perfect union it seeks eludes it in the outer world. It is only as it starts to seek within and act on its longings and desires for an inner unity and love that it begins to experience a deeper satisfaction. This Venus does not find satisfaction in anything but real love. It can enjoy outer love and be fulfilled by it for some time, and it can find a way to inner love through a devotion to that which it loves in the outer world, but as long as it thinks the satisfaction of love can be found through the fulfillment of its dreams in the outer world, it will be disappointed. And as long as its love is incomplete, it will attract what it tries to repel: situations and humans that cannot give themselves to love. It is only when it starts on the way of surrendering to the state of love that it can feel real fulfillment. As it begins to love everything in the outside and feel unconditional love for the one who has this Venus in the horoscope, it comes to a deeper and deeper experience of what love is. In the end, it will lead the bearer of it to a devotion and surrender to love itself. And through this process of becoming love, it will feel more and more love and more and more devotion to all that it meets, touches, and experiences in the outer world.

Mars and the Path to Enlightenment

It can sometimes seem strange that Mars is associated with enlightenment. Mars is, after all, the warrior god, fighting and using the sword and force to get his way in the world. But although troublesome at times, even Mars was one of the gods at Olympus. And as a god, he becomes a piece of the divine part of divinity and oneness as it is experienced by humanity.

Mars is associated with aggression and adrenaline and the will to fight for survival. Mars is also connected to the sperm of the male that penetrates the cell of the female and thus creates new life on Earth. It might be here that we can begin the journey of understanding the spiritual significance of Mars. It has the power and the will to penetrate and fertilize the embryo so that the potential for life can be fulfilled. In one way, the merging of the sperm and the cell is a representation of the alchemical merging and union of the king and queen, which makes it possible for a new consciousness to be born. And the creation of life in the physical world is in truth a way of bringing forth a new consciousness. On the inner level, Mars provides the stamina and will to walk the long path of the ovaries and to reach the holy goal so that the embryo can start its voyage.

In the solar system, Mars is the first planet that is farther away from the Sun than Earth. That tells us that its primary force is not directed toward the Sun and the inner world. While Mercury and Venus have their residences between the Sun and Earth and so constitute our interpersonal nature and experience, Mars is primarily a force that helps us to direct our power toward the outer world. The primary nature of Mars is to create and to reach for goals in the outer world. As spiritual beings, we have the need and we are driven to unfold our will and our force in the world, just as what created All That Is had this will to create and to go on imposing its spiritual force onto what was created. Even the story about the sperm that fertilizes the egg is a story about Mars being the force that longs to create and to assert its will in the outer world. It does have an instinctual need to create life and master circumstances in the world of form and time and space.

One spiritual concept is the idea of doing the will of God. Without a personal will, that would become meaningless. If we were unable to disobey the laws of nature and spiritual will, there would be no need to talk about the subject. So Mars becomes a very important tool for understanding the concept of free *will*. This will gives us the ability not just to choose, but also to act on what we have chosen and in this way become creators of our own destinies. We can fight with the world, or we can be a part of a fighting army. We can fight and act mindlessly and be governed by our aggression or survival instincts, or we can fight deliberately and be willing to do anything to achieve our personal goals and victories over competitors and enemies. Or we can align our personal will with a higher spiritual purpose. In itself, Mars is this inherent and unavoidable power and will within us. As much as we might try to stop having a will and a drive, as long as we are alive it will be there. We could stop taking responsibility for our will and actions and become mindless pawns in others' games, or we could use it to play our own small games. But we are born with this power to act and give our force a direction, and that is a divine attribute. It is a power that All That Is also wields, and it is used to create the universe.

Everything in creation has a will to live and exist; if not, it simply would vanish. And the spiritual path of Mars is to gain mastery over this will: neither to be governed by raw instincts, fears, or aggression, nor to be governed by the individual need for power and to be stronger, better, and more successful than other individuals. The spirituality of Mars is to align our power and will with the spiritual nature and to use this power and will to create love, joy, beauty, and wisdom and to create new consciousness and awareness. On the spiritual level, Mars is not used for fighting anything or anybody; on the contrary, it is used to further spiritual qualities such as love, joy, beauty, and wisdom. A spiritual

Mars is not fighting or competing, but rather using its force to empower all that surrounds it. In the end, Mars becomes the force of love, joy, beauty, and wisdom coming through us and into the world that surrounds us.

Mars and the Cardinal Path to True Power

True power is within the grasp of the ones who do not fear powerlessness. For the cardinal Mars, this is an invaluable understanding. As long as cardinal Mars fears losing—or fears losing its power—it will either stay hidden, too afraid to assert its will, or use its will to overpower others. As long as power is a fight between wills, this Mars will be caught in that battle of wills. If it tries to hide, it will be forced to defend itself. If it forces its will onto others, it will have to go on and bend others by its will until it meets a stronger force and becomes bent and loses the battle. If it tries too hard and pushes too much, it will deplete itself and become lost. And if it really becomes stuck within itself, the power will be self-destructive and the person will harm him or herself so that others can see how badly they have treated him or her (playing the victim).

To find true power, there can be no fear of failure or losing. In fact, one has to have the understanding that there *is* no failure or losing: it is just a rhythm of movement. One must be able to use the energy and direct it when the inner pressure and the outer circumstances come together. When the world is ready, a path will open, and the will can come out without harming or abusing anything. Then life becomes like a woman who longs for the power of the being having this Mars, and there will come a time to withdraw power from the outer world—a time to leave this woman, go inside, and renew the strength. In truth, you have a cardinal Mars in order to be a rainbow warrior in the world: to manifest and create and be led by the will of joy, love, wisdom, and beauty, to build up your creative energy and then release it in the world. If you cannot find the patience to let the inner force build until you release it, its power will be weak and ineffective. If you build and build and never release, the power will either implode or explode and in that way become inefficient or even destructive. To become a master of this rhythmic dance of will and power is to become a master creator and a true warrior of the heart.

Mars and the Fixed Path to True Power

When you have chosen to be born with a fixed Mars, you have chosen to learn how to hold a steadfast and unwavering will and focus in the middle of a seemingly chaotic world. This Mars is about becoming refined and more and more aligned with yourself by holding your power in the battle of life. How much do you become influenced by the way others use their Mars? Are you willing to lower your standards just because others have a lower standard?

In many ways, this Mars requires pressure from the outside; it needs to work through obstacles in order to learn about its own true power. It is not so much about resistance as it is about being challenged in a way that causes it to become aware of how much power it wields. To become conscious, it needs to step to the limit of what it can manage. If this Mars becomes stuck in one frequency, it starts to cling to the power it wields, and it will slowly begin to lose the power it has. This Mars is wise not to seek challenges, but rather to accept the challenges that come its way. If it does not learn how to transform its own way of handling things, it can become even more and more debased and will seek solutions that drag it more and more into power games and warlike situations. It has the challenge of using will and power without becoming stuck or blocking the will and power of others. In some sense, this Mars has to learn how to cooperate and see that people who are not fighting among themselves have a lot more power available.

On the spiritual road, it coordinates itself with other forces and the world at large by using the will to further love, joy, beauty, and wisdom. At the same time, it needs to use force to create circumstances in which those qualities can flourish. One important thing about Mars in fixed is that it needs to conclude business before it moves on to the next task, and the conclusion of business comes when the process has been finished, the situation is changed, and everything is in its right place. When this Mars begins to operate on its highest level and is connected with a person who is not afraid of losing, nor driven by instincts or the need to be better than others, it becomes a steady outpouring of love, joy, wisdom, and beauty. Do not misunderstand this, however, as it is not something you can just be and feel and think. For Mars, it is the *doing* that counts. Mars needs to manifest love, joy, beauty, and wisdom through the action and expression of the person having it.

Mars and the Mutable Path to True Power

One of the great challenges for Mars in mutable is the fear of not being strong enough, brave enough, or powerful enough. Mars in cardinal is about the dynamics of power, and Mars in fixed is a little like sumo wrestling. Who has the best balance and is the most grounded in body and soul? Mars in mutable is more about floating on the wind of power and letting oneself be aligned with the greater force. It is correct that as far as personal power and stamina goes, it is no match for the fixed or cardinal Mars. If an arrow and a sword meet in the air, the arrow will be crushed. But the power of the wind can carry the arrow so swiftly and powerfully on its wings that the sword becomes much too slow to catch it before it hits the bull's eye.

So, left unto itself, Mars in mutable can be very idealistic, and even single-minded, but however hard the person tries to win against or conquer the others, it will lose the battle. In truth, the supreme ability to be focused and concentrated gives the mutable Mars an edge, but it does not have the stamina to hold this focus for a long time, like the fixed Mars, or the stamina to try again and again and again, like the cardinal Mars. So the mutable Mars is here to learn how to use force itself to move on. It needs to align itself with greater forces and wills than the personal. If it does this without spiritual awareness, it becomes a follower and can easily misuse its power in the service of somebody with a stronger and more persistent will than its own.

As with everything in mutable, this Mars is there so its wielder can learn about choice and consequences. Does it choose the easy way or the hard way? And which force does it choose to ride on: the force of evil; the force of personal interest, power, and gratification; or the force of trust? On a spiritual level, this Mars chooses wisely, as it chooses to trust fate instead of fighting it. And when it chooses to ride always on the power of love, joy, beauty, and wisdom, this Mars, which by itself so easily feels weak and not fit for the hard fights of real life, starts to feel strong, focused, and unconquerable. It vacillates between being the eye that sees, the hand that holds and lets go, and the arrow flowing through the air—and the air that carries the arrow.

Mars in Earth and the Warriors of Beauty

Mars on the personal level is about winning (accomplishing your goals) or losing (not accomplishing your goals): On the spiritual level it is about enjoying the match or effort, just as much if you win as if you lose. It is also about having the right intentions, playing a fair game, and dealing with the result of the intentions. Sometimes bad intentions can lead to a good result, and it is quite common that good intentions produce a bad result. Mars is about both intention and result. To become a master of Mars is to have the right intention and to get a good result. And do not fool yourself: Mars is about becoming a master in the game of power and the handling of the outer world. Mars is about facing the challenge of life and living up to it.

With Mars in earth, you have the challenge to act on the intentions that are beautiful, not to act out of fear, guilt, or clinging. Even when you are forced to protect yourself from the onslaught of others, the protection needs to be led by the intention of serving and saving what is beautiful. Ugly action, or ugliness by and large, does not serve beauty. Also, the end result must be something of beauty if Mars is going to feel satisfied. Remember that beauty isn't necessarily an outer thing. Beauty can be beauty in the created form, but it can also be beauty in the way things are done. It can take the form of beautiful words, feelings, or actions. In fact, Mars used on a high spiritual level demands that the intention is more important than the person carrying the intention. Beauty in itself must be more important than you getting acknowledged for creating something beautiful or being beautiful. And this beauty is in many ways achieved through gratefulness—gratefulness for being allowed to serve beauty, for being able to create beauty, and for being able to make the world a more beautiful place by directing your will and power toward specific achievements. This willingness to serve and create beauty gives its owner abundance of beauty and richness. Not because he or she seeks wealth, but because wealth is a natural state to be in for what is beautiful. Of course, as with all other Marses, it does not help to have the best and most beautiful intentions if one does not act upon them with the will and force of Mars.

Mars in Fire and the Warriors of Joy

Oh, such a joy to have a will. Such an adventure to explore the world of possibilities with this will, to feel the rush of blood and heat rolling through the veins, and to feel the joy of life and enthusiasm and force that can make you dance, sing, fight, and express all that flows through your being. If you think that there is a competition between your joy and others, you will be caught in the web of fighting others. If you think that your freedom is threatened by others' freedom, you will fight for your rights, including your right to suppress the rights of others. If you think that the flow of power and the right to unfold yourself in the world is diminished by others who demand the same rights, you will fight and try to be the strongest, best, and most powerful.

To not fight the oppressor, to not fight death or defeat, is a key for this Mars. In fact, to not fight against anything, but just to fight for what is true to your heart, is an excellent way of handling this Mars. It is very good to be totally aware and focused in the moment of action, and at the same time totally aligned with your joyful intention and the joy of acting upon it and striving for the goal. If you can feel the joy of others using their power and can become more powerful through this, you are on the right path. If you understand that the more joy, freedom, and power others hold, the more freedom and power will become available for you, you are on the right path.

The intention of Mars in fire will be the intention of adventure and enthusiasm and being filled with so much energy and lust for life that you just have to express it. The achievement of Mars in fire is to create a space where all can express and feel this: a place where power and energy is available for all, and thus a place where the ecstasy of living can become stronger and stronger.

May the Force be with you.

Mars in Air and the Warriors of Wisdom

Mars in air is about using tactics to understand the interplay between people and the web of life at large. One of the first lessons to learn with this Mars is when to act and when to hold back. To be able to be in a situation and not act is just as important as to do the right thing. This is about precision in time and space. Mars in air needs to know the exact time and the exact place for spending its power wisely.

On the instinctual level, this Mars follows the rules of the game and tries to maneuver itself into the best possible position. On an individual level, it starts to understand the rules, and it learns either how to break them for its own advantage or how to change them. As a rule, Mars has to learn through trying and failing. There is no way you can find the true power of your Mars without making mistakes on the road. As it gains understanding and wisdom (if it does), it can start to see its own role in a new light.

The web of possibilities and opportunities is not just a playground for the personal Mars. The person with this Mars starts to understand that the play itself is more important than the player and that the web is the thing that is really worth taking care of. Spiritual wisdom begins with understanding that the better the web is created and the better all the players are, the more enjoyable the game becomes. And this Mars is curious and likes to enjoy meeting new players and finding new opportunities. If it does not understand this, it will be caught like a fly in the web of a spider, and life will become just a struggle to keep the position or to get away from where one is glued. To accept the play and the players as they are gives great wisdom. As it moves into the next level, Mars start to understand the spiritual rules underlying the web. The intention of its actions will be led by a deep understanding of the result it will create and a deep longing that the result shall form a better understanding among all the players, and even a better understanding of the nature of the game. It will see that even if there are a lot of players and a lot of games, at the same time there is just one game and one player. And as you realize that everything you do to others you also do to yourself, the tactics start to change; you start to do unto others as you wish they would do unto you. And as you surrender to your wisdom and the play of life, you start to delight in the game without being caught in the web. You become a free dancer who shows others how to be aware of every step you take on the road to wisdom and at the same time be absolutely free to move wherever you want and to do whatever you want in any given moment.

Mars in Water and the Warriors of Love

To learn to act out of pure and unselfish love, and to create more and more love with your actions, is the longing of this Mars. If it is turned around and becomes bent, it really does delight in taking away the love, and it just wants to satisfy its own emotional needs and not be bothered by the quality of those needs. It wants to be loved and to have its will; it wants to live out its dreams, and it doesn't care about the dreams of others. To move this Mars into a spiritual level, one has to start with changing the dreams. One has to begin with questioning one's own motives and then go on questioning them at every step. Is the intention behind the action truly an intention of love and wishing the best for those around you? Or is it a selfish play of your own emotion? When this Mars is disappointed, it may become sulky, bitter, and filled with lust for vengeance. This Mars can also lose itself in a twisted form of compassion. It becomes unable to handle the world, because it doesn't know how to cut the crap and deal with the suffering of others or the owner. Self-pity, cowardice, and emotional paralysis can block it.

But as it learns the true nature of love in action, it becomes stronger and stronger. And there is truth in the saying that no force is as strong as the force of love. No fear, guilt, or self-pity can hold this Mars back when it is aligned with the power of love. Every action of love creates love, and the persons challenging this love or trying to destroy it just become something more to love. As it learns how to manifest its intentions of love through actions that are filled with love, it starts to become more and more filled with love, and then it fights nothing. It just aligns itself with every resistance, attack, and fear by loving them. And as it continuously goes on acting out this force of love, it cannot help but create more and more love in the world.

Venus and Mars and How to Get Some Satisfaction

While the Sun and Moon constitute our basic inner nature, Mercury, Venus, and Mars are the tools we have to communicate with the outer world. Venus represents our magnetic energy, and in this it has some similarities with the Moon. Mars, on the other hand, has some similarities with the Sun, and it represents electric energy.

There is a great difference between the Moon, which symbolizes the basic magnetic energy that we *are*, and Venus, which symbolizes the basic magnetic energy we can *use*. The Sun is the experience of who we are as individuals, while Mars is an example of how we can choose to use the energy we have at our disposal.

As was already mentioned, the first energy we become "aware" of after birth is the energy of the Moon: our basic rhythm and needs experienced as an entity in the world. The Moon is the experience, but from the beginning it is not very clear that this experience belongs to you as a unique identity. This awareness of the Moon takes place more on the cellular and experiential level. So we have to move toward the Sun and identity to develop further. We are born on the planet Earth, and the first symbolic stop on our voyage toward the Sun and our identity is Venus. The first impression connected with Venus is our experience of comfort and discomfort. Through this, we get the understanding that there has to be someone (you) who experiences this comfort and discomfort. Already we have moved to Mercury, the conscious thought or understanding that there is someone who experiences this and the need to be aware of the circumstances that create this comfort and discomfort. So we go from the experience (Earth and Moon) to the evaluation of the experience (Venus and Mercury) to the experience of being the one who evaluates (Sun). In other words, we have moved inward through the solar system to connect with our individual core. From this core, the movement outward can begin.

As mentioned, the Sun needs Mercury to express itself and Venus to attract, and eventually repulse, that which is wanted and not wanted. It is important to remember that repulsion is just as much a side of magnetic energy as attraction.

If the newborn hasn't been allowed to feel and connect with its own likes and dislikes, the road toward the Sun has been blocked, and the identity hasn't been formed in a proper way. There can be still be a God connection to the soul and the spirit levels of reality, but the tool and point of focus that is needed to express the soul and spirit in the physical world will be dysfunctional.

Venus and Mars are situated on each "side" of Earth. Venus is the first step toward the Sun, and Mars is the first step toward the outer regions. On the purely egocentric level, Venus is what you like and dislike, and your natural way to attract what you like and repel what you want to avoid. When we have learned to master Venus, this works out very well. When we haven't, we have a tendency to become confused, attracting things we really would like to repel and repelling what we really would like to attract. A great bunch of psychiatrists earn their livings because of this confusion, trying to help people understand why they have so much fear of having a good time or are so accustomed to pain and rejection that it feels safe to suffer.

So Venus is about learning to use our magnetic energy in a way that is satisfactory for us. It is said that we should be careful with what we wish for, because we might just get it. This is true, but remember that Venus is not Mercury. It is not the thought or the word of wishing; it is the activation of our energetic field through our fear or lust. The mind—Mercury—can help us become aware of our real Venusian lusts and longings, but you have to use the energetic field connected to the aura and body to make this effective.

In a sense, Venus will also be connected to our inner feelings and longings in the same way, as Mercury is the mediator between our inner and outer worlds. Your thoughts will always be very private and personal. No one can really force you to think or to want something different. They can make you say something false, but your thoughts and your inner values are still your private little place.

Mars, on the other hand, is a different story. Mars is farther out from Earth and the Moon. It is not connected to our inner personality, but rather to the way we express this personality to the outer world. Since Mars is our actions, there is nothing left of Mars that is private or hidden if we do things that are contradictory to our beliefs; our actions speak for for themselves. You can see Mars as the force we have available to "push" ourselves out into the world. An interesting question surrounding Mars is this: who has the most influence on this planet, our inner world, as described by the Sun, the Moon, Venus, and Mercury, or the condition of society and the outer world, as described by Jupiter, Saturn, and the outer planets?

While Venus is attracting what we want or repulsing what we don't want, Mars is going out and fetching what we want or fighting another who wants the same thing we do. Working together, Mars and Venus constitute a dance that goes on in our individual field of energy. To learn to master this dance is the work we do when we connect and cooperate with other people and the outer world. We learn to give and take, to be open to what we enjoy and want to experience, and to push away and fight off what we do not want to experience. In this meeting, there is a flow of energy between us and other individuals. The charge in our field is very much an expression of our Venus-Mars energy, and the interplay between our individual field and the individual fields of others is what constitutes the human dance of attraction, falling in love, and so on. When we have repressed our own energy, we have a tendency to attract energy fields with an outer charge that reflects our inner. This is why people are often attracted and repulsed at the same time.

So, to believe that someone else can save you from your problems and loneliness and so on is necessarily an illusion. What you meet will reflect your own inner charging. When you have a balance, you will meet a balanced person. And if you think you are balanced and harmonic but you keep meeting unbalanced persons, you have to think again.

What you meet will by necessity reflect what you are yourself. There is no way to avoid this. And to accept it is an absolute necessity on the road to spiritual understanding and liberation. But despair not. If you are somewhat aware, you and a partner or friend can help each other to find a better balance and harmony. Yes, in fact, you need to meet other people so that they can give you a reflection of your own energetic condition. But you have to see that the other person is both a mirror and real in him or herself. This is the dance of Venus and Mars: to be intertwined but still separate, to merge and share but to still hold your own.

Mars is the will and the power that makes it possible for us to conquer the outer world and move into unknown regions. Without Mars, the inner planets would prefer to stay where they are, experiencing what they like, avoiding what they dislike, and remaining safe and happy in a world that would become eternally boring. Without Mars, there would be no way to express ourselves as individuals in a growing and changing society.

The Play of the Inner Orchestra

These five planets constitute our personalities. They give us a feeling of purpose and who we are. They are the tools we have arrived with on this planet. They show us the road to our inner light and purity and give us the way to express this in the world.

We could say that Mercury is the conductor of this orchestra. As we have seen, the Sun and the Moon are our core, and Mars and Venus our tools to express this core in the world around us. Mercury is, as mentioned, our inner conductor, the one we can use to become aware of what is going on. At the same time, it is our communicator, the tool we have to make others aware of what is happening within us, and the tool for stating our intentions and experiences to the world.

We could also split up this inner personality in another way. We could say that Venus and the Moon are about our values and needs and our feelings about being worthy and valuable in ourselves. Mars and the Sun could be said to constitute our self-confidence, or our belief that we are able to handle and express ourselves in the world.

Self-confidence is a Mars-Sun operation. The Sun is constantly beaming itself out into the world. Mars has the task of taking this life force and directing it constructively through the will. When they function together, we get an experience of being able to master and handle the world, to move in it through our own force and will. We become self-confident and feel that we are self-reliant and can make our own way in the world.

To find a balance between what we enjoy and what we need is a Moon-Venus operation. Through managing this balance, we create a feeling of being of value, as well as a feeling of being able to sustain ourself and fulfill our needs. At the same time, we learn how to enjoy ourselves and how to mix the enjoyable with the necessary. If we get too much Venus, we can easily become superficial and put too much value on the outer. We also can become fixated on enjoying ourselves. It would be like having too much cake and too little whole-grain bread.

The trick is to use Venus to attract also that which is needed by the Moon. If we are caught in the Moon, life is all about security and nurturing, and no fun. We need to use the Moon not only to nurture ourselves and others, but to nurture our own Venuses.

If Mars and the Sun are imbalanced in relation to the Moon and Venus, we are in trouble. There are a lot of self-confident people who have no regard for the feelings or needs of themselves or others. Taken to its limit, the Mars-Sun overdrive will create a ruthless and willful personality that does not care about anything but itself and its success and goals—a state that unfortunately is far from uncommon in our capitalistic society, which in so many ways is based on the Darwinian philosophy of survival of the fittest.

If we have an imbalance in the other direction, full of self-worth but lacking self-confidence, it won't last for long. As we experience ourselves as valuable but are unable to use our power to take our place in the world, we either start to feel helpless or we become exploited by others, and this process will erode our feeling of self-worth. It is like constantly giving, caring, and being nice and nurturing and getting no thanks: in the end, we will feel that nobody finds us of enough value to care about us. This imbalance is the road to becoming a victim.

The most unwanted position to be in is when both of these pairs are malfunctioning. Then we feel worthless and are without self-confidence. If we are in such a state, we had better look inward and start to work to change our perception of ourselves, rather than giving up or desperately trying to prove ourselves to the world.

We have to find new values, and new ways to value ourselves. And we have to set new standards for our goals and achievements in the outer world. The easiest way to do this is by gaining an understanding of the spiritual principles of love, joy, wisdom, and beauty and starting to apply these in our daily life and practice. This is one of the reasons why newborn believers often manage to drop their drug habits and low self-esteem. They have formed a connection with the underlying force of love and joy and see that they can start to unfold these principles with wisdom and beauty, and so their world changes from an ugly place with lots of stupidity and little love and joy to a beautiful place with love, joy, and wisdom.

Mars-Moon is about fighting for what we hold near and dear and being able to use our will and power to get what we need to survive. It is a bit like hunting for food in the old days.

Shopping is often a Mars-Moon operation these days. Venus is attracted to something, Moon reacts with instinct/intuition, and Mars goes to action, and then we come home from the sale as victors, because we proudly return with the loot. Of course, if it were just a Mars-Venus operation, we could become guilty for having spent so much of our resources (Moon) on something unnecessary (Venus).

And Sun-Venus is about attracting what gives us room to shine and makes us feel good about ourselves.

Mercury is the go-between that helps us find a balance and coordinate the efforts between all of these forces. On the inner level, this process develops self-knowledge and an understanding of what we really want and why we want it. On the outer level, Mercury is the tactician, the one who plans and schemes and uses the force of the mind to handle the outer world as efficiently as possible. On the spiritual level, the force behind all of this is the willingness and longing to experience and create as much love, joy, beauty, and wisdom in our lives as possible.

Jupiter, Saturn, and Our Spiritual Playpen

Jupiter and Saturn constitute the possibilities and boundaries of our little playpen in time and space. On the outer level, Saturn is the restriction of time and the structure that holds this world together. It is the limit and the boundaries. It is the mountain that carries heaven on its shoulders. It is the edge of the universe, and it is the cup that holds the water. It is the rules of the game and the foundation of the game board. Jupiter, on the other hand, is the joy of playing and the excitement of discovering new horizons and new games.

It is important to remember that everything we see, touch, smell, and hear is experienced in our inner world. We have an illusion of seeing things in the outer world, but the image is inside our head when we see it. The sound is also inside our head, and so on. So Jupiter and Saturn are our inner impression of the outer world and our individual experience of the borders between the inner and the outer.

Both Jupiter and Saturn are the law. Jupiter is the law of ever-changing and ever-renewing possibilities, and Saturn is the law of consequences. Saturn is the trunk and the branches of the tree, and Jupiter is the invitation to climb.

As beings, we are not just playing with ourselves or the endless vastness of All That Is. We are also playing together. This playing together creates what we call a society: a place that is created by humans for humans, where we find rules and games and test them out. And since Jupiter and Saturn appear in our personal horoscopes and are a part of our internal energetic systems, they can tell us something about our relationship with society. Whatever the size of our playpen, they can tell us about how we see the possibilities within this playpen (Jupiter) and what we need to do to utilize and realize these possibilities. They can also give us ideas about our relationship to our inner world and about what kind of restrictions and hopes we hold for ourselves. Saturn might be seen as discipline in the outer world and as self-discipline in the inner. Jupiter may be seen as opportunities in the outer world and as the hope and openness for opportunities in the inner. When we work on spiritual astrology, we need very much to be aware of the fact that the outer and the inner reflect each other. Everything that exists in the outer world is a manifestation of something that once existed in the inner world (of humans or of the ultimate creating force), and everything we experience in the outer world influences our inner experience of life.

Jupiter by itself would be hope and high beliefs, but no willingness to do the work. The grass would always be greener on the other side of the fence, and we would not be able to accept and work within the existing order of life and structures. Jupiter alone would be this eternal expansion, with nobody at home to hold together what is experienced together. All by itself, Jupiter becomes a windbag of empty promises.

Saturn by itself would become stiff and rigorous. It would be filled with the fear of losing what is. It would be death in the form of a regulated and unchanging life. It does not believe the grass is green at all, but clings to the brown and dreary life that is within the already existing boundaries.

The saying "As long as there is life, there is hope" is a statement of Jupiterian truth. Saturn, on the other hand, is the truth of how the energies are manifested in time and space right here and right now. Saturn is the truth of the moment, Jupiter the possibilities of the future and sometimes the fantasies of the past. To reach out to the spiritual lands that are connected with the outer planets and outer space, one has to move past Jupiter and Saturn. You have to master society and life in time and space in order to be able to reach the eternal. Jupiterian vision and Saturnian reality make a wonderful couple when they walk hand in hand.

When Adam and Eve ate the apple and got thrown out of paradise, there was only one way ahead. You can cry and beg and plead as much as you like, but there is no way you will be allowed to reenter that paradisiacal state without having eaten the whole apple with seeds and core. This was the apple from the tree of knowledge. So you have to learn, understand, and become wise. You have to understand how life in the physical world functions. There is no back door—only the front door of Saturn and Jupiter.

In many ways, Saturn is connected with magnetic energy. Saturn is holding time and space together so we can experience the moment of here and now. Through this holding, Saturn limits our vision of experience. In time, experiences are sequential and must be mastered in these sequences. In other words, you can't do everything at once. Jupiter, on the other hand, is the continual expansion of the moment. The universe is always moving and never standing still, and the same is true for every being on this planet. There is no way to avoid the concrete manifestation of here and now. This can be the cause for feelings of pain and lack of freedom, which are connected with Saturn. On the other hand, everything is moving, expanding, and growing, and this is the scary or joyful side of Jupiter. When those planets are a mess, we are scared of change. We want everything to be the same because we feel safe that way, and at the same time we are very unhappy because nothing really happens.

As Jupiter and Saturn work together, magic starts to happen. The playpen becomes a place full of opportunities and learning experiences. Saturn gives us a sense of reality and structure, while Jupiter gives the movement, hope, and possibility of widening our experience.

We understand that the law of nature and life in time and space is there to help us to understand the consequence of our actions, thoughts, and feelings. Society and the world become a place where this is shown so clearly that we cannot avoid understanding ... even if many of us take our time.

When we start to get a balance of this pair, our relationship to the outer world, society, and the movement of time becomes a blessing. We love the opportunity Saturn gives us to experience every moment and to be absolutely aware and present in the moment, and at the same time we appreciate and love every opening, change, and possibility that the Jupiterian energy brings to our awareness. There might not be any better training ground for eternal awareness in the universe.

If we compare them to the pedals in a car, Jupiter is the gas and Saturn is the brake. At the same time, Saturn is the structure of the car and the road we drive on; it is also the time we use on the trip. Jupiter is the experience of seeing the landscape pass by and the expectation of arriving at a new place. It is easy to understand that a car with no gas pedal will stay put and that a car with no brakes will get into accidents and great trouble, not to mention being a great danger to other cars.

To master these two energies, we first of all have to accept the rules and understand how things work in our playpen—society and the world. Then we have to reach out for the new and stretch ourselves against the unknown (Jupiter), and at the same time we must accept our limitations and reality as it is just now. We could say that there needs to be a healthy balance of hope and optimism (Jupiter) with integrity and realism (Saturn) if our adventure into time and space and society shall be filled with joy, love, wisdom, and beauty.

Jupiter and Expansion through the Cardinal Quality

In cardinal, Jupiter expands in bursts. It is like new doors opening, and we suddenly feel full of hope and optimism. In that moment, we need to let that optimism take us wherever it can. We have to use the momentum of possibilities. This is a bit like surfing on a wave of faith, hope, and possibility. But it is just as necessary to know when the wave reaches its crest and starts to withdraw. It can be difficult to stop and let the fun end for a while. A Jupiterian person has difficulty with letting good fortune go. It is like being on a lucky streak when betting on horses, and the trick is to know when to stop. If you do not accept that the ride is over, you may lose even more than what you have won. When Jupiter is weak in its influence, we have a hard time trusting the possibilities, and we keep holding back. Then the wave can pass us, and all we experience are the missed opportunities. Jupiter is also connected to the search for wisdom and understanding. It can be said to govern philosophy and the quest for understanding the universe through the mental faculty. It is said that those who seek shall find. But it is important to know when you have reached the endpoint of your possibilities so that you can hold on to what you have understood. Another consequence of this saying is that those who do not seek will not find so much. On the spiritual level, Jupiter is about this quest for spiritual insight. This rhythm of seeking and then withdrawing in order to digest and go deeper into what is found is the natural cycle for cardinal Jupiter. The hardest part of the Jupiter cycle is to maintain equilibrium in the turning phases: to let go when faith can hold you no longer and to be able to stay in the point of stillness when there is just stillness. In this respect, it is not how well you handle the cycle that determines your spiritual level, but what kind of expansion and experience you seek. The material seeker will find what is of matter. The spiritual seeker will find what is of spirit.

Saturn and the Handling of Reality through the Cardinal Quality

Saturn is the builder of form and structure. In cardinal, it gets an impulse and then goes out and tries to make this impulse a reality in the outer world. Everything concerned with Saturn is about understanding and mastering reality and structures on *all levels of reality*. It is to spend your effort and resources to build a boat, an empire, or just a sandcastle. When the energy is spent and the work has been created, you need to withdraw to regain power and to revise your plans and designs. To only press forward, with no regard for how much energy you spend, will deplete your energies. This cardinal Saturn is about doing what is necessary and knowing when you have done it or when you cannot do any more. At this moment, one needs to withdraw and accept the work as it has become. Then, in the next cycle of active energy, you can use the prior result as a stepping stone for the next, or you can switch your intention to something totally new. Often, Saturn is a place in your horoscope where you have to face your fear of not making it. Saturn is such a harsh realist that you can easily be fooled into thinking that you are not good enough. But in reality, Saturn is not such a harsh master. It just won't let you float in your dreams. It shows you where you are and what you have accomplished—no more and no less. In fact, it also gives you rewards in exact proportion not to your effort, but to the effectiveness and result of your efforts. A cardinal Saturn needs to face quite a lot of new challenges. It is important for it to meet new challenges, learn new skills, and master new situations. On the inner level, it needs to know the right time for asserting authority and taking control, as well as the right time for letting this go and accepting that whatever happens will happen. On the inner level, Saturn is about building authority and inner integrity. On the spiritual level, it is about building a vessel that can hold a higher and higher frequency. This can be on the level of the physical body, the emotional body, the mental body, or the spiritual body. We could call enlightenment the strength of the light shining through us. But it doesn't function if we become enlightened and the nervous system can't hold this amount of light, and all our wiring collapses. Saturn on this level has to become the form that can hold the light of God.

Jupiter and Expansion through the Fixed Quality

In the fixed quality, Jupiter is about maintaining hope and faith through all different kinds of situations. It is not so much about throwing oneself into the unknown as it is about never losing faith and hope. One name for the devil is Lucifer, which means "the bearer of light." And light is most needed when darkness prevails. In the same way, Jupiter in fixed can hold the light through difficult times. As it holds this hope and believes in unlimited possibilities, it creates those possibilities through cooperation with Saturn and the passing of time. Jupiter in fixed is about the steady and unwavering growth of understanding and possibilities. It is about having a steady direction and the guts to challenge the limits of the now. Through this constant pressure for expansion, the person with Jupiter grows and expands horizons. As fixed always is about moving energy from one level to another, Jupiter in fixed is about changing the world and the possibilities in it. When used badly, it might increase the opportunities but decrease the quality in society and one's own life. Cooperation with Saturn and its demands for quality and integrity is the key here. If this combination is right, the fixed Jupiter will increase the quality, wisdom, and hope that exists for the being with this Jupiter, as well as for the society he or she is a part of. In fact, if your consciousness is on a spiritual level, you will be a part of increasing and expanding the spiritual understanding and influence in all levels and energy fields in which you participate.

Saturn and the Handling of Reality through the Fixed Quality

This is really about mastering the task of having integrity, responsibility, and quality. Saturn in fixed is the Saturn that really has to stand like a cliff in the middle of the physical world and manage the pressure of the world. This is a testing ground and a laboratory for developing your sense of strength and trustworthiness. It is said that God only cooperates with equal partners. The meaning of this saying is that you have to take responsibility for every one of your actions, as well as all of your thoughts and feelings, and let God do his or her job without trying to take it over. To know your limits, and to know what is your responsibility and what is the responsibility of others, is of absolute importance with this Saturn. As you work with your own ability to handle the outer world, your inner quality changes. With this Saturn, there are no shortcuts to becoming a better person. As your actions and the manifestation of yourself in the outer world changes and develops, you grow, and as you grow in stature and maturity, the world around you grows in stature and maturity. As you take responsibility for yourself, all else follows.

Jupiter and Expansion through the Mutable Quality

Jupiter in mutable is not so much about creating all of your opportunities, but rather grasping and utilizing the opportunities that come your way. You cannot, like a cardinal Jupiter, push the doors open, and you cannot act like a fixed Jupiter and put your foot in the door so that it never closes. You have to go through the door as it opens. Jupiter in mutable may be a bit confused to start with, because there are so many opportunities and so much hope. Or, if blocked, there is just fate rushing by you and nothing there you really want to hold. As you flow and let yourself be led by the ebb and flow of life and the world, you have to be alert, because Jupiter in mutable is also about choice. You have to choose the possibilities that you want to do something with, and you have to choose the direction of your life by choosing which current you want to go along with. But after you have chosen, you have to let go and see where that current takes you. Mutable Jupiter is not so much about trusting your own ability to create possibilities for the expansion of understanding and to create other possibilities, but rather it is about choosing the flow and choosing the moment you will grab a specific possibility as it pops up in your life. At the same time, it is about letting go of what you have achieved and followed, and thus knowing when it is time to follow a new current and find a new opening. At the bottom of this Jupiter lies the task of trusting that life will always bring you possibilities and that you will be able to receive and utilize these possibilities.

Saturn and the Handling of Reality through the Mutable Quality

In some ways, having Saturn in mutable is a bit of a contradiction. Saturn is about being the rock in the turbulent sea of life, and mutable is about going with the waves of the sea. So what to do? Well, you have to understand that Saturn's control and structure isn't an outer thing. If a mutable Saturn tries to control and hold the outer world, it will become rigid, and eventually it will weaken. This Saturn is there to teach the owner to trust life, to see that life is in fact uncontrollable and that you as an individual are in many ways like a helpless cork floating on the tides of time and life. This Saturn is about developing inner authority and integrity. It is not about being the unchanging rock in others' lives, but about being true to yourself. Whatever life throws at you, it is a gift and it is also a test to see if you have this inner clarity and integrity. On the spiritual level, it is to become so secure in yourself that no fear can move you away from your true path. It is to trust life completely and at the same time be fully aware of your responsibility for doing the right thing in the right moment. This is about the courage to face life and stay in the tides without compromising what is pure and true, but at the same time letting go of control. When you really get the hang of it, there is nothing to fear, because you will have the inner strength and honesty that gives you the opportunity to go untouched and unafraid through darkness that others may fear. In the end, time, as well as the fear of death or having no control, totally disappears. And since you do not have any need to control the world, you are always in control.

Jupiter in Earth and the Fun of Form

With Jupiter in earth, being in form can be fun. To understand, sense, and expand through the experience of nature, the body, and physical activities is a joy for this Jupiter. In some ways, the understanding of spirit and the deeper meaning of life comes through enjoying life on Earth so much that it transcends the earthly. Jupiter in earth feels that the deep meaning for being incarnated on Earth is to experience earth and the kingdom and the glory of time, space, and the physical in all its power and richness. To create a more beautiful, more pleasurable, and more creative world is the hope and longing for everybody with this Jupiter. The spiritual longing here is never to escape Earth and find a heavenly paradise, but to do the opposite: to create heaven on earth. Jupiter in earth, as used on a spiritual level, believes in the possibility of creating a beautiful and creative society in which all people are nurtured and are given all opportunities to express and experience themselves to the fullest. Of course, this Jupiter can also lose all faith in everything but money and what can be seen, touched, and felt. It can create a very limited set of values and beliefs, or it can have the clear understanding that hope and dreams and beliefs only take on real value when they are put into practice.

Saturn in Earth: Contraction and Limitation, or Endless Abundance?

Saturn in an earth sign reveals that you have arrived to learn how life and laws function on the physical level. On the ego level, you can feel very constricted and fearful of not mastering the earthly existence. Things like money, values, career, and physical safety might be of great concern. You can fear loneliness, and you can feel shame for being unable to provide for yourselves and others—or work like hell to do it. On a spiritual level, you are here to understand how laws function in time and space and society. You are here to see the limitations, and also to transcend them. The fact is, as soon as you have really understood how the laws of responsibility, clarity, common sense, and action and reaction work, you can transcend them. On the spiritual level, you start to understand how, through integrity, clarity, and right conduct, you will get all that you need to have on the physical level. In fact, this is quite a funny thing. As long as you view Saturn as lack, limitation, and hard laws, you will experience this. As soon as you have learned the lessons and begin to see Saturn as the provider of all structure and form you need for any kind of experience you want to have, Saturn becomes a great friend and provider of all that you could ever have wanted. As Saturn reflects the ego, Saturn reflects limitation in form. As Saturn reflects the being, Saturn reflects endless abundance in eternity.

Jupiter in Fire and the Exuberant Child

With Jupiter in fire, you expand into new areas through bursts of enthusiasm and inspiration. Your energy expands as you are on the move, and you cannot make long plans or wait for possibilities. You have to seize the moment and grasp possibilities as they come by. There is a danger, however, that you will grab everything that comes by and will not learn to see the difference between real possibilities and fantasies or dreams. Jupiter in fire is lifted by spirit, and it can easily have so many ideas and hopes and so much enthusiasm that the bubble bursts and it falls down into despair and darkness. But the ability to see hope in darkness is maybe an even greater quality with this Jupiter. It has an endless reservoir of belief, faith, optimism, and joy. The only thing it really needs, then, is a spiritual connection and a workable link to Saturn and the outer world of reality in form.

Saturn in Fire and the Responsible Spirit

Saturn in fire is often connected with a bit of fearfulness and a lack of faith in life and circumstances. There can be a lack of spontaneity and generosity as well. One can become stingy and easily feel discouraged and disappointed. To have Saturn in fire is to have taken the job of building a fireplace for your own passion and enthusiasm. It is not as if the joy and fun in life comes free; you have to learn to work for the fun and enjoy the work. On the level of personality, this aspect is connected with some kind of self-discipline—not necessarily through inner constraint, but through building the form you need to bring out your faith and creativity. On the spiritual level, this aspect is not about having beliefs and faith. Your spirituality does not come from dreamy sensations and unclear longing. With Saturn in fire, you either *know* that there is spirit and are willing to take it seriously and work toward attaining some kind of spiritual liberation, or you are not especially interested.

This placement of Saturn easily creates a life in which one shifts from atheism to intense belief in spiritual reality. One also feels spirituality as a responsibility. It can liberate from the fear of death and old age (Saturn), but it demands that you take yourself and your spiritual understanding seriously and that you live up to your ideals.

Jupiter in Air and the Dance of the Sylphids

Jupiter in air is often associated with social grace. It provides friendliness and the knowledge of how to behave around other humans. To have connections and to belong to the right circles is important. Social expansion and new possibilities in life very often come through connections and the information and opportunities given by others. One with this Jupiter has a good ability to see possibilities in others and to help others bring out their best. Very often, there is great hope for the future. The hope and ideas for the future can be alluring, and like in the song from the sylphids, one becomes blind to anything but one's own hope and plans and does not see that the ship of life is headed for catastrophe. It is advisable, therefore, to have at least one eye on the now. On the other hand, the unlimited possibility for new ideas and inspiration can create a great flow of opportunities, novelties, and situations of great joy and pleasure.

Saturn in Air and the Connectedness of All Life

Saturn in air creates a personality that in some ways has a hard time in trusting others. There can be a certain coldness and aloofness in social situations. One often controls one's behavior in social gatherings and can become very lost if the rules for social conduct don't apply. On one end, one becomes a rebel who hates rules; on the other, one becomes an achiever who love rules and wants to be the one to get the best out of them. One can find it very important to know the right answer, and often one does not speak if one is insecure. This is a person who has to work hard to feel that he or she really belongs in the community, instead of just faking belonging. This is the person who needs to be on the inside but who easily feels lost and alone. The challenge is to really belong and to integrate one's true being with the collective on a deeper level instead of pretending to be a part of society, and so always placing oneself emotionally as an outsider. On the spiritual level, Saturn in air is about listening to the truth. This is to listen with the inner ear and to understand what kind of deep connectedness and unity exists between all lives, and in fact everything that is. By giving in to a deeper community, surrendering one's defenses, and allowing true togetherness on an inner level, the spiritual world and experience opens up and establishes a deep feeling of belonging everywhere and with everyone.

Jupiter in Water and the Wave of Love

Jupiter in water floods the inner world. One loves to love, to connect, and to feel. It is easy here to expand the emotions too much, to become lost in one's emotions, and to not know when to let go. In fact, it is easy to drown others in one's emotional waves. So much love, consideration, empathy, tenderness, and unity can be hard to handle for the receiver. The great gift of this Jupiter is the endless reservoir of love and emotional strength that lies within. Often, the strength of these people only comes out when the going gets really tough, and at these times they stay and hold and keep the love flowing through the most difficult of circumstances. On the spiritual level, these people are so full of love and the joy of others that they can give endlessly of their inner sea. As they expand their inner ability to encompass, they expand the outer world. As they remove all inner limits, they remove the outer.

Saturn in Water and the Art of Unity and Integrity

Saturn in water has often learned that intimacy is a risky business and that one should only involve oneself in that kind of risky adventure with the greatest caution and under very controlled circumstances. Those with this Saturn can often be very good at faking intimacy and getting very close to others, who feel there is an intimate relationship. But take a closer look. If you are the only one who really is vulnerable and who shows your weakness and neediness, is it then a real intimate relationship? On the personal level, this Saturn is about growing up and taking responsibility for showing and sharing one's real emotional states with others—to share insecurity, feelings of isolation, loneliness, and despair, as well as feelings of strength, dependability, and great quality and integrity. On the spiritual level, this is about using one's body and the high integrity of one's personal conduct and being as a channel for infusing the world with love. This is not a wishy-washy personal love, however, with neediness and fear of rejection. This is the sort of love that has the highest quality. This is trust and dependability. This is the love that can handle any situation, that never falters, and that takes full responsibility and supports you at the same time that it teaches you to manage by yourself. This is the love that empowers you and makes you stronger, not the love that makes you addicted and dependent. On the spiritual level, this is the highest quality of love, channeled down into the world of form.

The Outer Planets and the Endless Sea of Inner and Outer Space

Dane Rudhyar once called the three outer planets, Uranus, Neptune, and Pluto, the ambassadors of the galaxy. I have always felt that this was a beautiful way to look at them.

So what is the mission of these galactic ambassadors?

Without these planets, our capability of understanding spirituality and the deeper meaning of life had been very limited. I have written of the Sun and the Moon as that which is the core of our being and that which will be enlightened. But this enlightenment cannot happen without the transference of energy from the parts of our awareness that are found in the personal horoscope through the three outer planets.

If the sphere of Saturn limits our consciousness, we are only able to understand truth through rituals and dogmatic explanations and as an almost solely physical phenomenon. The idea of bringing your body to paradise, which exists in Islamic and Christian religions, is a consequence of this. Also, the idea that someone else can tell you the truth is a part of this limited view of the spiritual force. If we do not reach for the consciousness that is carried by the three outer planets, our mind and heart will be limited. We will be caught in the outer world and will only be able to understand what we can experience with our five senses.

The rest will become unexplainable miracles, and we will have to leave the understanding of the spiritual realms to the priests or the gods.

As we connect with the energy of the outer planets, roads open to experiencing and understanding the realms of spirit ourselves. We learn that we can find our own way to truth and inner freedom (Uranus). We also learn that it is through the inner that we can experience oneness in the outer (Neptune), and we learn to see that the force that has created All That Is is neither is good nor bad, but is beyond these descriptions (Pluto). The sorry state of religions and man's spirituality comes from the effort to understand God within the context of our outer world and experiences. As we change this understanding through integrating Neptune and Uranus, we begin to redefine and transform every understanding we have held about life and death and man's place in the spiritual game of the universe (Pluto). In fact, we die as merely humans, created and living in time and space, and are born as gods, living in eternity. So, it is by opening our hearts and minds to the outer planets that we can become free from being stuck in our personal and thus learn the impersonal. We learn to see that we can understand the real truth and can hold divine and unselfish love in our hearts.

Uranus and the Free Spirit

Uranus is the first planet outside Saturn. It was discovered around the time of the French and American revolutions. When a new planet is discovered, it means that the quality of that planet is ready to be integrated into the collective and individual fields of the human psyche. The slogans from the French Revolution—freedom, equality, and brotherhood (or sisterhood)—neatly sum up the essence of Uranus.

Uranus rotates differently than the other planets do. While the rest of the pack rotates around the belly, Uranus rotates sideways, so that one side always faces the Sun and the other always faces away from the Sun.

Nothing is an accident or without purpose or symbolic meaning in the universe. This oddity with Uranus can be seen as two eyes. One eye is connected with the real world, the individual, and the creative power that is focused on the freedom to become. The other eye focuses the energy toward the galaxy and the experience of universal belonging, togetherness, and brotherhood. In Nordic myth, the creator god Odin gave one of his eyes to get access to the well of wisdom. One has to be able to see the world from two absolutely different viewpoints at the same time to really understand Uranus. And to be able to do this, and to drink from the well of wisdom, one has to seek for understanding and answers from some other place than within the world of time and space. One has to give up something (one eye, or one way to see the world) to get something (wisdom, or a more universal consciousness).

To understand and master Uranus, one has to be able to live in two worlds: to be a being of the limited world of time and space and individual identity and to be an unlimited being of eternal freedom.

This is the first planet that is not bound by the already existing reality. This gives us a good idea about what kinds of freedom Uranus is concerned with. The first is the timeless idea about freedom within society and that which already exists. The other is the freedom to search outside the known and experience something totally new and unknown.

Remember that in Greek mythology, Ouranus (from which the name *Uranus* comes) was the creator god, the first being that gave the spark of consciousness to creation. Ouranus had to be overthrown and castrated so that creation could move on. So Uranus brings tidings about this uniqueness and creativity in us. But it also brings the understanding that we have to let go of the perfect world of ideas and possibilities in order to become real. The total intensity and perfection of being that Uranus strives for must be castrated in order to experience the world of time and space.

There is a fear of manifesting this creativity in form, in the same way that Uranus was afraid of losing his power to his son Saturn. As every artist knows, the idea and feeling of creation is always greater than the product.

There is another side to the Uranus story that is equally important: the rebel side. We could say that Uranus is a symbol for the spark of freedom, as encapsulated within the limits of time and space (Saturn).

And usually when we feel the influence of Uranus in our life, we feel this need to let the inner spark and fire burn freely so that the limitations and forms that hold us back can be burned away. On the mythological level, this energy is connected to Prometheus, Ouranous' grandson, who fooled the other gods and provided humanity with access to the fire. The first story is about unlimited creative energy seeking manifestation in form; the second about unlimited creative energy being "captured" within time, space, and physical reality.

On one side, Uranus as a planet represents the pure and unused creative force—energy that still hasn't been bound to a form. Uranus is the creative force that some mystics call the *kundalini* force. It can also be connected with *chi* and *prana*. As people, we are often caught between our need to feel some sort of control, safety, and belonging to the physical world of time and space (Saturn) and our need to just be totally what we are (Uranus). One problem that arises is that most of the time we don't have a clue about who we really are, so how can we expect to be able to be our unique and free individual self? Uranus has been called a higher octave of Mercury. In a sense, this is a fitting description. Where Mercury is about logic and the thinking process, Uranus is about using the mind as a vessel for exploring new territory. In many ways, Mercury is unable to think by itself. At its best, it can come up with new and interesting combinations of old thoughts, but while Mercury is bound by the past and the existing (Saturn), Uranus is searching for the future and what has not yet been experienced.

In fact, very many people who believe they think for themselves only use the Mercury function of repeating and rearranging old thoughts. Only those who have done the work of integrating Uranus as a part of their personal experience will become able to think for themselves. This is clearly connected to Uranus's quest for freedom: freedom of thought, freedom to love whom and how you want, freedom to find your own understanding of beauty, and freedom to express and experience joy on your own terms. Not everyone wants this freedom, however. Freedom means that you have all possibilities open, and then you have to take absolute and totally full responsibility for your own life, thoughts, feelings, and actions. Only when Saturn is fully integrated can

Uranus blossom fully. Only when you take total responsibility (Saturn) for yourself can real freedom (Uranus) emerge.

Acquiring Uranus consciousness helps us to get a new perspective on the reason for being an individual. For a person who has achieved this understanding, the world is not a playground for the immature individual to toy with, nor is it a Saturnian jail that some crazy god has created to test your ability to believe without using your head. The "I" has become a point of focus for the soul and the spirit. The individual center, as symbolized by the Sun, becomes this point of focus, which makes it possible for the soul and spirit to experience itself within the parameters of time and space—to become a creator, God manifested in form and individuality, walking around and meeting all these other faces of the same God, while all of them are unique and individual.

Aquarius and Leo are situated directly opposite each other in the sky, and their rulers are the Sun and Uranus. To be opposite also means that each one needs the other to make a whole, and this is true for the Sun and Uranus. This combination says that the only real togetherness that exists is the togetherness chosen by free and unlimited individuals, a togetherness that can be chosen or changed at any moment. Only what is given by free will has any real worth. This is one of the reasons Uranus is not associated with jealousy and is said to be bad for lasting marriages. Uranus says that you do not want anything that is not given by free will, and as we know, many marriages are based on a kind of buying and selling or a balance of threats, as well as a fear of losing and a fear of shame and sin.

Uranus is also about becoming a genius, or being a unique and outstanding human being. If there is an overdrive of Uranus, you may try to convince all others how unique you are. This need to prove your uniqueness is often founded on an inner lack of integrity and security. It is a bit like all members of a punk-rock gang coloring their hair red and thinking it shows the world how free and unique they are, while in fact the only thing it shows is that they are under the sway of group style and peer pressure.

In its basic form, Uranus is the pure energy that has created our universe. It is the inner force of the spirit working through everything that is. On a personal level, Uranus is connected to the individual awareness of this energy, the consciousness of being both creator and created. It is connected to the understanding that we all are equally unique and marvelous genuises: that each one of us is something that is happening now and will never be repeated, and that we are what we are because we have chosen to be so, and that we are absolutely free because all of our limitations are chosen by the soul and spirit, so we can learn and grow and drink deeper and deeper from the well of wisdom. The sign and house in which we find Uranus shows us the area in which we need to experience, explore, and express this individual energy and the way we need to do it.

On the spiritual level, Uranus is the freedom to be and to express completely what you are, while at the same time allowing others the same freedom. In fact, spirituality and life are freedom, and they cannot exist without it! Uranus is about finding your own way to spiritual understanding and wisdom. No collective religion or dogmatic truth will ever be satisfying for a person with an integrated Uranus. This person has to understand everything by him or herself. Authorities can be learned from, but not accepted as such. Uranus teaches us that the only way to true freedom and wisdom is to walk the inner road and to find the answers within ourselves. At the same time, it opens to us the road into the universe and what is called cosmic consciousness. In fact, it is the planet of the enlightened mind.

The Uranian Quest for Freedom through the Cardinal Quality

In this quality, Uranus has the task of learning when to use your freedom to act and when to use your freedom to withdraw: the freedom to say yes and the freedom to say no. Uranus is always about finding your own way through inner and outer life. As long as one is bound by other people's reactions and limitations one cannot be free. But at the same time, if one cannot take other people's reactions and limitations into consideration, one limits possibilities and loses the freedom. When to fight for your outer freedom, then, and when to protect your inner freedom? There is a time for expanding one's view and diving into the unknown, and there is a time to withdraw from new experiences and, through reflection and digestion, make those experiences a part of your inner being. Of course, as your connection with Uranus grows, the difference in inner and outer freedom diminishes. And when you have total inner freedom, your reactions in the outer world are always a consequence of your conscious choices. Uranus has a lot to do with becoming conscious and making your own choices.

Uranus in cardinal tells you that you have arrived to use your will in new and different ways. Remember that freedom for you is dependent upon the freedom of other people. Your freedom will suffer and go up in smoke if you use it to take away the freedom of others. So before you stands the task of using your free will without creating conflict with other people's right to use their free will. In fact, you have to become so free and tolerant that you can tolerate the intolerant. As you master this quality, the direction and form of your will changes. Your choices will be new, because they will not be based on the past, but rather on who you are in the moment. Freedom can only exist in the now, and as you start to deeply understand this, you will become a person who is not boring. Your actions, choices, and understanding will change and will surprise others and even yourself. A true Uranian person is in some ways unpredictable, because they renew themselves constantly.

The Uranian Quest for Freedom through the Fixed Quality

Here you are learning to stand apart from the crowd and be true to your own inner nature. You learn about who you really are by expressing this nature. To find your inner freedom, you have to test it in the outer world. Often, you will be in situations that seem "unfree" or constricted, so this outer pressure can give you a deeper understanding of what freedom really means for you. The point of this is that by relying on yourself and your power, you learn to change oppressing and restricting situations. In doing this work, you not only set yourself free, but others at the same time.

You can do this in two ways. Either you can "choose" to feel caught and limited and then change the energy by getting out of the shackles, or you can have an idea about possible ways of becoming freer that do not yet exist in your life or the world. By making these possibilities into reality, you are a part of creating new space for human unfoldment. The three outer planets are not purely personal. Freedom and the right to be totally yourself is an inherent power underlying everything that is created. In fact, one of God's most important attributes is the freedom to be and create without restrictions. As you start to liberate yourself from the chains of Saturn, you also become a part of a collective movement toward greater freedom and understanding. At a very deep level, Uranus is about connecting with the mind of the universe and absolute truth. When a fixed Uranus gets this connection, it becomes able to see the truth in every moment, and as the saying goes, the truth shall set you free. By seeing the truth, this Uranus learns to speak the truth and do the truth. And then freedom and truth become one, and the person with the fixed Uranus becomes the living truth of freedom.

The Uranian Quest for Freedom through the Mutable Quality

With Uranus in mutable, you are on a quest for truth. But of course you have to find your way through the thick jungle of lies yourself. Often, you will have to create your own path, and the direction is determined by your choices. So this is not about the freedom of the will (cardinal) or power (fixed) but about the freedom of choice. To make your own choices and take the consequences of them is important. Many people believe they choose for themselves—in fact, almost everybody believes this—but in my humble opinion, most people choose very little.

Their choices are determined by the past and genetics and environment. To really choose, you have to leave the paved path and find your own direction through the unknown. As a person with Uranus in mutable goes on this journey, he or she learns to connect with the truth behind the illusion, the great mind of All That Is. There is no way to undo your choices, but there is always a possibility for new and different choices. On one level of development, people with mutable Uranus think that freedom is not to be bound or hampered by anything, to have no restrictions or obligations. This is not freedom, but fear of freedom. Included in the package of freedom are, of course, the possibilities of choosing that which binds and holds you. If you know you have chosen that which limits you, you are limited by choice. If you do not understand this, you will blame others, society, or God for your lack of freedom. One challenge for this Uranus is to stay in the endless sea of possibilities and change. Some grab the first truth they find, and then think that their freedom is to align with this one particular truth. The result is a very limited understanding, of course, and in worst-case scenarios fanaticism and lack of tolerance toward others. This balance between the great truth and your personal truth, as it appears in the moment, is necessary to reach for mutable Uranus. In a way, truth is eternal and unchanging, and at the same time, truth manifested is temporal and always in flux. By applying this understanding, the mutable Uranus moves toward becoming that unique and genial being they have the capability to become.

Warning!

You may think that you are free to choose whether you want to learn about freedom. You could hardly be more mistaken. Since the quality of freedom is inherent in life, all life will seek this in one way or another. On the level of the body, you will seek freedom in the material world. On the level of emotions, you will seek emotional freedom. On the level of personality, you will seek freedom for the personality. And on the spiritual level, you will seek the freedom of soul and spirit. According to sign, house, and aspects in your personal horoscope, Uranus will confront you with your lack of freedom and lack of understanding of the truth. And Uranus does not have a gentle hand. It strikes like a lightning bolt and tears down your house built on lies and lack of freedom. So unless you want to be jolted into freedom, you had better start to seek it by your own will, power, and choice.

Uranus in Earth: The Freedom of Creating

Uranus in the element of earth is about seeing the beauty in all life and, through this appreciation of beauty, finding freedom. Gratitude for being allowed to experience life in physical form is also a part of this freedom. As long as one does not see that all life is free, even in the physical, one is trapped in the illusion of limitation. Another part of this freedom is to experiment with one's talents and resources in order to find a unique direction for how one wants to live this life and how to spend money and earn money. Nature and the laws of nature are also of great importance. Many may see nature as "unfree" and limited, but Uranus in earth needs to understand that nature in itself is absolutely free and that it carries the truth—not by thinking or feeling the truth, but by being the truth.

One with Uranus in earth has a need to create oneself as a living example of the true and natural, as well as the freedom in just being allowed to be what one is. At the same time, this Uranus will keep you trapped in experiencing life being unfree and limited, until you understand the true nature of spirit and soul that flows through All That Is.

On the purely practical level, Uranus in earth is about having the resources to live as you like. On the personal level, this Uranus is about being able to utilize your talents in a creative way. On the spiritual level, the freedom comes from understanding that your soul has freely chosen all of the circumstances and limitations that exist in your life. This is exactly what you needed to find your inner freedom and truth. To apply the freedom of Uranus, you must find your own values, your own ways of living your daily life, and your own visions and ways of making your impact on society at large. Freedom does not come from trying to escape time and space and form, but rather through becoming free as you live within time and space. When this is achieved, you will be able to connect with the greater purpose of time and space, and you will start to behave in accordance with this greater purpose. As you move further ahead on this road, life on Earth becomes rich and filled with gratitude, everything becomes a pleasure, and life is filled with unending grace and abundance.

Uranus in Fire: The Freedom of Living

Uranus in fire is an explosive combination. It does not like any form of restrictions. This Uranus creates a contradiction. It wants to be a flame that burns absolutely free, but at the same time it needs something to burn and a place that can hold the fire. Saturn is this holder of the fire, and if Saturn does not function in the horoscope, the person's fire will either be stifled or burn out of control. This Uranus sees freedom as the right to follow any impulse or instinct, to express the owner's true nature just as it is in the moment. It doesn't take a great mind to figure out that this person can become very dysfunctional in society and a real pest for his or her surroundings. The being has to learn to achieve more and more functional ways of obtaining and expressing his or her freedom.

At the bottom of this Uranus lies the need to express joy and live every moment of life fully. It knows that only the moment matters, and it can easily forget past, future, and consequences as it is caught in the moment. Uranus in fire enjoys experimenting and gets a kick out of experiencing something new. It has the task of making the most out of life. When it does get caught up in a new idea, it just blazes with enthusiasm and joy. There is a risk, however, of burning too hot, being too wild, and not taking into consideration the limitations of body and the material world. It can crave freedom so much that it loses it because of an unwillingness to accept the realities of life. And if it gives away too much, it will become depressed and explode in meaningless actions of stupid rebellion. As it really moves into the spiritual realm, it starts to give the owner a taste for ecstasy. The person becomes so filled with the joy of life and the devotion to spiritual truth that life becomes nothing but an eternal party.

Uranus in Air: The Freedom of Thought

Uranus in air loves to understand. The freedom of thought and the search for wisdom penetrates everything. We must remember that the Greek god Ouranos was the god who created Earth. And in Christianity, it was the thought of God that created the universe. To get new ideas, and to know the joy of playing with ideas, is freedom for this Uranus. To experiment with people and to test out all of these new possibilities is a party. Uranus in air does not like to follow the normal social restrictions and rules, but it does love to experiment with them and create new ways of living together. It is concerned with the freedom of the individual within the context of society. With this Uranus, there is a great need to be free in social situations. This goes for the freedom to be social when there is an urge to do so, as well as the freedom to with-draw from the social life when one wants. It has also a great need to speak the truth, and it has a bit of impatience with conventions, slow thinking, and bureaucracy. If this Uranus is governed by the personality or instincts, one can easily become beseiged by the ideas of telling the truth, shocking people with opinions, and always being in opposition to the existing norms.

There can also be intolerance, that the owner of the horoscope will demand great tolerance from others but will not have any tolerance for those who seem to inflict limits on his or her freedom. In a way, it can be a little like eternal puberty. On a spiritual level, this person can be a great example of the courage to speak the truth and live up to one's own ethic, whatever the consequences. This Uranus will also give the mind access to a high level of understanding what really goes on be-tween people—not to be caught in words and arguments, but to go di-rectly for the essence and truth of the situation. There will also be a great ability to create peace, to experience togetherness and equality, and to see all living beings as brothers and sisters.

Uranus in Water: The Freedom of Love

With Uranus in water, the great task is to love without shame or guilt: to be free to love whatever you want whenever you want. There will be a reaction here against all attempts at manipulating one into love. At an immature level, this person will demand the freedom to love on his or her own premises but will not grant others the same right. You are born with Uranus in water to let go of jealousy and the belief that you can own what you love. Throughout your life, you slowly or quickly learn that only the love that is given freely and without conditions can last. Still, on the immature level, you can use all kinds of manipulations to get love on your own terms, without being willing to give unconditional love to others. As you mature, you begin to understand that only freely given love is true love. As this truth of love starts to take hold, you be-come freer and freer from the old concepts of love. In fact, you begin to understand that being able to love and to give this love freely is the greatest gift of all. To be loved becomes of little importance; the freedom to show one's love becomes more and more important. In the immature person with Uranus in water, love feels like restrictions and rules—a dangerous thing that could remove your freedom. There is a great fear of really becoming attached to somebody, or on the other end, that other person becomes your whole truth and you desperately fear losing what you love. In the mature person, the possibility of totally loving and letting yourself be captured by this love becomes the freedom. There are no restrictions or limitations in this kind of love, because all you really want is to love and to express this love. You could say that as truth emerges in this way, you become devoted to love. And not just personal love, as the devotion stretches until it encompasses All That Is. In the end, the freedom you choose is to be one hundred percent devoted to the essence of spiritual love.

Neptune and the World of the Soul

The three outer planets can be seen as stepping stones on the road to galactic consciousness. They can also be seen as stepping stones on the road to birth and earthly consciousness. The creative spark of Uranus is associated with the moment of conception. Suddenly, out of this meeting of the egg and sperm, a new and unique union rises. The one cell starts to multiply into thousands. All of those cells are unique, and they have a perfect organization and group consciousness that creates this fantastic and complex organism called the human body. Isn't this a beautiful example of perfect cooperation between Aquarian and Leonine principles? With this process, the body goes through the entire physical development of life on this planet, from single cell, to fish, to mammal, to human. This is one of the reasons that our collective history is accessible by every human being: our body has been through all the stages, and it remembers them with its perfect cellular remembrance.

Neptune is connected with this remembrance, from the time we laid in the amniotic waters in our mother's belly. The world we experience before we are pushed out into the light of the physical world is the inner world, and Neptune is our connection with and our remembering of this inner world.

As a spiritual planet, Neptune is about oneness and the inner world. It is often connected to the concept of unselfish love. In many ways, Neptune dreams of the perfect world: of love without any stains, pure joy, absolute beauty, and the truth that is born of knowing in the center of soul and spirit. As Uranus is the freedom of what we could call the mind, Neptune is the freedom of what we could call the heart. It is the inner portal that gives us access to other dimensions and beings and ultimately the essence of spirit. In astrology, Neptune and Saturn are often seen as opposites. Saturn is the so-called outer reality of time and space; Neptune is the inner reality of dreams and unity. Saturn is limitations and borders; Neptune is the all-encompassing and unlimited. Very often, Neptune is associated with dreams, fantasies, and illusions—in other words, what does not exist. But this is only a question of perspective. One of my favorite quotes comes from something Robert Hand said when he held a speech at an astrological congress in Norway. It goes: "Saturn is the illusion that there exists a reality. Neptune is the truth that it doesn't." Seen from the inside, Neptune describes the reality of what we feel and how we really experience the world within.

On a primitive level, Neptune becomes all of the dreams and longings of the body, the instinctual search for the perfect place. On another level, it will be our dreams and ideas about paradise. On a spiritual level, it is the portal into that state of being that can be called paradise. It is to go beyond the outer world and the form and to visit the realms and experiences that touch on the eternal. In Neptune's sphere, time is not cut into pieces or measurable like the time of Saturn. Neptune is time as unity, time as the movement of one single being, and time as an experience of flowing in an eternal moment.

For the ego, Neptune is the ego's longing and dreams and its experience of unity with the world. In many ways, Neptune can be confusing and strange for the ego. It has these dreams, and it wonders if they are just fantasy—or even the dreams of a crazy man—or if they carry something that is attainable and real. We could call Neptune our inner mirror. If we are foggy and unclear and our dreams are mostly born of lust, fear, and greed, this is what will be seen in Neptune's mirror. If we are clear and aware, we will start to see better and truer dreams and not be led astray by the fog and unclarity of our own inner workings. If you believe in illusions, Neptune will confront you with these illusions and will let you play with them in the mirror until you see through them. If your dreams are true to your own nature, Neptune shows you the way to these dreams and gives you the longing to make them real. As mentioned, everything that exists in the outer world has first existed in the inner world and mind. So we could say that Neptune connects you with the template that lies under the physical world of form and time and space.

Neptune is connected to the remembrance of oneness. Symbolically, it is the longing for the Garden of Eden, Shangri-la, and eternal bliss. Physically, it is the remembrance of unity with our mother, being a part of her rhythm and heartbeat through the umbilical cord, and floating around in the amniotic waters. When Neptune is afflicted in the horoscope, this dream of the perfect world was filled very early with different snakes and other monsters that destroyed the idyllic scenery. The dream of bliss is still there, but the feeling of pain, danger, and "evil" is very strong.

Through the house and sign in which Neptune is situated, we can find a way to experience this inner world of dreams and longings. To go on the quest for the real essence of Neptunian reality is like walking through veil after veil. And if you have cleaned away all of your illusions and can open your eyes to the real magic of Neptune, you will experience an inner meeting with that reality which lies behind all other realities: the true reality of spirit.

Neptune in Cardinal: The Dream of Will

With Neptune in cardinal, you have a need to act on your dreams and to try to manifest them in the world. As you engage in pushing out your energy for reaching the goals of your dreams, you meet both the limitations of the outer world and the inevitable unclarity of your own inner world. To act on Neptune is a risky affair. You do not really know if what you feel and believe in is just a fantasy or if it can become reality. Often, Neptune's influence sets us in a state of high expectations and unrealistic idealism. As you act on these ideals, you learn which ones function in the world and which ones were only your imagination. You also learn to see the difference between the ideal state, which Neptune dreams of, and the limitations in the world. You will meet two hindrances on the road to realizing Neptune: the first is the condition of the world; the second is your own shortcomings and inability to live up to your own ideals and standards. A cardinal Neptune tests the ideal against the possibilities of the world. As the dreams reach the potential they have for the moment, one has to withdraw and move inward again. Some people become so disappointed by themselves and the world that they lose hope and the will to try to live up to their ideals anymore. Others learn to go in and find the balance between ideals and reality. In some ways, Neptune inspires us to try our best and go for the highest. The cardinal Neptune can become stuck when it fights for a futile and impossible dream that does not work in outer reality, and it can also become disillusioned and give up the whole business of reaching for those ideals. Through the rhythm of testing out your dreams in the world (outgoing) and aligning your dreams with possibilities (ingoing), you will slowly learn more and more about manifesting dreams in reality, and you will find dreams that give you energy and have the capability of becoming reality. To not be led away by illusions or give up because of disappointment, but to stay on the steady flow and never lose faith in your dreams and ideals, is the task of this Neptune. As you go on your road, you will be able to manifest more and more of your highest ideals about love, joy, beauty, and wisdom in the world. And as you do this, you will become more and more in tune with the force that lies behind the world. As you act on your highest and best, you will become what you act upon, and in the end, you will experience oneness with those ideals and dreams that you carry within your soul.

Neptune in Fixed: The Dream of Power

This is not about having outer power, but rather about having the inner power to manifest your ideals in the world. Neptune in fixed is concerned with inner conviction and staying power in the work of manifesting one's dreams and ideals. Adjusting the methods and ways for letting the energy flow from the inner to the outer is necessary. If one gets stuck in a method or dream that is not possible to live out in the world, one becomes a Don Quixote and fights windmills. As with everything in fixed, the person with Neptune in fixed needs to understand that it is the quality of the result that shows how well you are attuned with Neptune. Having high ideals with no practical consequences doesn't create growth. The other way to become stuck with this Neptune is to give up and feel that you have a hopeless task. In some sense, the ideals will still be there, but they will just be a frustration, since you will not believe that they in any way can be applied in your life or contribute to really changing the world. This happens when you do not really understand the relationship between the ideal and the manifestation. With this Neptune, your work is not to reach the goal and create the perfect world, it is to hold the ideal of the perfect in your heart and to go on striving to manifest as many as possible of these ideals. As you do this work, your inner world will become transformed, and you will have a steady increase in the energy you pour out from your heart into the world. The quest is not to fulfill the job, but to go on doing it no matter what happens. As mentioned, however, the result is important. But it is not necessarily the outer result that matters most, but rather the effect your work and idealism have on your own heart and the hearts of those around you. As you come closer and closer in your heart and mind to the ideal state of your dreams and you become more and more able to give freely of the gifts of your heart, your influence on the world grows, and you become a true transformer of energy on the planet—a transformer that rides on the unending wave of true love and thus makes the world a more loving and spiritual place through your own being and efforts.

Neptune in Mutable: The Dream of Truth

With this Neptune, you may alternate between enjoying traveling in your inner world of dreams and becoming preoccupied with a single idea from or aspect of all of your dreams. This Neptune presents an idealistic search for the truth. If you do not find it, you may become disappointed and stop looking for it. You may even become the greatest skeptic, thinking that there is no truth. On the other hand, you may think that you have found the truth, the whole truth, and nothing but the truth, and so become a single-minded missionary for this truth. As with everything else in mutable, you have to learn to make choices and stand by them. In one sense, you have to trust that your inner longings, dreams, and world will lead you to fantastic experiences. On the other hand, you have to choose what dreams and longings you want to follow. On an instinctual level, you take the first and best dream that pops up. By meeting the reflection of this dream in the outer world, probably by confronting your own lack of realism and your tendency to be blinded by illusions, you start to learn about the difference between inner truth and ideals and what already exists in the outer world. On the personal level, you can float away from meeting your own false self-image and never take a stand. You can also try to live up to your personal ideals and confront yourself with your shortcomings and lack of perfection in the outer world. As you walk through this web of illusions, dreams, and longings, you learn to separate what has truth in it from what is only a way of escaping the truth. Remember, Neptune is just as much about our ability to fly away from the real world through our fantasies and imagination as it is about using fantasy and imagination to create a better and more loving world. As you find the balance, you learn to trust the universe and the force of love, idealism, and perfection that underlies All That Is, and at the same time you become a speaker of truth who is willing to stand up for your belief in what is possible. To be true to your own inner truth is important. At the same time, however, you must learn how you, through this devotion to your inner self, can be a part of manifesting the dream of unity, unselfish love, and spiritual essence into the world. With Neptune in mutable, you are the dreamer, and you need to see that your dreams are an important part of creating reality. By taking full responsibility for your dreams and inner world, you start to become a vessel for manifesting the true Neptunian force of oneness and love on the planet.

Neptune in Earth: The Beauty and the Beast

Neptune in earth may have a difficult time coping with the ugliness of the world. Those with this Neptune have ideals about beauty and can feel pain from all of the ugliness created by humanity. They can also experience life on Earth as very brutal and feel repelled by sickness, death, and the fact that life has to eat other life to survive. Some with this horoscope will have a hard time accepting the conditions that exist in this region of time and space and they will fight this ugliness. Others may just try to avoid what they dislike.

But with Neptune in earth, you have not arrived on this planet to be disgusted by earthly life. On the contrary, you have arrived to be delighted by earthly life. As long as you fight ugliness, you will be caught in ugliness, and you will suffer. The trick here is to build an unconditional love for the physical realm—to really appreciate that the power behind All That Is has taken the bother to move so slowly that we can taste, smell, feel, and hear this manifestation. Feeling this unconditional love for this world, as well as an unconditional gratitude for being born into it, is a good trick for opening your being to the love of Neptune. As you start to experience earthly life through the pure lens of Neptunian love, you begin to see the beauty in everything. Instead of understanding life from the outside, you start to perceive it from the inside. And then you see that one being giving up its life so another can live—be it a carrot, a salmon, or a moose—is something beautiful. You will no longer be repulsed by and feel pain for the lack of perfection in the physical, because your love and your gratefulness has made you understand that in fact there is no ugliness and that the physical world is a perfect paradise. As you start to live in this paradise, you are one of those who helps others to see that this planet is a paradise, and as time goes on, it will become a paradise for more and more of us.

Neptune in Fire: The Search for the Golden Castle

Neptune in fire is very often a true idealist. The person with this Neptune has great hope and faith, but when this faith and hope are tested out against the harsh realities of the world, there may be some disappointment. This

Neptune really searches for the dream, and it might have a hard time accepting limitations. At the outset, it wants everything to be free and all beings to be able to express themselves freely. It can become caught in fighting against oppressors, or it can become caught in one ideal about how life should be lived and then become intolerant toward other solutions. In fact, it can become a quite gloomy Neptune, and the carrier of it may lose a lot of the joy of being in the world, because there are too many compromises and too little enthusiasm. As it understands that it does not create more love or joy by being gloomy, it starts to change. In fact, as it learns that the journey and the joy of traveling over the earth is more important than reaching the goal, it can begin to let the joy and love for life flow. This Neptune is not about reaching your dreams, but rather is concerned with holding the dreams in your heart and traveling toward them. Then, it suddenly knows that the goal is already here, because what it sought was that pure joy and burning love of being and living. It does not have to reach the goal of the outer dreams, but just be fulfilled by the power of the dream. Love can be a good example. You can dream about and find love in the outer world, but it can just as easily be lost and disappear. Neptune is much the same. The only way to really reach your dream (love), is to become your dream, (love), no matter what the outer circumstances are. And then one lives in the golden castle and walks on the earth at the same time.

Neptune in Air: Dreams of Peace and Perfection

This Neptune is quite a dreamer. It is like the contestant in Miss Universe who says that her hopes for the future are peace, love, and happiness for everybody on Earth. It wants to create harmony and goodwill among all men. It does not like conflict or discord. This Neptune can make the owner quite wary about human behavior and the conflicts and aggressions that flow between men. At the outset, it wants to create peace and understanding. It has high ideals about love and togetherness, and it can become very disappointed when reality kicks in and disturbs its illusions about love and its ideals about relationships. On some levels, the one thing this Neptune easily forgets to take into consideration is the not-so-developed condition of humans and society. When it goes sour, it either gives up on humanity and becomes a compromiser and trader of love, or it clings to its ideals and fights everybody who tries to get some reality into the person with this Neptune in the horoscope. But as it learns from reality and keeps its ideals in the heart, it starts to be a channel for the wisdom of love. And you do not have this Neptune to experience ideal love and peace. You are born with it to become a person who through the wisdom and compassion in your love can start to create peace and harmony on Earth. This does not happen because you fight what is not peaceful and harmonic, but because you develop the wisdom of love in your heart and, at every corner and conflict, understand which way to choose to make the world a more loving and peaceful place to be. As you do this work, you become an example of the peace, love, and wisdom that builds a new society. And of course, you yourself become filled with the peace, love, and wisdom you share with the world with every breath and every action you take.

Neptune in Water: Longing for Love Without Limitations

All you need is love, love is all you need. This Neptune gives a deep longing for unity and totality. As love unfolds itself, the person with this Neptune may become unsatisfied and never experience that it can be total enough and have enough unity and connection with everything around it. It is a beautiful Neptune for falling in love, as well as the feeling of being totally devoted to this love. Love can easily take you to heaven, but then if something goes a little off track, you can fall deep down in despair, because once again the total love you seek slides through your fingers and harsh reality announces its arrival. On the psychological level, this Neptune often creates codependence. When one person has the task of fulfilling your perfect dream of total love, you easily move from unselfish love to lack of independence. Here, it is like a hunger never satisfied. It might learn to live with limited and divided love, but there will always be a longing for something better. This Neptune can get deeply dissatisfied when it gives in and accepts the limitations of earthly love, or it can be a bit like Romeo and Juliet and choose to suffer in the eternal immature quest for the perfect situation.

As it matures and becomes conscious, it begins to learn that it is not on Earth to experience the perfect love, but rather to learn to love as wholeheartedly as it can. When the person does not look for love from the outside, but rather dedicates him or herself to express and experience the love as it rises from the inner, without becoming disappointed if the outer result isn't as perfect as the intention, the change begins. Then the Neptune learns to become devoted to love, not to the object of loving, nor to the result of the love. As this happens, the deep hunger miraculously will be stilled, and the person will be more and more filled with love. This fulfills his or her spiritual purpose of becoming one who loves totally and without hesitation. And as this goes on, the dreams come true. Love has no limitations, because the capacity for love is without limitations.

Pluto and the Law of Eternal Change

Many things can be said of the ruler of the underworld. Pluto is associated with our fears and taboos. It is the dustbin of our consciousness, the place where we put all that we do not like about ourselves. It is the master of life and death, a fact that gives it so much power over human lives. And since the power of life and death is the real power, Pluto is about our relationship with power and powerlessness. But all this is looking at Pluto from the viewpoint of our bodies and egos. Pluto is in many ways the natural instincts that flow through our bodies, and since we have suppressed so many of those, Pluto becomes the holder of fear: fear of our own sexuality and mortality, fear of our savageness, and fear of our inherent ruthlessness. On the ego level, Pluto is again what we have to face to accept our own mortality. And as true as it is that humans hold power over life, it is just as true that we are powerless in the face of our own death.

With all of this power and fear swirling around Pluto, it is quite understandable that it has a reputation for manipulation, power games, and ruthlessness. On the ego level, we often gain a sense of power, and even immortality, by having command over others.

So Pluto is connected to power as well as powerlessness—both the power to make things happen and to make sure that they don't, and the great powerlessness the individual can experience in the world, especially when confronted with things like aging, death, catastrophes of nature, and so on. In many ways, it can be seen as the garbage bin for everything that is scary for the individual "I." In this garbage bin, we often put everything that makes us feel badly about ourselves. We could say that a Pluto-repressing person tries to avoid and forget all parts of life that feel bad or are scary. A Pluto-possessed person, on the other hand, is fascinated by the contents of the garbage bin and can't help but to wallow around in it.

In many ways, Pluto is a very simple influence in our lives, though a very powerful one as well. Pluto represents the interplay of magnetic and electric forces, the dance of holding things together and letting go, the push and pull of attraction and repulsion. When we meet Pluto on our way, the challenge is to find a way to create a balance in this dance—that is, when to let go and when to receive, when to accept powerlessness and when to accept power. And it represents the necessity of change. Without Pluto, we would experience an eternal standstill in an unchanging world. We would have a kind of existence, but no real life, since life is characterized by movement and change. The real death comes when we stop being alive inside and just exist, when fear of death and fear of life has broken our spirit. So the closest we come to an experience of death is when we try to suppress the function and influence of Pluto. It is like trying to use silicone to preserve youth instead of flowing gracefully into new ages.

True enough, Pluto often comes and rips out of our hands what is near and dear to us. But remember, this is not out of evil, it is out of necessity. An old proverb says that nothing will get into a closed hand. So we have to be able to let go in order to receive. Death is an absolutely necessary ingredient in life. Thus it is true that fear of death also is fear of life. When we get a real understanding of this process, we start to see that everything the Plutonic force takes away from us is a gift disguised as loss. Seen from the soul's level, the main force moving the universe is the force of love, joy, wisdom, and beauty. This force is by itself benevolent. This naturally leads to the conclusion that whatever happens happens because we need it to happen. Every occurrence in the universe is an expression of love. If we are killed by raping murderers, this in its basic essence is connected to love, because this is what we have asked for and what we need to move on. From the soul level, the individual existence on this planet is like a stage play. And few would call the writer an evil man, even if somebody in the play got murdered and tortured. Every occurrence gives us an opportunity to become wiser, more loving, more joyful, and more beautiful. When time passes by, many people can look back at their most difficult experiences and times and see that these times were what made them wiser, more whole, and more loving human beings. To really get to this total acceptance of everything that is and that happens, one has to experience the world as built on the force of love (Neptune) and one has to have the wisdom to understand why things are created as they are. Christianity is an example of what happens when one tries to believe in love but ignores the necessity of wisdom and understanding (Uranus). Without this understanding, the idea of calling everything that happens perfect and an act of love would be absurd, and we would have to call the world a kind of absurd freak occurrence or say that evil is just as strong a force in the universe as good. The planet that gets to carry this notion of evil and the absurdity of death and loss is Pluto.

As we start to look at Pluto from the angle of the spirit, all of this starts to change—and the ability and necessity of change is the spiritual key to Pluto. All that exists in the world of time and space is always changing. Nothing can stay the same. As this spiritual principle becomes internalized, all fear and power games start to dissolve. Pluto has been called the will of the universe. This will is not an outer will, but the will to change and transform that is inherent in all that exists. Seen from a spiritual angle, all transformation and change brings what is changed one step closer to regaining unity with All That Is. Even the fall into darkness or the death of the body and the ego is a beautiful step on the road to enlightenment. In many ways, the most Plutonian and toughest experience in life is to be born. To come from the unlimited world of the soul and be pushed into a confined human body and out into a limited world of time and space is not always fun. And you are even subjected to more or less total amnesia so that everything you know is forgotten and has to be learned anew! So when this act of courage is over, everything else is easy in comparison. Of course, Pluto is about ruthlessness, even the ruthlessness of love, because as you internalize and accept the true nature of the world, you seem to be ruthless to all those who fight change and think love is a kitten you can do with as you like. Love is just as much about stripping away illusions and showing you the true road to divine union as it is about cuddling and being nice and supportive.

For the ego and the body, accepting Pluto is accepting the unavoidable and accepting change as it manifests all of the time on all levels of reality. For spirit, this change is what makes the ride through manifestation such an interesting, enjoyable, and adventurous experience. For spirit, Pluto is the dance of opposites that makes life possible... and what a beautiful, enjoyable, and fulfilling dance.

Remember, Pluto and its ferry moon, Charon, are the outermost known planets of our solar system. They are the border between the solar identity and the galactic identity. We could call them the guardians of the door to enlightenment and the cosmos. As our individual center and life-giver to our solar system (individuality), the Sun represents our ego. To move beyond ego and become a true member of the universal brother or sisterhood, we have to pass through the gate of Pluto and join the galactic brother or sisterhood. We have to accept the death of our old ego and the birth of a new being, and this cannot happen as long as we have any fear of change, life, or death. Keep this in your mind when you read these sections about Pluto. The spiritual aspect we talk about is not so easy to understand if we are caught in the web of our ego, daily games, and earthly life. This is the last step in fulfilling the work of having built an ego and made it into a transparent lens for the love, joy, beauty, and wisdom of the soul and spirit.

Pluto in Cardinal: The Will to Live and Die

Pluto in cardinal can also be called the will to change. If you do not have the will to change, you become stuck in what exists and lose your power and ability to create new circumstances in your life. If that happens, fate will come by (fate = the will of the universe) and force you in its ruthless ways to let go of the old and bring in the new. In cardinal, this is about willingness to trust fate. It is to be created by your fate and at the same time to create your own fate. If you get stuck in a helpless situation, you will hold back from accepting and living your fate and will be forced by life either to embrace it or to die or suffer because of your refusal to move as life changes. If you get stuck in the outgoing position, you will be caught in the hopeless job of having control, through your will, of everything in life. And as you work harder and harder for this, your efforts will become more and more futile and you will have to either die trying to control everything or let go and relinquish your grip on your own destiny. As you stop fearing death and powerlessness, you accept what you cannot change and also accept responsibility for what you can change, and hopefully life teaches you to see the difference between outer control and inner power.

Pluto in Fixed: The Power of Life and Death

Here, Pluto has to be integrated in the person. The personality has arrived to learn to surrender to the power and, through this surrendering, to wield the power. This mastery of power comes through learning and understanding the power of transformation. Fixed energy is in the outset about transformation, and Pluto is the master teacher of that. In a way, Pluto in fixed becomes very personal. The transformation is about transforming the holder of the energy—in other words, the person with a fixed Pluto in the horoscope. As long as this person resists change or resists holding the power of change, Pluto will exert pressure and force the person to let go of him or herself. As the vessel that shall be the channel for change and the cosmic will accepts death—and new life—the current of power coming through that person becomes stronger and stronger. When this person gets stuck in the Plutonian energy, he or she either becomes a power maniac who does not see the difference in personal power and the power of the universe, or becomes a powerless victim who is helpless in the face of life, death, and change.

The ability to accept any change life has to offer, and at the same time be an agent for change and renewal in the world, is the attitude and work that gives persons with Pluto in fixed access to that dimension of life that lies outside the sphere of the ego.

Pluto in Mutable: The Acceptance of Life and Death

This Pluto is about accepting both separateness and unity. If it only feels the unity with All That Is, the person with this Pluto has a hard time experiencing him or herself as an individual. They feel caught in a flux of events outside their control. Fate is a merciless thing that just rolls ahead and deals out death and life and good and bad fortune in a seemingly random manner. If this person becomes stuck in the separate section of life (in the particle stage, as a disconnected ego), they will feel very alone and will try to survive as best as they can while they sail over the endless sea of dangers and murky, deep water that threatens to swallow them. In many instances, both of these feelings occur at the same time. Then these people feel utterly helpless, but they are in the same boat as the rest of powerless humanity.

As the people here learn both to go with the flow and to accept life as such, and learn that they hold much of their fate in their own hands, the prospect of being alive becomes brighter. As a particle (ego), they can choose what current they want to flow with and how they want to react to the fate and will of the universe. They cannot avoid being changed, but they can choose when and where they want those changes to take place. As a part of the flow, they learn to accept fate and the tide of life and death. And when they learn to combine these two stances, they learn when to become a particle and when to let go of themselves. There are times when the right choice is to surrender and go with the game that is being played, and there are times for asserting your own rules and games. To know which is appropriate and when it is appropriate is the trick that opens the door to galactic unity for people with Pluto in mutable. In a sense, they already know that the difference between having an ego and not having one is quite small. If they try to hold on to the ego's particle nature, they will inevitably lose it. If they try to avoid the formation of the ego's particle nature, they will be forced to have one. As they become masters in the flux of being both a personal point and an impersonal force, they change on a very deep level, and the true nature of their spiritual being will emerge.

Pluto in Earth: The Changer of the World of Form

This is a Pluto that has the challenge of mastering the life of the physical. One of its tasks is facing the fear of illness and the death of the body—to accept the ravages of time on the body and the inevitable end of physical life. It is to master the fear of the sick and the rotting in life. It is to let go of the need for power and control over the physical and at the same time assert your power in the physical. In one aspect, it is to face the fear of lacking anything in the physical and to let go of what you have acquired, to let go of outer beauty, richness, and power so that inner beauty, richness, and power can grow. It is to see the physical as an agent of change and to see life on the physical plane as what makes enlightenment possible. In some sense, it is to be of this world and still have the anchor of your being in the spiritual. It is about letting go of the old and the past and constantly creating a new future. It is about absolute gratefulness for experiencing the cycles of death and rebirth, and it is to stand fearless in front of life and death. It is to bow to the beauty of life and to see the great plan and purpose running through everything that is created. It is a total acceptance of life, and it is to fully hold the power of creating new life. It is to have the courage to consciously choose change and new life. It is about seeing the love behind the ruthlessness of all life and embracing everything that is natural and part of love with absolute gratitude. It is to feel gratitude for every single step and occurrence that happens in your life.

Pluto in Fire: The Courage to Live Without Fear

This is the Pluto that calls for bravery and heroism—the bravery to be ruthlessly true to your own spirit. All fear, reluctance, guilt, and shame are to be tossed into the flames of your burning spirit. In a way, the first enemy of Pluto in fire is your own fear and need to control life. This is about facing your own fears, devoting yourself to the inner flame, and risking death to find life. If this person never risks the death of what he or she is or has, he or she will not reach new life.

In one sense, this Pluto is about the willingness to sacrifice your own small goals and ideas for a higher cause. In another sense, it is about following the voice of your spirit and always seeking the fullest possible experience of joy. Do you fear life, or do you have the guts to live your life to the fullest? Do you fear ecstasy, or do you dare to move into the flames of ecstasy and burn yourself clean? This Pluto challenges the owner to live fully and totally in the now and to trust that spirit will carry him or her through any difficulties. This Pluto is also about power. Stuck in itself, the ego wants to have control over life and death and to have power and influence over others and life in general. As it moves into the spiritual, it does not want to have power over anybody or anything, but rather learns to accept all power that is bestowed upon the person. It takes just as much bravery to risk becoming an egomaniac through wielding power as it takes courage to face the powerlessness in oneself. One has to take the flame of life and lighten up all of the inner areas that are filled with lies, fear, and unconsciousness.

As this happens, these people learn to surrender to the flame of life, and through becoming this flame, they understand the true nature of life and see that there is no difference between what burns and the flame it burns with. And alas, the soul is no longer bound by the solar consciousness.

Pluto in Air: The Power of Absolute Truth

Air in itself is about wisdom and rules and how the interplay between humans and all others is conducted. Those with Pluto in air have arrived to change all of this: not what wisdom is in itself or the game as such, but they have arrived to challenge the rules (and maybe to change the whole way we play together), to fight for what is fair and just, and to let go of rules that might have been fair and just at one time, but no longer are. As humans and society change, so does wisdom change, and the way we play has to change too. Pluto in air is about ruthlessly seeking wisdom as it is now. It is about not fearing leaving old truths behind, not fearing the emptiness of not knowing what is true and just, and not fearing to embrace the new truths and rules as they rise from the eternal wheels of change that move everything created on its way toward becoming more and more conscious. And Pluto in air is not just about seeking the truth; it is also about applying it so that the world can change. It is not to let fear stop you from being true in your speech and actions, nor to let guilt stop you from changing the world.

To make this happen, you have to start to be true to yourself. You have to see through your own small games and plays and take the chance of showing your naked truth so that everybody can see it. This is not to manipulate words or truth to get it as you like, but to tell what is true and pure without protecting yourself from the consequences of this truth. As truth becomes more important than the speaker of truth, you come closer and closer to alignment with the absolute truth. You start to understand the underlying wisdom of the game, and you no longer play to win or impress or just to be nice and loved. You play the game of wisdom and use every opportunity to open the mind and the heart of other beings to their *own* truth. As you advance in this game, you are not the game nor the truthsayer, you are the channel of truth. The difference between ego and not-ego dissolves, and your consciousness leaves the pull of our solar system and becomes filled with the wisdom of the cosmos—which some refer to as cosmic consciousness.

Pluto in Water: The Courage of Ruthless Love

Here, we have to meet our deepest fear of becoming lost or alone or being eaten. This seems maybe more like Scorpio than Cancer and Pisces, but remember that we are dealing with Pluto, the god of the underworld. To have this in water is to have given ourselves the task of learning to know the deepest layers of our emotions, or else to be governed by our unconscious feelings. Here, we have to face our fears of dependency, or we will become codependent and caught in a sticky web of feelings ... or we will stay alone. Pluto will every now and then make our hidden and unconscious feelings rise from the deep, and if we are not prepared, they will take control over our lives. It is said that what we repress is what in truth holds sway over us. This goes for Pluto in all of the elements, but even more so in water. The fear of not being able to love lies here, as does the fear of not being loveable enough.

The element, quality, and sign we have Pluto in is something we are on Earth to change our relationship to on a profound level—or to learn the consequences of not changing this relationship. A spiritual approach to this is, of course, to change, since spirituality is to be changing always and at the same time to be in contact with the force behind all change.

And how do we approach a Pluto in water? Well, there is only one way to master this challenge, and that is to choose love: love rather than security, love rather than hate or indifference, and love rather than convenience and power. To master this, we must let go of all clinging and all power games connected to love. We have to be ruthlessly honest toward our own feelings. We have to go on cutting away all of those feelings that come from our lower selves, and we have to stay true to the path of true love. To do this, we have to start by trusting the force and power of love in itself. This is potent stuff, and it is easy to try to bend and manipulate it. But if we try to use love to force or manipulate someone, even just a tiny bit, we will lose our direction and lose the true power of love. As we align with this force, we become unable to do anything other than show and live our true love. The force of love starts to work through us, and as this happens our personal love becomes like a tiny feather floating in the sea of love. And the difference between personal love and impersonal love becomes unimportant, and after a while non-existent. As this happens, we move beyond our ego consciousness and become a part of that force of love that lies behind the creation of all of the galaxies in the universe, and our love will have no end and no limit.

Involution and Evolution

The development of human consciousness is clearly mirrored in the organization of the planets in our solar system. The planet that best describes the experiences of a newborn baby is the Moon. Old esoteric doctrines said that the human soul entered Earth through the Moon. And you will remember that before it is born, the fetus has gone through the exact same process as the development of life on Earth. This is one of the reasons that our cellular remembrance can allow us to feel and experience unity with all forms of life: we have been that life, from the single cell to the fish and on up to the mammals, before our birth into the outer world.

Our journey in the body starts with integrating the principle of the Moon. This is the infant who is completely trusting and helpless. The next step in the process of consciousness is to develop some sort of values. For instance, the child likes yellow, that which shines; tomatogooey better than carrotgooey, and so on. It has moved into Venus and started the work of getting some sort of values, and then it comes to Mercury and experiences this strange thing called communication—that sentences, sounds, gestures, and all those other crazy things we do in fact have a meaning. And from there, the consciousness moves into the Sun and the first identity is formed. The Sun at this stage establishes identity and the first experience of "I," but it also affords an experience of separation and the first conscious anxiety for something outside this "I."

Seen from a spiritual point of view, one could say that one has to have an "I" before one can transcend the "I." In some people, this early forming of the "I" has not taken place in the proper way. If this is so, the person will have a problem with identity and can easily become schizophrenic. There can also be a great connection with the spiritual and selfless side of consciousness and a poor connection with time and space and the earthly personality.

So, when this center of identity is formed, the journey outward can begin. The "I" has to learn to express itself (Mercury) and to communicate with others (Venus). It has to be able to express its own values, to share with others, and to express affection and gratitude (Venus). Then it starts to become earthed and becomes able to cope with the flow of its own and others' emotions (Moon). In this way, it learns to feel a part of the family, the community, and humanity (the Moon and Earth).

So, it has arrived on Earth as an individual being with its own values, opinions, feelings, and personality. And now the time has come to learn to express all of this: to act on it and to unfold all that is in the personality (Mars). As the will and the ability to handle intention and power are developed, the ability to expand into the world (Jupiter) and to handle responsibility and create structures (Saturn) is growing. Eventually, the young person through this process becomes a member of the larger world and works to create a better future for him or herself and maybe mankind (Jupiter). So, as the ability to function in society and be and act in the world of time and space is mastered (Saturn), there is a natural longing for more freedom and new consciousness (Uranus). This search for more and more freedom and consciousness is in fact the creative instinct that is embedded in all life (Uranus). And as the same force that guided the Greek creator god Ouranos propels one, one passes through the sphere of Uranus and reaches the deep inner sea of Neptune. One then becomes immersed in what one longed for: unity, love, and oneness (Neptune). As one yields to this, one starts to let the old ego slip away. One gives up the old self-centered life and accepts what happens. One becomes at one with existence and totally present in every moment of life and death. And so, through total acceptance and celebration of All That Is and all that happens, one passes through the gates of Pluto and becomes a realized being instead of a limited ego. One opens one's eyes to the galaxy and the "spaced-out" consciousness of the awakened ones. And so the journey ends, and the personality has remembered its true nature and celebrates life as only true masters can celebrate.

The Planets in Houses

Sometimes an astrologer describes you as if your life were only concerned with the houses and signs where your axes and planets are. It is important to remember that every person has access to all of the energies in the universe. This means that you have access to the energies from all twelve star signs and you operate in all twelve houses. To say something else would be as stupid as saying that you don't need to sleep if you do not have planets in the fourth house.

But if you see the houses as small prison cells that confine the planets to live under their jurisdictions, this might become the case. So what does it really mean to have a planet in a house? In my opinion, it means that I have to work with the area of life that this house represents in order to get access to the planetary energy. If I have the Sun in the tenth and avoid all issues about my need to be seen, to have a career, or to get acknowledgment, I will have very little access to my own solar energy. You have to go to the house of the planet in order to get access to the planetary energy. But when you have access to that house and the planetary energy, you can use it wherever you want in the horoscope. We can use the Sun as an example. You need to use the energy of the Sun's sign and do it in the Sun's house. This is like igniting the fire of the Sun. If you do not do this, you will lack energy, individuality, self-confidence, and so on. But as soon as you get access to the solar energies, your self-confidence and energy will start to radiate throughout the other parts of the horoscope and your life. That is, you have to light up the wood in the fireplace, but when you have done this, you can use the fire to warm up other rooms and the whole house. As we start to develop, the houses will define us less and less in our birth chart. An advanced being has managed to raise the energy level of all of the planets to such a degree that they can be used in all areas of life. To use another analogy, the light will be so bright that it will be more and more difficult to say that this is a green or a blue or a pink person—one would achieve what I like to call a rainbow personality.

Rulerships

The man of meditation is playful, he is not serious.
He cannot be serious: the whole of life is a divine play,
and he is part of it. He is just playing a role.
He acts the role as beautifully as he can, as perfectly as he can,
but he knows that the whole world is a big stage,
a great drama, but nothing more.
So he is not serious about it.

—OSHO

The idea of rulerships is old and has followed astrology for a long time. It is especially connected with horary astrology, where there were rulers for every hour of the day. Using mythology, we can gain an understanding of rulers by seeing the gods as rulers of different areas of life: Mars was the warrior god, Demeter a fertility goddess, and so on. This provides an understanding of the planets as rulers of houses, or mansions, as they were called.

But what does it mean when a planet rules a sign? Does it mean that the planet sits on a throne and decides how that sign is going to behave? Personally, I would find it more natural to think of a planet as a servant of a sign, and that the connection between sign and planet arises because the energy of the sign can easily be expressed through that planet. It is natural for Gemini to express through words and the mind—in other words, Mercury—and it is natural for Leo energy to express itself through the Sun. So it seems it is more like a connection than a rulership. As I see it, it is the quality of the sign, and the house that is occupied by the sign, that naturally expresses itself through the house and sign of the "ruling" planet. But note also that while the main stream of energy has a tendency to move like this, it is not the only way. Gemini can express itself through feelings and the Moon, even if it takes a little more work than using the Mercurial shortcut.

One interesting and puzzling thing about esoteric astrology is that it operates with different sets of rulers depending on your level of development. The rulers normally worked within astrology, and they are esoterically connected with a person or horoscope operating from the level of ego consciousness. If you start to operate from a level of soul consciousness, there will be a change in rulership for most of the signs. Does this mean that there is a kind of revolution in which one king or queen dethrones the other and grabs the ruling scepter? My point of view is that as your consciousness grows from ego to soul level, the way you express and understand sign energy will change. When the more beautiful and selfless sides of a sign become expressed, it seems that this activity and energy naturally will be more and more directed through this esoteric ruler.

Aries

Mars normally rules Aries. The pulsating and creative Aries energy is channeled through the body and action. There is an instinctive outgoing and conquering impulse that is expressed through the use of bodily force. As the consciousness develops, the pulsating energy and the will start to become a tool for the mind. The first one is a bit like the wild and unpredictable Greek Ares, while the structured Roman god Mars is moving toward the second level. As the soul awareness grows, the creative force of Aries becomes a tool for the quest to create what is seen as good and beautiful through the mind. The Aries energy will no longer be invested in a competition with other individual wills, but rather will be guided by the wisdom and knowledge of the soul toward what is better for everybody.

Taurus

On the ego level, Taurus is ruled by Venus. This signifies the sign's need to experience its physical senses, as well as the individual appreciation of beauty, wealth, comfort, and harmony. On the lower individual level, it is associated with a person who wants to have everything for him or herself, a greedy glutton who cannot let go of anything. As the consciousness is raised, the Taurus isn't solely occupied by the world of form, and it starts to understand the flow (overflow) of energy between the created and the uncreated. In esoteric astrology, Vulcan is the soul ruler of Taurus. Personally, I have a problem with accepting an invisible planet as a ruler of the earthy Taurus. For those who cannot work with a planet that hasn't been discovered, I suggest you see a more refined and advanced Venus as the soul ruler of Taurus. But Vulcan is the smith god connected with the creation of beauty, as are gnomes and dwarfs. On the soul level, Taurus is occupied with taking the raw inner material and transforming it into something beautiful. On the soul level, Taurus can see the inner beauty of all form and is not blinded by the outer. So as the consciousness rises, the Taurean energy will be expressed through this overflow of creation and beauty and will manifest through the house and sign where you find the esoteric ruler—Vulcan.

Gemini

On the ego level, Gemini is ruled by Mercury. It is this curious mind, wanting the answer to everything but having a hard time going beneath the layers and seeking the depths of anything. The ego is a collector of knowledge. Maybe it wants to impress others, or maybe it just wants to have something to do so that the dullness of the world doesn't feel too painful, or maybe it sees that knowledge can be used in a search for wisdom and thereby becomes more than merely entertainment and movement for the sake of movement.

As the focus starts to change toward the soul level, Gemini becomes more and more occupied with the value of knowledge and the value of any movement and question. Instead of just doing something, Gemini starts to want to do something that is good and benevolent and valuable—and not only for him or herself. It begins the long road of wanting to be of service and to use all of its knowledge, ideas, and connections for the betterment of humanity.

As the soul level begins to establish itself, Venus becomes more and more a natural place to express the Gemini energy. In a deeper sense, Venus is connected to the ability to value, and in an even deeper sense, to love. In Gemini, this becomes the ability to see everybody as having a value and being worthy of love. It even means the ability to love everybody. So as the Gemini energy becomes expressed on the soul level, the person starts to love everybody and wants to bring beauty, harmony, and togetherness to all mankind. This energy will then be expressed primarily through the house that has Gemini on the cusp and the house where Venus is situated.

Cancer

The normal ruler of Cancer is the Moon. The Cancer show of emotions is easily expressed through the Moon. On the lower level of development, Cancer is possessed by one's personal feelings and has very little distance from one's own need. That need may be to feed or be fed, to love or be loved, and it's always changing and moving in accordance with the outer reactions to one's inner needs. As the person develops, the feelings become more and more a directed force that is connected with the will and the mind. One starts to use feeling consciously instead of being a "victim" of every feeling that pops up.

As this develops further, Cancer starts to be an outpouring cornucopia of love. Instead of being associated with each single wave, the inner is now, through the soul, connected with the ocean of love. As Neptune, the esoteric ruler of Cancer, starts to work through this sign, the outpouring of love becomes more and more unconditional. One loves because one loves, not because one wants something back (such as others to love you in return).

Leo

Leo is Leo, and the Sun rules both the ego and the soul. The difference is the perception of the ego. As long as the ego thinks it is the main character and the most important one on the stage, the soul level is blocked. As the understanding of the "I" changes, the soul becomes more dominant. The more one sees and *uses* the "I" as a point of focus for the universal spiritual force, the more one operates from the soul level. In the world of Luke Skywalker, the overly egocentric way to use the solar power accessible for Leo would be a fast road to the dark side of the Force. One of the reasons *Star Wars* has made such an impression is Luke Skywalker's striving to reach a point where he becomes a vehicle of the Force. The ego wants to shine to be recognized and appreciated by the world, and the soul wants to shine to give warmth and light and energy to the world.

Virgo

On the personal level, Virgo is ruled by the mind and Mercury. The Virgo personality is occupied with analyzing, always seeking ways to improve whatever it touches. On a lower level, it can be very occupied with, even a little possessed by, what is imperfect. It can be extremely critical and negative, and it can wield a logic that becomes very destructive. An egoistic Virgo energy is in many ways just as self-occupied as Leo, only the Virgonian energy is directed inward. One is totally occupied with one's own imperfections, and one finds these deficits the most important thing in the world. As Virgo energy evolves toward the soul level, it becomes less and less complex and more and more simple. Instead of filtering everything through the head, it starts to "see" and understand the world through the heart. There is a rare and simple innocence at the heart of Virgo energy that is allowed to surface as the soul becomes the point of focus, and this simple combination of wisdom and love will easily be expressed through the Moon. Here, the true purity and humility of Virgo energy is inevitably expressed without any fuss. The Zen story about the monk who chopped wood and carried water before he became enlightened and also chopped wood and carried water after he became enlightened is the Virgo story about enlightenment. The whole difference lies in the attitude.

Libra

Libra has a need to see its individuality reflected in someone else. It needs to be recognized and approved of. There is a need for social approval and company. On the lower scale of development, Libra does everything to be loved and gain approval. It can do the most horrendous things to get affection and affirmation from someone else. As Libra develops, it becomes more centered on the relationship, and the search for beauty and value starts to go below the surface. As the understanding of real togetherness grows, Libra moves toward the soul level. When Libra starts to understand that it has to give itself affirmation and affection first, some of the job is done. When it starts to realize that to be loved or liked for something that isn't genuinely real is worse than not being loved at all, much of the job is done. As the soul perspective grows stronger and stronger, Libra gets a clearer and clearer understanding of freedom. An advanced Libra will only give what he or she really wants to give—there will be no flattery and no nice words to get one's will. This Libra wants only something given from a totally free will and heart. There is no jealousy, no manipulation, and no fake friendliness—only the true and sincere love and joy of one person meeting another. And this is the point at which the Libran energy will flow through that point of focus shown by Uranus placement in sign and house.

Scorpio

Scorpio's old ruler was Mars. The most used ruler today is Pluto, and the esoteric ruler remains Mars. It becomes very clear here that it is the way you use the energy that is important. The old Mars was very much associated with using your inner psychic will to get your way. Through Mars, the person was able to manifest the inner need and emotions in the outer world. With Pluto as the ruler of Scorpio, we see a great need for transformation of this energy. On the lower level of Pluto, Scorpio energy is possessed by the emotions and needs of the inner personality. You could say that this individual is possessed by his or her own needs and feelings. The consequence of this possession will with time and pain necessarily lead to a transformation.

Through these Plutonic experiences, the soul gradually emerges, and the motivation starts to change from the compulsive need of the ego to a consciously directed energy from the soul. Scorpio energy works with this deep magnetic and compulsive force. When a person is able to "become possessed" without being possessed by the possession, the soul level starts to emerge. By this, I mean that the individual is able to handle the energy of falling in love, or other very strong emotions, and at the same time is able to hold this energy without having to act. Then the action becomes a choice, and it becomes possible to act from the soul level. And when one in fact acts from this level of wanting the most love and grace for everybody involved, Mars becomes a tool for the love force of Scorpio.

Sagittarius

Sagittarius is ruled by Jupiter, the planet that almost forgot it was a planet and nearly became a sun. This exuberance, joy, and lack of restriction are a part of the Sagittarian nature. This great wish to expand forever and see and experience everything flows easily through Jupiter, the traditional ruler of the archer. On the individual level, there is a great need to move up and away, to reach the next goal and find the next vision, and there is an inner feeling that the grass is always greener somewhere else. As Sagittarius develops, a strange calm comes over this sign. Instead of seeking heaven, paradise, and wisdom out there in the heavens somewhere, Sagittarius starts to look down on its own two feet. Through the feet and the feeling of walking and belonging to the earth, Sagittarius connects with its soul. It must be found within and then directed outward. As Sagittarius develops the ability to be in the moment and at the same time to connect with and care for all of its surroundings, the soul level starts to appear. Everything that seemed so complicated starts to become simple. Everything that seemed so far away suddenly appears in the palm of the hand. The Sagittarian energy starts to become expressed through the planet Earth. In one way, one could see the Sagittarian energy as the real guardian of the planet, because no one can understand the holiness of nature like Sagittarian energy. Earth is said to be located directly opposite the Sun in the horoscope. This opposition says that when the Sagittarian energy operates from the soul level, the balance between the earthly and the heavenly becomes more and more perfect. The understanding that everything is holy—and that holiness in form and holiness without form are equally important—is self-evident for the soul-operated Sagittarian energy.

Capricorn

Capricorn, in older days, was sometimes described as a sea goat, something like an animal mermaid. This picture of the sea goat can provide some clues about the soul-centered Capricorn. But whatever disguise Capricorn uses, there is no way to avoid Saturn, which is both its traditional and esoteric ruler. On the individual level, the world for Saturn is something to conquer and master. It is important to be higher and better and to avoid weakness and vulnerability. There is a need to be able to master everything alone, so loneliness will of course be a problem. The world is a hard place; it is a rat race, and if you don't run, somebody will squish you under their heel—so better to be a squisher than to be squished. As one becomes tired of the burden and allows the soul level to become more important, the perspective changes dramatically. Seen from the soul level, Saturn gives us an opportunity to experience and express our soul and spirit through form. Form becomes a great gift, not a prison or a test. It's like God has taken the trouble to move so slowly on the energetic scale that we can touch and smell and sense God within the space of time. By appreciating and sharing this fantastic gift of being alive and being part of the crew of the cosmic starship called Earth, one develops more and more of the true understanding that everything is a blessing, and it is a gift that is given *freely*. And then one starts to give one's life as a gift to the universe, and one can see life as the fantastic and exciting adventure that it truly is.

Aquarius

Until Uranus was discovered, Saturn ruled Aquarius. Saturn's rulership tells us about the feeling of being caught in form that often accompanies Aquarian energy, and it also gives an idea about the rigidity that may haunt the sign, which after all is fixed (stale) air. Uranus provides us with a clue about the more developed Aquarian need to be something unique: to break out from the masses and to be something that is recognizable and remembered as different from everything else. Still, this is the individual need to be something special, the need to be more and better and more clever than other men. On a lower level, the Aquarian energy can provide a pure lack of ability to conform and find a place in society. It can be the delusion that society ought to conform to *your* standards: in other words, a hidden tyrannical factor that somehow gives the person a justification for doing whatever he or she wants. In one of its lowest forms, Aquarian energy becomes terrorism. There is no respect for those who are innocent or for personal lives. The idea is more important than anything else. As this possession of one's own rights and freedom wanes and one starts to see deeper into the world and other people, the soul-centered Aquarian energy becomes visible. This energy is connected with and easily expressed through the esoteric ruler of Aquarius, which is Jupiter. The Aquarian then starts to become a true giver of hope and that which is good to all men. There is a generosity in Aquarius, an ability to love without condemnation or any wants for oneself. To feel the joy of togetherness—just the joy of being together and having fun—is reward enough for the soul-centered Aquarian energy. There is a sense of celebration, hope, and idealism that is shared with everybody, and the ideals are more important than oneself. But everything is done with love. One has a deep respect and acceptance of other people's values and needs, and still one really knows how to love and share what one has, even with those who think they are that person's enemies.

Pisces

The old ruler of Pisces was Jupiter. When Neptune was discovered, the Piscean energy easily became expressed through this planetary energy. On an individual level, the Jupiterian Pisces believes in its own inner world. It is operating under the delusion of its own sense of right and wrong, and it has a hard time finding a distinction between its own feeling and longing and the true state of things in the world. There is an inner confusion. The Neptunian delusion may be even more grandiose than the Jupiterian. Ego-centered Piscean energy is very occupied with one's own feelings. The most important thing is this inner state, and everything that can lead to redemption or feeling good is seen as good. In this state, immediate satisfaction is always chosen, and the result is longtime suffering. As Pisces starts to mature and get a better understanding of its own longing, the more difficult way of renouncing and letting go is chosen more and more often. And the strange thing is, the more the Piscean energy chooses the hard road, the easier it becomes. The esoteric ruler of this sign is Pluto, and truly, when Piscean energy starts to operate on a soul level, everything is transformed. The search to find a back door into heaven is traded for the great joy of being in the imperfect world. Every little experience of love is seen as a blessing, and to be allowed to find the way to oneness through the path of aloneness becomes a gift of love. When Pisces stops feeling sorry for itself and stops chasing after its own inner need to be a savior and a loved one, it in truth becomes a vehicle for the love that is the nature of the soul. Such a force will naturally express itself through Pluto, and by its own momentum it will start to change everything it touches. That is one of the reasons why enlightened beings always have been a threat to the existing society. By the pure power of their presence, they start to change things, and those who do not allow themselves to be changed will react strongly against them. When the Piscean energy operates from the soul level, one is not ruled by any fear of the reaction of others; one is transformed by the "merciless" power of love.

A Little Remark on the Way

I thought I would mention that it is very difficult to have some of your planets operating on the soul level and others on the ego level, at least for any length of time. This is not a question about planets moving into other levels of awareness, but about you moving into deeper contact with your real self. You are not a fractured mass of astrological data. You are one: a whole being who becomes more and more aware. As you move into the soul level of awareness, the way you express and manifest the energies in your horoscope is changing. The energy starts to flow in different directions and manifest in different ways than you are accustomed to.

This transition may happen rapidly, or it can occur slowly over many years, as it does for most of us. In times when the progress is especially speedy, one might become frustrated. One would like to think that as you develop, everything becomes smoother and there is less resistance. This is not the case in times of transition. As you will see, when your flow of energy, as it is astrologically shown by the horoscope, starts to change, you become confused and bewildered and may even become sick. This happens because the old energy patterns and waves become disturbed and destroyed as the flow is going into new and unknown directions, like a river leaving its old banks and seeking a new path. There can be small or significant feelings of despair, hopelessness, and frustration. This is what the old mystics called the "dark night of the soul." But if the process that goes on is a true movement toward greater soul consciousness, you will always come out on the other side of the dark night and see a new day that is brighter and more joyful than the day you left behind.

I will also mention some wise words from Alan Oken. He once said in a lecture that there is no use in interpreting a horoscope on the soul level for a person existing on the individuality or ego level, but what is possible is to use this understanding of a horoscope to tell the ego-focused individual what his or her greatest potential is, and so give an idea about where the road to soul consciousness lies.

ASPECTS

You are to live and to learn to laugh.
You are to learn to listen to the cursed radio music of life
and to reverence the spirit behind it
and to laugh at its distortions.
So there you are. More will not be asked of you.

—HERMAN HESSE, STEPPENWOLF

So now we move into aspects. One of the questions surrounding this topic is about which points can be aspected. In some traditions, one draws aspects to the lunar nodes, MC/IC axis, and Ascendant/Descendant axis. Personally, I might be influenced by my Taurus Sun, since I only draw aspects to planets and other bodies that have mass. I count conjunctions to other important points but do not use the other aspects. This comes from my understanding that points as Ascendant and the lunar nodes do not really contain anything. It is just an empty space that is given a certain meaning in the astrological horoscope. For me, aspects are lines of energy, and there can be no real contact in this manner between a real object and an imaginary point; there is nothing there that can reflect and turn the energy back. Conjunctions, on the other hand, do exist in the same space as the imaginary point and will influence the energetic charging of this area. In a way, you can think of the quality of the sign when you look at the relationship between a planetary body and a point as the Ascendant. Every planet in Leo will have some of the qualities of the square to a Scorpio Ascendant, no matter the degree of the planet and the Ascendant. We could say that the fiery Leo planet has a hard time expressing itself through the filter of the watery Scorpio Ascendant. In the same manner, every planet in the two other water signs, Pisces and Cancer, will have a bit of the trine quality in regard to the Scorpio Ascendant. It just means that the energy of a planet in Pisces or Cancer has easy access to expressing itself through the filter of the third water sign, Scorpio.

I will begin by giving a short description of my idea of planets in the last degree of one sign, or the first thirty minutes of a sign. These planets are in the doorway, and they seem to be a bit confused. The soul has chosen such a position in order to learn to achieve balance and a deeper understanding. At its worst, you experience the planet as borderline and schizophrenic. At its best it is like being bicultural and getting the best of two cultures. Then we are back to the energetic picture of ourselves that magically appears when we draw up the aspect lines in our horoscope.

Houses, planets, and signs are, as mentioned earlier, in many ways just the background—the setting of the stage. The play begins as we start to look at the aspects.

You could say that the aspect comes forth through a division of the circle into smaller and smaller parts. You could also say that aspects follow a numerological sequence, dependent on how many aspected points you have. The number one signifies a conjunction, the number two an opposition, three a trine, four a square, five a quintile, six a sextile, seven a septile, and eight a semisquare. You could also say that the major aspects come through a division of the zodiac into twelve, so every thirty degrees make an aspect. Then we also get the semisextile and the quincunx.

In addition, you can divide the zodiac into nine and get a novile, and into ten and get a $36°$ aspect, which can also be called a semiquintile. It is also possible to get aspects by adding up semisquares, septiles, and quintiles. Then we get the sesquiquadrate—or 135° aspect; the biseptile, which is 144°; and the bi- and triquintile, 102°52" or 154°18".

In other words, there are a whole lot of aspects, and for every aspect there is a question about orb. How accurate must that orb be to be taken into account?

I like to see the horoscope as an expression of a living whole, not as a cake sliced into small pieces that have to work hard to keep in touch through the aspects. I like to think about the horoscope as a piece of music or, as in an old Greek description of the planetary movement over the sky, as the music of the spheres. If we think of the natal chart as a piece of music the astrologer can listen to, the orb of the aspects is dependent on how good we as astrologers are at listening, and of course how much of the symphony of the horoscope is available for the consciousness of the horoscope's "owner."

In fact, *any planet in the horoscope has some kind of aspect to any other planet.*

To even think that there can be no connection between, for example, the Moon and Mercury in a human being is absolutely absurd. There is always a connection. An aspect only gives an idea about the special quality or importance of the connection. It is like how any instrument in an orchestra is connected to any other instrument in the same orchestra. To an untrained ear, there might seem to be no link between some of the instruments, such as the drum and flute, but to a trained ear, every bit is a part of a connected whole. The aspects we use only signify either a connection that is very audible and stands out from the rest of the sound picture or a connection that is very important to be aware of if you want to understand the hidden message in the beautiful piece of music that every human life is. When a planet has none or very few and weak aspects, it may seem like there is little or no connection between this planet and the rest of the horoscope. To an untrained ear, it seems like either you hear the music of the single planet and not the rest of the horoscope or you hear the rest of the gang but can't hear the single planet. So you start to listen to the music of the life of the person with this unaspected planet in new ways, and voilà … the connections start to become audible. It's like you have to hear the finer tunes and then have to be able to listen a little behind the outer noise so that you can find the chorus of the finer tunes, and then you will start to understand how the music of the seemingly unaspected planet blends in with the orchestra.

So generally, I am saying that the orbs get wider as you learn to listen to the depth of the music that lies in your heart and soul. Also, as you evolve toward the level of soul, the nature of the planets involved becomes more and more important, and the nature of the aspect less and less important. In an evolved being, the energy of a square is manifested in the world with the same ease as a trine, and a trine is manifested with the same vigor and power as a square.

I have found it interesting to note the difference between aspects that are on their way to becoming exact and aspects that have become exact. The person with the aspects that haven't reached fulfillment are always seeking a situation and experience as is described by the aspect. It is like this is something new and unknown that he or she really longs to experience; you could say that the person intentionally moves into the situation. When the aspect has completed, it seems that the person already experiences the circumstances described by the situation. He or she is already in the energy and tries to use the momentum of this energy to move out into the world in new ways. I will use the Moon and Saturn as an example. When the Moon is approaching an exact aspect to Saturn, it is like the person is seeking circumstances that can give limits and structure and order to the Moon, so these circumstances can give the person a clearer and deeper understanding of everything connected to the Moon. If, on the other hand, the aspect has been exact, it is like the person already experiences the feeling of restrictions and limitations that Saturn sets for the Moon. It's in some ways already inherent in the psyche. This person has a need to use these already existing circumstances as a basis for going out into the world with the resources of the Moon. By accepting and using these inner and outer Saturnian restrictions, new experiences and achievements can be reached.

Another way to describe the difference is to say that an aspect that has been exact in many ways is internalized, while one moving toward fulfillment seeks manifestation in the outer world. To give another example, when Mercury is moving toward an exact aspect with Uranus, there is a great interest in the unusual. One is intrigued and puzzled by unusual points of view, statements, thoughts, and so on. When the aspect has been exact, one does not need to look to the outer world to find unorthodox points of view. Instead, one naturally thinks in different ways than expected, and so all of the "crazy" ideas just pop up from the inside. The same principle can be used to understand how transiting planets function when they "hit" the natal planets. Up to the point of exaction, there is a need to experience the transit as something coming from outside, moving within. This doesn't necessarily have to be an outer event; it can be like new feelings, consciousness, or intuition entering the personal field of experience. But after the aspect has been exact, there is a need to express this new energy into the world and to see what results that brings. When the aspect in radix is fairly exact, it signifies a condition that is a part of you almost always. You are the state described by the aspect and the planets and houses involved. You experience life through this angle. You could see it like a permanent home, instead of a place you visit and leave.

Aspects create a special relationship between two or more planets. The natures of the aspect and the planets involved define the quality of the exchange of energy between the two planets. This exchange between planets also creates a field of energy between the two planets. On one level of consciousness, the energy from one planet creates trouble for the others, or it gives the other planet help and inspiration. As long as we are at war with ourselves or a bit unintegrated, these energies will be experienced as something happening between two parts of our self. As we start to move on the spiritual path, we begin to understand that nothing is separated. We are whole in ourselves, we are in unity with the created world, and we move toward unity with All That Is. Having a spiritual understanding of an aspect between planets is to see that this aspect gives us the task and the opportunity to create a synthesis between the energies represented by the planet. This synthesis is on the inner level, but it will also emerge as a synthesis on the outer level of reality. Each aspect has a unique way of creating this synthesis.

And with the danger of repeating myself, I will say that each aspect gives us an idea of how we have to proceed in order to stop experiencing separation and become whole in ourselves.

Individual Aspects

Conjunctions

When two planets align, the aspect says something about *totality*. In fact, there is the possibility for a total merging, so one cannot be separated from the other. Through this merging, there is a possibility for acting with total focus and *concentration*. Of course, the power increases greatly when the combined forces of two or more planets work in total unity.

Semisextiles

This humble little aspect is about *attention*. We could even call it attention to detail. Here, you are given a chance to find and use talents and possibilities that are a bit difficult to see. In some ways, the possibilities are a bit too close to see. There is an old saying about not seeing the forest because of all of the trees: attention to what is close, but not obvious, is the trick for starting the synthesizing process between the planets in semisextile.

Novile

Noviles are about *faith and magic*. When there is a total trust between the planets, and a total trust from the person with them, faith starts to create wonders and indeed magic happens.

Semisquare

Semisquares are about *tolerance*. Planets in semisquare easily get frustrated and irritated by each other. If the irritation is allowed to rule, one tries to avoid the other and both planets can become very blocked in their expression. As they learn tolerance and even start to feel joy or love for the other, or at least start to see the wisdom and beauty in the other's approach, one begins to master this task. As those with this aspect learn tolerance and acceptance instead of having frustration and irritation toward others, they learn to accept and tolerate themselves as well. And if they learn to accept and tolerate the different qualities in themselves, they develop the same attitude toward others. Then the frustration and irritation become free energy that can be used by the two planets in unity, toward accomplishment and growth rather than blocking and stagnation. On the spiritual level, it creates an inner ability to accept and hold and meet frustration and irritation and use this energy to create something filled with love, joy, wisdom, and beauty.

Septiles

This aspect, which is not often used, is about *alignment*. It gives a unique opportunity for perfect coordination between the two planets. In fact, this aspect only kicks in if you are on the spiritual level. It is concerned with the two planets working in perfect harmony as they align themselves with the will of the universe. Here, there is no trying and no resistance when it operates. And until this alignment is done, the aspect just lies dormant.

Sextiles

Sextiles are about *inspiration and utilization*. The task here is to make the best of your gifts. This may seem easy enough, but it can be just as easy to slide by. The exchange between the two planets flows easily, and the energy from one inspires the other. To create a synthesis, the inspiration from one must be utilized by the other, and vice versa. Through realizing the promise and possibility in the sextile, the synthesizing and unity between the two planetary energies is achieved.

Quintiles

This aspect is about the *creativity of the genius*. The number five is very connected to humans and our movement through time and space. We have five fingers on each hand. This is not just about creating, but about creating something that has not been created before. The synthesis between the two planets will create a distinctive and unique field of energy.

Squares

Squares are about *transformation*. Each of the planetary energies has to become transformed in the meeting with the other. As this transformation happens, they become more and more coordinated; in the end, they are transformed into a powerful unit, and the energy created by the dynamics of the aspect becomes available for the whole personality. We could say that this aspect is given so that we can find a resolution of our inner conflicts.

Trines

Trines are about *receptivity*. It is to be open to all opportunities as signified by the houses and nature of the two planets. It is about saying yes and accepting all that the world has to offer. The first step in the trine is to see how the two planets automatically support and reinforce each other. The second is to see how they can create new opportunities and possibilities. The task is to do your best instead of being satisfied with what works. On the spiritual level, this is to go with the flow and to really enjoy it and use it for the good of All That Is.

Sesquisquares

This aspect is about *patience*. Inherent in the sesquisquare is a tendency to use too much force and pressure to accomplish things. It is a frustration between the planets involved that creates a push. It is a bit like they are annoyed and easily irritated with each other, and they can easily start an internal quarrel and competition. To be able to hold off this frustration and have patience is the way to go with this relationship. Both planets have to learn tolerance for the other, and as they learn to have consideration for each other, they can start to cooperate. As they do this, they both get stronger, and the combination of the two forces creates an energy field of stamina and patience.

Inconjunctions

Inconjunctions, or quincunxes, are about *awareness*. They create a link between two planets that reside in quite different signs. In some way, these two themes have to be woven into each other. We could say that differences have to be seen and solutions have to be found. Both planets need to become aware of the *modus operandi* and perception of life as it is expressed through the other. When a synthesis is found, the person becomes very good at connecting two sides of life that at the outset seemed to have little or no connection to each other.

Oppositions

Oppositions are about *integration*. In many ways, the opposition is the aspect that most easily will have to be faced on the outer level of reality. In fact, it gives us the opportunity to make an inner integration by meeting and seeing ourselves in the outer mirror. This aspect seemingly forms a contradiction. It is like being on both sides in a rope-pulling contest, either on the inside or with the outer world. The trick is to become aware of this and to change the rope to a line on which we can dance like trapeze artists in a circus … and the name of the circus is Terra, and we are the trapeze artists.

A Little More about the Septile and the Quintile

Astrologers generally seem to have difficulties with understanding these two aspects. Maybe this is because there is so little written material about them, or maybe it's because they are seldom used. The quintile, which is derived from a "splitting" of the circle into five, ought to be a major aspect. Five is a low number, and a very important number for human beings. Four is the number that describes form, or the existence of matter in time and space. As demonstrated by the great pyramids, you need to have four corners if you want to make a structure with an inner content. Three corners will give you breadth but no height.

Five is the number for soul moving through time and space. And that is what humans do for fun: we move through time and space. I guess there is no coincidence that we have five fingers, five toes, and five extensions from our torso (arms, legs, and head). I believe one of the reasons the quintile is less used is that 72° is such an awkward number compared to the neat 30 series. But to be fair, the quintile aspect is far from the big drum in the orchestra. It is easy for the energies in the quintile to be drowned by everything going on in the squares and oppositions and trines and sextiles.

As long as you are too caught up in the world of conformity, the quintile will have very little influence on your life. As you break away from the standard measures and become more and more unique, the quintile will grow in strength and influence. You have to be a creator in form, instead of just created in form, in order to get access to the quintile energy. If you search in horoscopes, you will find a great influence from quintiles in the horoscopes of artists and madmen. Hitler is an example of a person who dared to rise from the masses and visualize his dreams in a unique way. A scary example like this gives us an understanding of what kind of potential for misuse and misery might be hidden in the quintiles. But they also have the same potential for joy and creativity. The basic concept of the quintile is that it gives you something that is uniquely yours, a talent or possibility that exists only in you. The combination of the two planets and their house and sign placement tells you about the nature of this special gift.

It is possible to open an untapped field of energy and to create new and special circumstances in which this energy can be used. A person who is afraid of standing out from the masses and who tries to blend in and be normal will find it almost impossible to utilize this energy.

The septile is another kind of animal. It is maybe even more difficult to pick up on than the quintile. The septile requires a certain amount of silence and calm if you are going to understand it. It is concerned with a special form of harmonizing between two planets. If one or both of the planets is too noisy or too occupied with squares quarreling or trines having a good time, there is no room for the relatively shy septile. Seven is an old magic number for fulfillment. There are seven days in a week, and in ancient times, astrology operated with seven heavenly bodies. The septile strives for this perfect balance. You could say that it has some of the pointedness of the conjunction and some of the stimulation of the sextile. When you are silent and ready for the septile, the movement and coordination of the two planets involved will be flawless. It is like a dance between telepathists. Everything is in deep harmony and perfectly timed. There are no differing opinions about what to do or where to go between the two planets. They are moving as one, and still they have the benefit and joy of being two different planets. If you have a septile between Mars and Pluto, it is like your personal will and the cosmic will have a capability and natural talent for perfect harmony. When you are listening to your deep inner voice and have the calm to wait for the inner knowledge, what you want to do is exactly the same as what your fate moves you toward doing. There will be no struggle and no resistance, only this perfectly coordinated use of power and will. You could say that while creative expression is a good way to open up to quintile energy, meditation is a good way to open up to septile energy.

The Cycles of Waxing and Waning Aspects

If the two planets are in a stage from conjunction to opposition, we call them waxing. When they are moving from opposition toward conjunction, we call them waning. These two series also operate differently when seen from the spiritual angle. To put it as simply as possible, when they are waxing, the experience has to come first, and then consciousness can follow. We could say that action creates awareness. When the aspect is waning, consciousness comes first and then the action.

On the spiritual level, a waxing aspect is about having an experience that by its nature gives us the capability to increase our spiritual awareness. When the aspect is waning, we have to gain an understanding and awareness of the spiritual way to use the aspect before we can put it into operation on the desired level. This rule is not only applicable for the aspects in the birth horoscope, but also for the aspects created by transits.

When aspects are waxing and you act on the impulse of the aspect, and if your intention is spiritual, the result will be an increase of spiritual awareness. If you just try to act on the impulse of a waning aspect without having spiritual awareness about the energies involved and what you want to accomplish and why, the action will not take you to the intended place. Very often, the aspect will not even generate any action before you have an awareness of the situation. In other words, the understanding comes first and then the action for the waning aspects.

Planetary Groups

I like to divide the main astrological bodies into three groups:

- Group one is the inner planets: the Sun, the Moon, Mercury, Venus, and Mars.
- Group two is the planets setting the limits for our human society: Jupiter and Saturn.
- Group three is the outer planets: Uranus, Neptune, and Pluto.
- The centaurs seem to have a little to do with all groups, while the asteroids seem to be mainly in group one but branch also into group two.

Aspects can happen between planets within the same group or between planets of different groups. Seen from a soul level, the significance of the aspects is very different depending on which group the aspects connect.

Aspects Between Inner Planets

Aspects within the personal planet group are primarily concerned with a need to work out issues on the ego or individual level. The growth that happens will be through a clarifying of how to use the ego correctly. In this instance, you are given a fixed set of parameters that constitute your experience of being an individual, and you try to work with these parameters to function as well as possible as an individual. Having many aspects in this category says that you have decided to do a lot of personal and internal work in this incarnation.

Aspects Between Inner Planets and Jupiter or Saturn

Aspects between the inner planets and Jupiter or Saturn are there to give you lessons and possibilities concerning being a part of human society and togetherness. Many aspects in this category signify that you have chosen to learn a lot about how to make a society function in this incarnation. You are here to learn about and use the possibilities that exist in the structures and forms that humanity builds as it evolves.

There is a great need to manifest your personal inner world into the outer world of society and culture.

Aspects Between Jupiter or Saturn and the Outer Planets

Aspects between the outer planets and Jupiter or Saturn seem in many ways to be the most fated of the aspects. You have decided to come down and do a special job relating to the development of society as a whole. Seen from an individual level, this might be experienced as fate, and sometimes as bad luck or lack of choice. Seen from the universal level, it is like doing some kind of service—a need to be a part of the ongoing process that is called humanity. To do certain things without thinking about personal gain, recognition, or reward is wise when one has these aspects.

Aspects Between Inner and Outer Planets

Aspects between the inner planets and the outer planets signify that you want to work with the relationship between the soul and the personality. Having many aspects in this category signifies that you have arrived on Earth in the hope of making a major step forward in your development as a spiritual being. What matters here is not the result or the outer achievement, but the inner process. You can experience great loss and difficulties and grow in your inner understanding through this, or you can have great success and grow through that. Depending on your soul's choice and your level of development, you can grow through experiencing the pain of lack—the pain of not belonging and the lack of love, beauty, joy, and wisdom. Or it can be a process in which the individual learns to let go by experiencing more and more joy, wisdom, beauty, and love.

Aspect Combinations

In this section, we will go into all of the combinations of outer and inner planets and look into the soul's intention by being born with those aspects.

We will not go deeply into the nature of the aspect itself, but we will have a look at the energy theme that comes to the surface. When two planets are connected with an aspect, they become a couple. It is not just that one planet has an influence on the other; the aspect creates a new field of energy, which is the field of the two planetary energies combined. This is a little like a composite horoscope. Something that didn't exist when the planets were separate has come into existence. It is like a marriage. On the one hand you have Mike, on the other you have Edna, and together you have Mike and Edna, which is something totally different.

The reason I choose to delve deeper into this group is twofold. Aspects in this category seem to be predominant in people working hard on the phenomenon we call self-development. The reason for this should be obvious. I also believe that this transition from ego consciousness to soul consciousness is extremely important now. Symbolically, the discovery of Uranus, Neptune, and Pluto in the three last centuries of the second millennium gives us a clue about the importance of incorporating the principles they are associated with into our consciousness. If we do this, we can manifest their energy with awareness instead of being "victims" of the powers they represent.

Humanity has developed and refined its understanding and experience of the individual ego in the last five thousand years. You could say that in this time humanity has distilled the ego from the group and collective consciousness. Today, the ego is in dire need of reconnecting with the collective consciousness and thereby understanding itself as a part of the whole. Only a thousand years ago, your life was totally dependent on your belonging to country, family, race, and culture. In fact, you had no life as an individual, because your being was defined by your relations. In Nordic mythology, it was far more threatening to be declared "varg in veum," which literally means "a wolf in the wilderness," than to be killed. When dead, you lived on in the memory of the family and in the eternal realms. When expelled from family and society, you ceased to exist.

The idea of equality and an individual's right to freedom was partly tried out in Greek civilization, but it then went underground and didn't really surface until around the time of the French and American revolutions (also around the time of Uranus's discovery). Today, an expanding number of individuals experience their individuality as the foundation of their lives. No more are society or family the most important, but the experience of oneself. This has given rise to feelings of deep loneliness and lack of roots, because when your major identification is with your own individuality, you are all by yourself and are not really attached to a greater oneness.

Seen from a global level, the amount of selfish individuals has reached such limits that the ecology of the planet and life in general on Earth are threatened by their "weight." It is of crucial importance for individuals on planet Earth to move to the next stage and to regain their consciousness of being a part of the whole without losing their sense of individual worth.

To come to an understanding that one chooses by free will to make the "I" a tool for the soul rather than using the world as a private playground for the ego. Aspects between inner and outer planets are the astrological signification that one is working with the process of learning how to let the personal/I/ego become a point of focus for the impersonal/soul.

The following walk-through is valid both for aspects in radix and for the same combination made by transits. Seen from the level of the soul, every transit is perfectly timed. It brings you the challenges, gifts, and insights you need at exactly the right time.

Pluto

Pluto is the great teacher of letting go. It lifts all of the energy that lies within us to the surface, the hidden and subconscious and buried. To live with Pluto is to live with total intensity. This energy gives us the possibility to fuse yin and yang and to transform through the melding of our magnetic and energetic energy. The full force of Pluto is like a possession, because it is the total mobilization of life energy, and the trick is to be so focused that you can handle this pressure. A way to work with Pluto is to allow yourself to become possessed without being possessed by the possession. This can mean allowing yourself to totally and absolutely fall in love without needing to act on the feeling—to be able to hold the enormous pressure inside so that you can be transformed by it. The trick is not primarily to avoid the action, but to keep the balance so that you have a real choice. This pressure and inner focusing begin the transformation that opens up your ego so that the soul intention can come through.

Pluto-Sun

With this aspect, you have chosen a life of major growth, as well as confrontation with old karmic patterns. There is a search to gain a deep understanding of power and worth. You will learn that the only way to ensure that you use power correctly is to stop fearing powerlessness. You will learn what happens when power is used to overpower or control others. The process your soul has chosen is to learn how to empower others and to confront your deepest fear about being worthless. By giving up the false egotistical pride and opening up more and more for the ego as a tool for the soul, you will learn to handle the strong and fantastic force that flows through a person with such an aspect. It is important to remember that the person who always feels sad and depressed because he or she is possessed by his or her own negative self-image has just as big an ego as the person with an inflated self-image. Instead of being focused on the fight for power, you need to become aware of how your power can be used for creative transformation. With this aspect, life is really about life and death; everything is important, and accepting both life and death as two beautiful sides of the same coin, your life can become a flower of change. Because this aspect really pounds it into you that life is change, every time you stop to go with the flow, you will get pushed—maybe gently at first, but quite soon life will push harder and harder, until you learn that you are here to use your transforming power correctly.

Pluto-Moon

This is a deep confrontation here with inner angst and demons. There are themes of nurturing and fearing that there isn't enough, but on the other hand there is a theme of emotional dominance. There are difficulties with finding emotional boundaries. The inner ego seeks security through a total fusion with something outside, either by filling oneself with it—like food, sex, or cigarettes—or by being what totally fills somebody else. Every form of rejection will seem like abandonment.

To be emotionally alone is difficult. Most often, there will have been a lack of respect for emotional boundaries. There can be much fear and strong feelings of rejection and separation connected with such an aspect. When one starts to move deeper into it, one understands that one has chosen this connection in order to learn about trust. In the deepest sense, what you will learn is to accept and embrace what you are given. On the soul level, what you get is what you need. If people humiliate you and go way beyond your emotional safety and comfort zone, you need this experience to be able to learn never to do the same to others, and you will repeat it until you learn to put up healthy boundaries for yourself. As you start to heal yourself and at the same time see the necessity and gift in all that you have experienced, your fear and insecurity start to change, and you learn to know that you are always safe, and are always given what is best for you. The trust is total, and since your trust is total, there is nothing in your ego that blocks the soul intention and energy from coming through. You achieve the ability to be totally present in every moment of time.

Pluto-Mercury

You have chosen to do some real serious thinking when you are born with this aspect. Your ideas and thoughts become very strong, and you tend to be possessed by your own ideas and opinions. In your early experiences, viewpoints have a tendency to be black and white: you are either right, or you are wrong. You have been presented with seemingly undisputable facts, and you have a tendency to present your own opinions in the same manner. It is as if the sheer force of conviction and a one-track way of presenting it makes it right. With this aspect, there can be no easy solutions. On the soul level, you have chosen to operate through a mind that wants to cut through all the wrappings and directly into the bone. As you start to become obsessed by truth and essence instead of opinions and being "right," the whole picture changes rapidly. You become more and more of a person who is not fooled by outer appearances or what seems to be obvious. You become more and more capable of seeing behind the obvious, and you start to speak with the voice of the soul. You become a courageous spokesperson for deep and eternal truth, instead of someone caught in the belief that fleeting opinions and shifts in thought from day to day have something to do with truth. You see that truth lies beneath the surface and is connected to an all-pervading universal essence.

Pluto-Venus

This aspect gives you an exceptionally strong charge of magnetic energy. Very often, this is associated with intense passion and sexual encounters. This force can make you irresistibly attractive or attracted, or it can make you just as strongly repulsive or repulsed. You do not know how to be indifferent, except when you are totally indifferent. You have chosen to be born with this aspect in order to learn to handle this strong flow of magnetic energy. This aspect can easily manifest in a way that what you really want manifests, but it is also the same force that often makes reality out of your nightmares. There is a need for passion and intensity that can make normal life dull. In many ways, you want to dive below the surface, to get solid ground under your feet, and to get in contact with the core feelings in life, and to do this you often have to move beyond normal rules and taboos. On the individual level, you break taboos just to have fun and avoid boredom. You can also be possessed by your likes and dislikes and be sucked into love affairs and other passionate "crimes." As you move into the soul level, you understand more and more of what is going on. You have this strong inner passion, but you are not a slave to it. Your soul starts to use this magnetic force to manifest the circumstances you need to develop. In this process there will be a deep transformation of values, in which you move from the need to satisfy your ego to a need to create beauty, closeness, intimacy, and love between yourself and whatever you are surrounded by.

Pluto-Mars

This is one of the most potent and powerful combinations of inner and outer planets. You have this combination because you have wanted to learn about the correct use of power. Since the output of energy is so forceful here, there is no way that your way to get your will and related activity will go unnoticed. If you try to force your way through life, you will meet strong opposition. The ego will be confronted with situations in which your choice seems to be either to overpower others or to be overpowered. There seems to be a limited amount of energy accessible, and you have to seek power or be powerless. As long as you move along this line, you will always be caught in power struggles or be alone and depressed. As long as you fight against something, you will make what you fight against stronger. One way to move out of this trap is to put your power into what you see as good and benevolent. You will still have opponents, but through this change of motivation, you will start to experience this in a different and less personal way. As you let go even more of your attachment to the outcome of your actions, you will feel that more and more of the pressure is released. When you really start to master this aspect of life, your power and your will are an expression of your soul energy. Pluto-Mars is in a way always ruthless, but your ruthlessness can become the pure power of love.

Neptune

Neptune is the great bringer of dreams and inspiration. It is your door to the inner world, and all the mystics have stated that the way to nirvana, heaven, enlightenment, and so on is the inner way. Nothing is more natural for the soul, because Neptune is the home of the soul. One important thing to remember, though, is that the inner world of Neptune is much bigger than the outer world of the body. The body and the physical world, then, are embedded in the inner! This great feeling of holiness, mystery, and oneness is the domain of Neptune. The illusion arises when we think that the inner world is the outer, or that the outer world is the only one that exists. The great pain associated with Neptune appears when our inner world can find no meaningful reflection in the outer. Every human being has a capability for total and selfless love. If you are told and you believe that this love is an illusion, your inner world becomes absurd in relation to the outer so-called reality. What Neptune urges us toward is to create heaven on Earth—or even better, to realize that Earth already is heaven.

Neptune-Sun

Reality does not live up to your expectations. As with every Neptunian aspect, this brings a great longing for the sublime. One seeks the archetypal form of the ideal, not the flawed manifestation in time and space. Women with this aspect often start out idealizing men, while men start out idealizing themselves. Another possible starting point is being the victim. Since life does not live up to your expectations, it is easy to believe that you are an unlucky victim of unfortunate circumstances. You have chosen to have this aspect so that you can always have an inner vision of the ideal. There is a longing for unity with this ideal that can lead you far on the road of spiritual and artistic exploration. This aspect creates a profound feeling of loneliness, and only contact with the inner realms of soul and spirit can heal this loneliness. Perfection is not to be found outside. But as you cultivate harmony, love, and oneness within, you start to create the same circumstances without. The heaven that you long to manifest in the world lies dormant in yourself. As you wake up to the true clarity and awareness that Neptune can bring, you will start to manifest your soul's love and experience of oneness through your ego identity. The house and sign of Neptune show where the inspiration and experience of love and peace come from, and the house and sign of the Sun show where and how you can manifest this inner beauty into the world, using yourself as the focusing point. Remember, it's the inner and personal planet that needs to learn to handle the energy flow from the outer.

Neptune-Moon

This aspect is like an open channel from the soul to the heart. And for those who have not learned to protect their heart, there will be trouble. When one is born with this aspect, one has chosen to work with the essence of love and vulnerability. There is a great longing for oneness with the source. This can have the effect of trying to give away something that one does not yet possess oneself. One tries to comfort and take care of other people's need for love without taking care of oneself first. The commandment "Thou shall love thy neighbor as thyself" becomes important. One of the reasons this love thing has gone so astray is that people start with their neighbor. However, it says, "as thyself," so one has to start with loving oneself. This aspect can make you a victim, but it can also teach you how to receive love in a proper way. You can learn that you are worthy of love, whatever you do. And when you accept this with your heart, you start to become a giver of true and unselfish love. Since you yourself already have enough, you can give without wanting back. Your soul wants you to learn to be in the flow of love at the same time as you remain an individual. Remember, what you want is to be in this stream of love, not to feel badly for every kind of suffering in the world or to feel guilt if you feel love when others do not. To make the world a more loving place, you should nurture it with your love, not pester it with suffering and feelings of guilt and inadequacy. To learn to trust that you are loved and have a lovable soul, and to inspire this trust in others, is what your soul had in mind when it chose to be born with this aspect.

Neptune-Mercury

This is a great aspect for those who want to walk into hidden and mysterious places. The mind is connected with the great inner world of the soul and fantasies. This aspect urges you to think in pictures and images, and it is a gift for those who seek synthesis. You want to use your mind to see behind the curtain. You have a need to understand, and often to express, what is beyond words. Music and poetry may inspire this kind of mind. Deep down, you have a longing to be a messenger for the elf king or elf queen on Earth: to be a channel that can translate and make understandable the wisdom and experiences from the hidden and unseen realms. In some way or another, you have chosen this aspect because your soul wanted to be a messenger. The mind has a need to make a connection between the logic and coherency of the inner world and magic as it works in the outer world. As a consequence, you may become confused, because the inner and outer world may become mixed up. You are here to see how fantasy and reality are connected. What we call reality is fantasy manifested in time and space. And through your contact with the essence, you will be able to see the world as a fairy tale, and you will see how the road leads from fantasy to reality and back. As you manifest more and more of this energy, instead of confusing truth and lies, you will begin to be a spokesperson for the truth of the soul.

Neptune-Venus

I once saw this aspect described as the divine discontent. It gives one a great longing for the perfect state of bliss. It is like seeking perfection in eternity and time and space at once. One wants to hold and have beauty forever, but one also wants to eat the cake here and now. There is a conflict here between satisfying the ego and the soul, or there is a mutual striving to satisfy both at the same time. This aspect gives a great longing for the beautiful and delicate. Many of those born with this aspect search to become aware of their soul's longings through becoming artists. Others become servers of humanity. There is a conflict going on here between satisfying oneself and being selfless. There seems to be a very small balance beam to walk on, with ditches on both sides. And you know, with this aspect, one really would prefer not to be dirtying oneself in a ditch. On one side of this balance beam lies the ditch of guilt, because one has been selfish, and on the other the ditch of helpless victims, because one has been too unselfish. One needs to learn that a rich person has something to share and that a person who deprives him or herself of richness has little to share. This richness is something a person with this aspect should learn to enjoy, both on the material and on the spiritual level. There is a great naivety combined with this aspect. One really has a tendency to believe in the fairy tale and to feel somewhat deceived when one experiences the harsh reality of mundane life. One really doesn't feel well equipped for real life and long days in the coal mines with this aspect. One feels that life should be easy, that it should fulfill your dreams and treat you as if you were royalty. To be born with this aspect is a signal from your soul that you are here to bring more beauty into the physical world. You seek to take some part of the eternal and make it real. Since the world seems harsh, it can be easy to try to flee to some sort of otherworldly heaven. Escapism is always a possible solution for Venus-Neptune people. But what your soul longs for is to manifest a bit of heaven on Earth. In the area and manner that is shown by house and sign, your soul wants to manifest some sort of beauty and grace in order to create a link from this world to the pure essence of the spiritual. This is an aspect of surrender—a surrender to the joy and glory of the spirit and soul as it dances joyfully over life.

Neptune-Mars

At the outset, this makes your Mars energy more of a worrier than a warrior. It can be difficult to use your power and will, because you seem to be overly sensitive to other people's reactions and pain. In its extreme, this aspect can make you a fearsome coward who always shrinks from challenges and battle. Your soul has chosen to be a warrior of love. It would like to learn to use its will for the ideal rather than the short term. There is a great deal of idealism involved here. There is an ongoing process of refinement and deepening of the heart. As long as you use your will against something, the road will seem very difficult and hard, because you do not have the necessary ruthlessness. To thrive, you have to fight for what is good and just. You have to be noble, honest, and caring. You have chosen to really learn to love your adversaries and to forgive everybody the pain and seemingly the evil they do against you. As long as you are stuck in your own negativity, you will be stuck in the outer world and will feel the pain and loneliness in your soul. Your soul wants you to be able to hold the pain, sorrow, and anger of others in its heart without being destroyed by it, and to understand their pain, feel it, accept it, and then forgive and release it. In fact, through this you are realizing your own negativity and lack of compassion for yourself and others that has been built through many lifetimes. As you perform this act of letting go, your force becomes guided by compassion and love. You are no longer a wimp. Neither are you, as some with this aspect prefer to be, totally frozen in self-pity or indifference toward others.

You move forward in the world with great courage, you are fully aware of pain and fear, and because of that, you do what is necessary as your soul seeks to manifest love and oneness on Earth. You become a true rainbow warrior for the sake of peace and love.

Uranus

Uranus is very much the planet that inspires and moves us to become our true selves. It inspires us to move beyond what is cliché or only a repeated cultural pattern. Uranus is the liberator that seeks to release the unique creativity and individuality within each and every one of us. We could say that Uranus is the planet of geniuses, and we could also say that everybody in some way or another has the potential to be a *genius*, because genius means "one of a kind." Remember, this fantastic universe never repeats itself. Just look at snowflakes.

While Neptune is very much the magnetic glue of love that holds the created universe together, Uranus is the electric spark of creativity that makes the universe grow and develop into something new. How aspects to Uranus are going to work is a bit difficult to predict, because Uranus moves us beyond what is and into the unknown, beyond what we are and into what we may become. That is the fantastic thing about being on this adventure. We are given the Uranus spark of uniqueness and free will, and nobody really knows what we are going to do and where the universe is moving. We might know that we come from a source of eternal spirit and love, and that we will return to this source, but what happens in between is open for debate. So Uranus is the alarm clock shaking us awake from our deep sleep. It can awaken a sleeping ego or, if the ego is already fairly up and going, it can awaken the ego to the consciousness of the soul. Uranus is like a fire in the blood, like a rush of energy and expectation. It is the fire in our hearts, the flight of our minds, and the feeling of exhilaration as we drink from the well of wisdom and swim in the energetic sea of life.

Uranus-Sun

On a soul level, you have chosen to be born with this aspect in order to learn to realize more and more of your unique potential. This aspect urges you to break free from the limited shells of ignorance that surround you on different levels. There is a need to release the inner fire, which is the inner spirit, and direct it out into the world. By connecting with this inner spiritual core, you start to realize that you yourself are a spark of the all-encompassing spirit. On a more psychological level, this aspect urges you to be more and more of what you already are and to understand that creation has made no error: you were created both as a soul and as an individual human being, because the universe wanted, as fully as possible, the experience of being you. Uranus operates through the consciousness and the active element of expressing. Your conscious-ness is creating your actions, and your actions create new conscious-ness. In experiencing this flow between action and consciousness, you have the capacity to get more and more understanding of your own real essence and the way it seeks to manifest in the outer world. Uranus makes you aware of the flow of energy in yourself and around you, and it urges you to work with "higher" and faster-moving energies all the time.

There is a need to learn to handle this fast and highly charged en-ergy. Uranus is in many ways seeking perfection. It seeks to reestablish the perfect union of the soul and the body to create the link between what is above and what is below. This aspect is there so that you as an individual can be a transformation station for the divine energy. This energy moves in two directions: you are channeling down the divine energy and distributing it into the physical world, and you are working with liberating the divine energy encapsulated in the illusion of separa-tion and imprisonment in time and space. In short, you have chosen this aspect so that you can be reminded that the purpose of your life is to become fully what you are.

Uranus-Moon

In many ways, this seems to be a strange combination. With this aspect, you want to learn, on a deep and instinctual level, what freedom really is. It can seem confusing, because there is a strong need for belonging and at the same time a strong need for distance. This helps you very much to develop what in spiritual theories is called the observer. There can be a conflict between what you perceive as freedom and what you perceive as feeling secure. The big question is how to belong, share, and experience empathy and at the same time be free. This aspect helps you to understand how you can be close and still not lose yourself in this personal closeness. If you become too dependent, the situation starts to become uncomfortable, yet at the same time, too much independence makes you distant and aloof. As stated earlier, the magic that this aspect helps you to learn is to be close, affectionate, and caring while at the same time not losing your energy in dependency. It is by meeting and mastering the energy inherent in this aspect that you learn that safety and freedom are one and the same. Real freedom is choosing what you belong to. It says that real freedom is not the freedom from belonging or sharing or closeness, but the freedom to choose your belonging and responsibilities. You have chosen to learn to trust the deeper and instinctual layers of your being, and so you, in the end, will instinctually respond in a way that is true to your inner nature. You have chosen to trust a consciousness that is beyond words. When you totally and absolutely accept your own inner rhythm and move effortlessly in accordance with this rhythm, you have received the gift of an aspect between Uranus and the Moon.

Uranus-Mercury

This speeds up your mind and makes everything within your mind move faster. There is no way you can depend on others' thinking or easily digestible ideas with this aspect. It is there so that you can learn to think by yourself; nobody will be there doing the thinking for you. Through the development of an independent mind, you learn to see through illusions and find the truth. In this joint effort, Mercury and Uranus have different functions. To find truth, you need to be able to see through lies and to perceive truth. Mercury is the partner that sees through what is illogical and false. By itself, it can tell that something is wrong, but it cannot perceive what is right. Uranus, on the other hand, has this ability to see into the essence of the matter. It can bring up a deep and subjective experience of truth, while Mercury can look at this experience from an objective angle and translate it into a language that can be expressed so that your personal truth becomes understandable for other human beings. This aspect creates an energetic link between the personal human mind and the cosmic mind. Your job is to be aware of which is which. It is possible to become confused and believe that the perceptions of the human mind are the cosmic truth. Through awareness, you have the capacity to correct these misconceptions and thereby go on growing in wisdom and awareness. The development of understanding happens through an opening of Uranian inspiration that becomes accessible through the functions of the Mercurial mind. To see and speak and perceive truth is what the soul seeks to manifest when it has chosen to be born as a human being with this connection in the horoscope.

Uranus-Venus

Here, the soul seeks to delve deeper into the understanding of values and joy in the reality of time and space. One seeks to understand eternal values, as opposed to changing values, and to find a way to express pleasure and joy in the physical world. One has a tendency to experiment and seek many ways of finding beauty and joy so that through these experiences one can get a deeper understanding of the true nature of love. This gives one an understanding that love has to be freely given and freely received. In the cultural settings in which most people in the world live these days, this aspect can be a difficult one. Love is confused with need and dependency. True joy disappears very quickly, when what is joyful and beautiful becomes something forced and constrained. This aspect creates a highly charged attraction. One can really be compulsively drawn into energy fields; the trick is not to become stuck there. One needs to learn to handle this strong energizing of one's magnetic currents. As a result of this, one will hopefully learn the difference between short-term satisfaction and lasting values.

In the beginning, the strong force of the inner current will easily lead one to seek momentary release. In other words, one wants satisfaction and joy, and one wants it now. There is little patience inherent in this aspect. Through experiencing the results of moment-to-moment living and satisfaction, one learns to perceive the underlying values and one learns to separate truth and real values from fleeting and unstable ones. As one masters this aspect, there becomes less and less difference between eternal values and the momentary satisfaction. One learns to live in the world with true joy, and there will be no missed chances for enjoyment and happiness. Every moment is seized, but in such a way that joy begets more joy, not separation and coldness or confusion. The soul has chosen this aspect in order to learn that joy and freedom are connected to an inner state. As long as the focus is on the outer, real satisfaction can never occur. And this aspect is about satisfaction. When one lives in accordance with one's inner joy and is free enough to give and receive true pleasure, one flows with this highly charged current of life. By letting go of such notions as sin and shame, and by understanding that the essence of spirit in human form is joy, one fulfills this aspect. The Venusian urge is expressed into the world with Uranian consciousness of the true nature of spirituality.

Uranus-Mars

A soul born with this aspect has chosen a life with a need for action. The strong flow of energy here has to be directed and manifested as action in the outer world. Often, the current is so strong that one barely manages to keep one's head above water, and the river of life can seem to be full of torrents. The movement is often rapid, the flow going so fast that one hardly manages to adapt to the abrupt changes. One has chosen this aspect so that one can learn to handle the freely moving energy of life with the will. This is not an aspect for peace, at least not in the beginning. Often, one seems to have more energy than one is able to handle, and that is exactly the lesson the soul has sought. One is thrown into the rapids and has to learn to swim. A common factor for the Uranian aspects is that one has to learn to handle things by oneself. This is not an individual who goes from walking to running; rather, this is someone who starts with running and eventually, as time goes on, learns to control the situation so that they can also walk. Patience and control are the result of trying again and again. And there is no way to avoid the challenges.

There is a need here to direct the inner truth and the fire in the heart through the will and the power of focusing. Those with this aspect are given a large amount of freedom. It can seem like they are tossed helplessly by their own inner energy. But as they get more control, they can direct this energy where they want. This freedom of action is there so that they can learn the consequences of their own actions. What happens when they are unaware of their own and others' situation and needs? By having the freedom to do everything "wrong," they have the capacity to learn the connection between the action and the wanted result, as well as the price involved. When the deeper connection between truth and will is made, they understand that real freedom is making every act a manifestation of truth. As consciousness rises, the truth is not only their individual truth: action becomes an expression for the truth of the soul and the reality of spirit.

Retrograde Planets

Easy is right.
Begin right and you are easy.
Continue easy and you are right.
The right way to go easy is to forget the right way
and forget that the going is easy.

—CHUANG TZU

A retrograde planet seems to be moving backward instead of forward. This fact in itself should give us a clue about how it functions. The non-retrograde planet follows a line that becomes a circle as it moves around the Sun. Retrograde planets make a loop, which can be seen as a place where the normal rules for time and space seemingly don't function. In reality, the planet moves nicely ahead in its path, but since we observe it from Earth and not from the Sun, it seems like this strange loop really happens. Since we are on Earth and are encapsulated in time and space, the retrogradation tells a story about our viewpoint of reality.

Time and life on Earth seem to move forward in nicely ordered sequences. B follows A, and we come from the past and move into the future. A retrograde planet has problems with functioning in this ordered flow of time through space. Time moves in different directions: the effect sometimes appears first and the reason later, or there seem to be holes in time where things happen simultaneously or time seems literally to be standing still. Everything can seem to be a repetition of the same. This is especially the case when the planet is close to the turning point. One thing often forgotten by astrologers is that a direct moving planet can also be a part of this time loop: a planet that has moved direct will participate in the retrograde loop until it has reached the point from which the retrogradation started.

When a planet in transit moves retrograde, we move collectively into a period where time and space don't behave as they are "supposed" to. A retrograde planet in a personal chart seems to be dancing to a different drummer than the direct planets. A direct planet can follow the rhythm of the world and be manifested directly into the world. A retrograde planet has greater problems with understanding this rhythm, and the timing will of course be more difficult. A common feature for retrograde planets is that they are slower to manifest and blossom in the world. They can't just follow the stream and see what happens; they have to make up their mind and know where to go before they can go there. This orientation process takes time. In other words, you could say that a direct planet moves first and gets the understanding afterward. A retrograde planet, on the other hand, has to have the understanding first. Action is a result of consciousness, while consciousness is a result of action for the direct planet. Having many retrograde planets in a chart makes it difficult for the individual to adjust to the world, at least in early years. Their perception is not adjusted to the outer flow of events, and often what they want and seek is seemingly inaccessible in the outer world. They can also become unfocused and be occupied with things that seem irrelevant. While the direct planet takes one step at a time and eventually gets an understanding of the big picture as a result of all its smaller steps, the retrograde planet seems to need an understanding of the bigger picture before it is ready to put the pieces together. One consequence of this is the rapid movement that happens when the retrograde planet finally gets going. Since it has the whole picture sorted out, it doesn't have to stop and think every time a new step ahead is needed.

Sun and Moon Retrograde

If you have the Sun or the Moon retrograde, you definitively belong to those who have arrived in the wrong solar system; you may even have missed the exit to your home galaxy. Probably you come from a bipolar solar system, and the best you can do is to fix that destroyed double-carbonium tricord accelerator and go home.

The truth for the rest of us is that we are on exactly the right planet at exactly the right time. We even did an excellent job of choosing the right parents, nation, and place to be born. So even if this place feels a little weird every now and then, this is home … for now. You might as well connect with your soul's intention for being here and enjoy the situation. You are a traveler in space, zooming away at tremendous speed on the spaceship Earth, a great adventurer and explorer of unknown regions where no humans have gone before. And just so you don't get too lonely, remember that you are part of a multiorganic organism that lives inside and shares the same gaseous womb, called air. May the Force be with you!

Mercury Retrograde

When Mercury is retrograde, it is your mind and thinking faculty that exists in this strange time zone. Most often, people with Mercury retrograde are very curious. But their questions and thoughts seem to go in other ways than what is expected. They don't think in straight lines. In a way, these are minds that want to see a picture from all sides. They aren't satisfied with how to move from A to B. They want to know all of the other options, and they also want to understand everything involved. Like the movement of a retrograde planet itself, they sometimes have to move backward to find a turning point so they can go on to move forward. Every Mercury-retrograde person knows inherently that one who doesn't know history has to repeat it. So sometimes they get so caught up in the history and corridors of their minds that they don't move out into the world, where new history is created. They ask seemingly unimportant or strange questions, but the questions are quite appropriate for the quest they are on. To find a solution, an answer, or an understanding, they have to see the whole picture.

This longing to see the whole picture may be confusing, especially in a society that is so hooked on sequential thinking. Your experiences in childhood determine how your Mercury works later in life. If your questions have been called stupid and your thoughts and efforts to formulate your thoughts have not been heard, you often become silent and think that speaking is of little use, since no one will understand you anyway. If you have been allowed the freedom to explore the world of your mind, the opposite will occur. You will be a very talkative and highly communicative being. A Mercury-retrograde person has to understand and know the thoughts he or she is communicating in order to be able to express them clearly to others. The thoughts and ideas have to be processed on the inner level first. As with all retrograde planets, one has to go within to get without. A good thing about retrograde Mercury is that you have to think for yourself, if you are going to think at all. The only alternative to thinking is to be a mindless parrot that repeats seemingly interesting sentences but doesn't really understand what it is saying.

Mercury retrogrades are known to have a wandering mind. They seem to disappear from the subject, while in reality they are moving along another road or possibility connected to the subject. If Mercury retrograde doesn't manage to knit things together, they may become lost and caught in a web of thought that seems illogical and disconnected. In reality, they *are* logical, but the strings are not woven together as they should be. When they learn to do this, they become very good at synthesizing, and they can combine seemingly unrelated ideas and thoughts and merge them into a new and deeper understanding.

The soul has chosen to be born with Mercury retrograde precisely to learn this ability of synthesizing. In many ways, every person with Mercury retrograde has a fair share of the philosopher within. They are just as much concerned with why they should take that next step, as with how and where they can do it. As mentioned earlier, this Mercury can get a little lost in the outer world, because the mind is turned toward the inner regions, not toward finding the road. But when the synthesizing factor works, the mind becomes able to see the details and find the way, and at the same time they can see the bigger picture. They do not only understand the outer workings of mind and communication, but they also have an understanding of the deeper and broader picture. Mercury-retrograde persons have a hard time planning for the future. Since time doesn't work "properly," they have a hard time seeing where the future is moving. In a way, they can just as well reexperience the past, but can that be called future? The unfolding of life is more like a growing understanding of both life and the moment that also encompasses the future. It's like their mind is inside this ball, which grows and includes more and more stuff as the ability to perceive and think grows, instead of walking on the line from past to future as "normal" minds do.

But they can become very good at handling the future when it comes, since they are instantly able to include what happens now with all that has happened before. To picture time as this growing and expanding moment that includes both the past and the future is a nice exercise for Mercury-retrograde people.

Venus Retrograde

The ego could easily ask the soul with a complaining voice why it chose to be incarnated with Venus retrograde. Sometimes it is very disappointing and confusing. What you really want seems to elude you, and all that you get seems to be of little interest. If you try to get this Venus to function as if it weren't retrograde, you are asking for confusion and a lack of satisfaction. Sometimes it seems that the life you really wanted doesn't exist anymore, as if part of you were caught in a time warp in the seventeenth century.

A "normal" Venus is more or less in tune with the everyday world and the changing flow of values, taste, and morals. Not so with the retrograde kind. It seems to seek eternal values, and since eternal values seldom are the hottest of the year, it seems to be out of tune with the rest of society. To get a firm grip on this Venus, you need to work in two directions at once. You have to gain both a deep understanding of underlying principles and a clear understanding of what makes you feel good while doing it and what makes your soul feel uncomfortable. You also have to be very precise with what you want and ask for. To have a normal Venus is like coming to a buffet and saying, "Oh, I will try a bit of that and have a taste of that." And if you don't like it, you just leave it on your plate and go grab something else that seems better. Not so when the goddess of love, sensuality, and beauty is retrograde in your birth chart. If you persist, you will find a menu hidden behind some old papers on the table. You will have to work a bit to get the attention of the waiter, and you will have to know exactly what you want before you order. Most of the time, the waiter is a bit like a strict mother. You will not be allowed to leave the table before you have finished your meal.

This rule also goes for the love life of most Venus retrogrades. They have to know exactly what they are looking for, in sex as well as in long-term relationships. If not, what is inside the package seems to be very different from what the text on the box said. Or even when the contents are the same as described, you suddenly realize that this doesn't really do it for you. So Venus retrograde has to keep the tongue straight in the mouth and try to get it right as fast as possible, because the method of trying and failing does not work very well. On the other hand, when Venus retrograde really makes the right choices and is true to its own deepest truth and values, there are few Venuses that give more lasting satisfaction. The deep love from someone with this placement will always have a touch of the eternal and timeless, and they will have no interest in all of the so-called possibilities that pass them by. They are not interested in men, but in one particular man. They are not interested in food, but in one particular kind of food. Their soul has chosen this position of Venus so that they can learn to divide the important from the unimportant and to see and choose what has value and depth and quality. So a maturing Venus retrograde feels no despair if there are very few around that they appreciate: one is enough. The bottom line is that Venus retrograde has to be true to its own sense of beauty, value, and love. There are no shortcuts that give satisfaction and love. But when they get it, it is the real thing.

Mars Retrograde

Mars retrograde feels a bit like backing your car down the streets of life, instead of driving normally. It is quite exhausting at times, and you don't move very fast. Every now and then you just have to stop and wipe the sweat from your brow. Mars is associated with the will and your ability to manifest yourself in the world through action. But somehow it may seem that you were born with the brake on. Often, you do not know where you want to go or what you want, and when you eventually decide, the train has left or someone has already bought the thing you wanted. Mars retrograde is often a problem with timing in action.

At its worst, you gain the understanding of what you want only after it is too late. It is like not having and not doing makes you aware of your destiny, will, and direction. So by experiencing the results of non-action, you start to learn that proper action in the proper moment also has some advantages. In a world where non-action is the ideal, as in certain Buddhist societies, you would be a hit. But in a world where will makes the way, and action the day, you seem to be in trouble.

The retrograde Mars learns an enormous patience, which is very good when you finally understand that you have to use your power in the world. Many people go around trying this and that and pushing on because they are so afraid of not getting anywhere. Not so with you. When you have learned the game, you know how to wait for the right opportunity and then grab it and give all you have, because you don't want a little of this and a little of that. You want exactly what you have set your will on. You can be very single-minded and goal-oriented, and there is almost a relentless quality that keeps you going, whatever the price. This gives you a fantastic staying power, but remember, if you do not move, your staying power will root you to the spot, and your life will seem to go nowhere.

You have chosen to be born with this aspect so that you can learn to direct your will and power in a precise and finely tuned manner. Most persons with retrograde Mars have no need to show off their power or will. They are more often introverted observers, but when they move, it will be with a swiftness and precision that is surprising, even to them. It is important to be clear on where you want to go, why you want to go there, and how you plan to do it. What seems like non-action is often the planning stage. Then you become like a driver who goes through the whole race in your inner vision before you sit down behind the wheel. And since you are prepared for every turn and surprise that may come, you will drive with a swiftness and confidence that is amazing. Very often, Mars retrograde comes up after a (former) life of introspection and some sort of inner work. You could say that the inner power and will have to be anchored if the outer power and will are to function in a proper way. You also have to learn that the way you act is more important than the result. You need a strong code of honor to make this Mars work at it best. This Mars is the sign of the warrior, one who has to understand the timeless laws of right action and clarity of will and mind. When this is done, you will have a deep freedom and sincerity, an understanding of your purpose in life, and the will and wisdom to fulfill this purpose.

Jupiter Retrograde

With a "normal" Jupiter, you have chosen a life in which opportunities often present themselves. It seems like you see a road, and it's up to you how good you are at walking. Retrograde Jupiter is another story. As with the other retrograde planets, you have to get access to and do the work on the inner plane before the outer doors open. Jupiter is very much concerned with hope, possibilities, and having a position. With Jupiter retrograde, you have to fill out the inner position first. If you take on a position or try to reach out for possibilities without being ready, the results will not come. In many ways, you do not grow with the job. You have to grow first, and thereafter the job will appear. There is a great saying that when the pupil is ready, the teacher will appear. And it is even more true for the retrograde Jupiter person that when you, the teacher, are ready, the pupils will appear.

Very often, Jupiter retrograde has difficulties seeing the possibilities in the surroundings. They have to enlarge the inner space first, and then they can extend their energy to a bigger outer space. Therefore, things may, as with all retrogrades, take longer before they blossom. If you try too hard to change outer reality so that you can change with it, it will go very slowly indeed. The inner reality must be changed first. One good thing about Jupiter retrograde is that it carries an enormous ability to have hope in difficult times. Jupiter direct sees the possibilities and goes on a ride when everything is bright and full of possibilities. In the beginning, Jupiter retrograde might be a bit naive, and it doesn't really understand what is happening when life gives it a slap in the face—or fifty. But in the darkness and desperation, there is a kind of almost unbelievable optimism that makes these people go on and gives them the hope and guts to face seemingly impossible obstacles. An unaware Jupiter retrograde is easy to discourage, as far as their dreams and hopes are concerned. In other words, they can easily lose their unfounded dreams and beliefs for the future. But it is almost impossible to take away hope itself from these people. And when they have done their inner work and know exactly what they want to explore and why they want to expand, their belief will carry them a very long way.

When Jupiter retrograde finally understands how this works, they might not care very much about position and power in the outer world, or they may see it as a tool that can give them the opportunity for manifesting their inner world. They have learned that opportunity and position in themselves are of little interest, but that it is necessary to have position to be able to share your inner world, and hopefully your wisdom, with the rest of the world. Jupiter retrograde forces the person to go deeper into the questions of why they want position and influence and why they want to expand and enlarge their horizons. In this way, Jupiter retrograde, as do all of the other retrograde planets, forces you to become more aware of yourself and what motivations you have, thereby giving a strong need to search and find your deeper intention, and to connect with the soul's motivation for seeking whatever Jupiter has to offer in the world. Noble ideals, and a wish to use your own position and fortune to make life better for others, makes it much easier for you as a retrograde-Jupiter person to accept and attain the possibilities that Jupiter offers in life.

Saturn Retrograde

Saturn retrograde can show up in two seemingly different ways. One is through the lack of limits and rules. You just don't see what is possible or where there is a wall. That gives you a tendency to get some bumps on the forehead, because you walk right into the walls of outer reality. Another possibility is to see walls all over the place. There seems to be so much limitation and restriction attached to being born in this time and place that you hardly feel free to move at all. Space seems limited, and time some kind of strict schoolteacher that demands too much discipline. There seems to be a shortage of ready-made structures and forms that you can move into. It's a bit like a hermit crab that has a hard time finding a shell that fits: the one you have is either too small to get into or too big to drag around, and there are no new ones available at the market for the time being. The sooner Saturn-retrograde persons understand that they have to build their own shell, the better.

With Saturn retrograde, you will have problems with discipline. Either you are fearful of everything and try to follow the book, like a priest in fear of being condemned for eternity, or you resist every attempt to discipline you. A very good word to learn for Saturn retrograde people is *self-discipline*. That is the only thing that works. You have to build that inner structure that gives you enough strength to handle the outer world on your own grounds. Saturn is the doorway to the outer planets, what you have to master before you can move on into the realms beyond Saturn's limits. And when Saturn is retrograde, you have to meet and conquer the inner demons of Saturn first.

When these people face difficulties in the outer world, they will seem to have an enormous amount of stamina and inner power that allow them to overcome great difficulties ... if they have understood the purpose of the inner work. Eventually, they will learn that the outer world is a reflection of the inner, and by accepting both the limitations and demands that exist in the inner, they will eventually be able to change and mold the outer world. Saturn retrograde often starts out as a feeling of not knowing why one is in this strange world of form. One can easily lose interest in the outer world and retreat to the inner—a strategy that works well for a while but eventually goes wrong, giving a feeling of sinking too deep into oneself. After all, Saturn has to do with being in time and space. It is connected with what is here and now and with changing your circumstances by working with the existing structures. The advantage of Saturn retrograde is the ability to form your own reality, if you have done the inner work and have a good understanding of how the laws of time and space operate.

Saturn retrograde often starts out with impatience. You do not really understand that things take time in the outer world, and you have to learn to see how your inner work slowly takes form and becomes what we call reality in time and space. Having Saturn retrograde is like coming down to Earth to do some alchemical work. It is you and your ego that are inside the magical flasks and fumes and flames of earthly existence. By understanding the processes and learning to listen to your inner voice, you will eventually learn when it is the right time to act. And you will also learn what the right temperature (balance or harmony) is that gives the necessary heat or cold that allows the process to continue. The soul has chosen this position so that you can learn to use this visit in time and space as a tool for understanding what is beyond time and space. You are your own alchemist, and it is up to you to use the magic that transforms your ego from lead to gold—the process that opens your heart and your soul while you are in time and space so that the energy from the eternal source can flow freely through you and into the realm of the world.

Outer Planets Retrograde

When Uranus, Neptune, and Pluto are retrograde, you belong to those who have to choose and find their destinies. The role you play in the big game of life is not obvious. You belong to that group of people who have a great capability to create something new in the evolutionary journey. Another possibility is that the greater meaning of life escapes you. There is a mystery there, and you either feel tormented because you don't understand, or you couldn't care less.

Uranus Retrograde

With Uranus retrograde, you can feel very common. You are just one of the foot soldiers; there is nothing remarkable about you. Or you can feel very strongly that you are special, but you don't know how to get it out in the world. There can be a tendency to hide your eccentricity and to have a deep-seated fear of being different. All of those qualities that make you unique and special are hidden somewhere. You might seemingly accept the truth of the crowd and walk through life as if this were the real truth. But somewhere deep down, you feel like a zombie. Another possibility is that you demonstrate your uniqueness and your freedom at every opportunity in which it doesn't function very well. So until you dig deeper, you seem to have the choice of being a nonfunctioning rebel or a well-functioning bore.

With Uranus retrograde, you have to dig deep into themes like freedom, truth, and uniqueness. In a way, your longing for freedom, and a place in the world where you could just be yourself, is not there. You have to find a deeper understanding of what freedom is for you. In this respect, it becomes very important to learn that freedom isn't freedom *from*, but freedom *to*. To choose between fifty tubes of toothpaste is of no interest to you. You have to understand that freedom is an inner state, not something dependent on outer circumstances. To be true to your own self is the greatest freedom. To become unique is to become what you already are. And to be what you already are is freedom. In many ways, Uranus says that freedom is to choose what limits your freedom.

Freedom is not having no responsibilities, obligations or boundaries. Freedom is not to have thrown out everything that holds you, but to have integrated everything, so you are free to be exactly that which you are. Without the ability to love, be close, and belong, freedom is just an escape from fear of intimacy. So Uranus retrograde is the great teacher of achieving freedom of the soul—not by throwing away what matters in life, but by containing it. A really free person will be free and true to him or herself, even if he or she is in jail. As stated, the most important lesson for your soul with Uranus retrograde is the understanding that freedom and uniqueness is an inner state, not something dependent on your situation in the outer world. And the good news is that when you have achieved this inner state of freedom, your life in the outer world becomes very free. Since you are true to yourself, nothing can take away your freedom. Hurray!

Neptune Retrograde

People with Neptune retrograde can easily feel that life is absurd. It seems like the outer world in no way has room for their inner longings. Spirituality and belief can be really hard to hold onto, since the world of your dreams seems so far away, in a fairy-tale land that you are told is just a fairy-tale land. So you easily lose your belief in what exists inside yourself. You could also become some kind of fundamentalist, trying to force your inner world onto the outer. Anyway, there seems to be an unbridgeable gap between the inner and the outer, and deep down you feel the absurdity of an outer Saturn world that doesn't have room for your inner Neptunian landscape.

With Neptune retrograde, you have to find your own understanding of religion, spirituality, and the world of spirit and soul. I can guarantee that following some kind of established religion like a sheep follows the shepherd will lead you nowhere except to the slaughterhouse. There is an inner landscape you have to discover and explore yourself if you want to harvest the benefits of Neptune. One of the benefits you get by making this effort is getting in contact with your dreams and visions, which allows you to become aware of what you really feel a great longing toward. Neptune is also associated with love, but a more encompassing sort of love than Venusian satisfaction. Through working with Neptune, you start to understand that everything that exists in the outer world first has existed as a dream in the inner world. And the reason that the world seems so absurd is that the dream you carry is one that doesn't already exist in the outer world, but rather one you have been born to create as well as you can. Neptune gives you a contact with the dreams and purpose of your soul. In a way, it cuts through the illusion of the outer to see that inner reality is the one reality that really exists. Through manifesting and encompassing your Neptune, the inner world becomes tangible and meaningful, and the gap between outer and inner doesn't seem absurd. Instead, this gap becomes a doorway from which you can channel your dreams, love, and soul intention into the world.

Pluto Retrograde

Pluto is the joy and fun of every horoscope, whether it is retrograde or not. That was a joke—or maybe it wasn't.

Pluto is concerned with fate and the law of life and death on the physical level, and the law of change and eternity on the spiritual level. As individuals, we seem to be more or less fated. But there seems to be a difference in how much slack we have with this thing called fate. When Pluto is direct, it is like fate comes and drags you along and you have to do your best on your way in life. With Pluto retrograde, it can feel like fate has passed you by, and you start to wonder why nothing of real importance happens to you. In simpler terms, Pluto retrograde says that you have to create a lot of your own fate. This gives you a greater freedom, but it also gives you a greater chance of missing possibilities. Pluto direct is like a life in which loads and burdens are put on your shoulders and you have to deal with them. With the bugger retrograde, you have to unload first so that you can get a new load and go somewhere with it. People with Pluto retrograde very often spend much of their early life going inward. They know there is a great treasure somewhere inside, but they have to follow the treasure map, find the place, and do the digging. When that is done, it seems that the "real" life can begin.

So having Pluto retrograde can be very confusing: you don't know where to go or why, but as soon as you have found the treasure, the direction sorts itself out. The story about the count of Monte Cristo is a good example for retrograde Pluto. Pluto represents both karma and dharma. Karma is the engraved patterns you carry with you from former times. Dharma is the possibilities of what you can become in this life. With Pluto retrograde, your first task is to understand, and eventually to change, your karma, and the second is to create and carry out your dharma. With Pluto direct, the two go more hand in hand.

You meet old karma at the same time as you create new karma and strive to accomplish your dharma.

Something that is important to know for everybody, but especially for Pluto-retrograde people, is that when nothing happens, great changes can occur. Pluto-retrograde people can also feel that they have no power or influence in the world. A common reaction to this is resisting: to show their power and will by resisting both their fate and the power of others. But as soon as they get a better understanding of their inner power and authority, these people start to move out into the world with great presence and determination. So Pluto retrograde is a strange fellow. You have to dig out the old, rotten stuff before you can really understand the light. You have to work with fate and accept fate. But the more you accept fate and what you cannot change, the more you get freedom and the ability to change.

A good thing for Pluto-retrograde people is to acknowledge and encompass their inner feeling of powerlessness. Through losing their fear of losing power, they arrive at a place where they can handle power in the outer world in a good way. The inner fear and insecurity must be faced first, however, so that they will not be misled into abusive or self-destructive behavior when they meet their own fear reflected in the outer world. The soul has chosen this Pluto position so that it can learn surrender and how to trust fate enough so that power will not be misused. By accepting and becoming what is their fate, these people can become real transformers. When spiritual law is understood and internalized, they can become movers and changers of fate and destiny. Their influence and power will be a steadfast pulse. Since they are here to learn to let go, to fight against outer adversaries will never work for them. They have to learn that to fight against something is to empower what you fight against. Instead of negativity and destructiveness, they should cultivate the ability to use their power for everything that is good and valuable. The right use of power for these people is to use their power to empower others and to support what is moving the now into the future in a harmonious and good fashion, without fighting against the negativity of the world. To be able to do this, they have to have cleared out the negativity in their inner landscape. And if they have a fate, it is to be confronted with their own negativity, so that they can get rid of it. The soul wants to clear out the old garbage from earlier times and move on to what really matters: the transformation of matter into more beauty, light, love, and wisdom.

ASTROLOGY AND TIME

We live in a world that is confined by time and space. Of course, we also live in an eternal timeless world, but it is hard to remember this when you have to handle the world of time and space all the time.

Science has made great developments in our understanding of space. We have explored a bit of outer space, as well as a bit of inner space, through psychology and other means. What science still has is a very poor understanding of time. And since astrology is the science and art of understanding the quality and movement of time, astrology is the missing piece in our minds' understanding of the world we live in.

Astrology is the science of time, not only psychologically but also on a physical level. The movement of the planets creates time. The daily rotation of Earth creates day and night. Earth's movement around the Sun creates the year. The development and understanding that astrology can bring to science will be the missing link for bringing our understanding of the reality of the time-space that we live in to a whole new level.

We live in a time in which the very experience of time is changing. In the beginning, everything seemed to repeat itself endlessly. If you have to stand in line for the next development for some millions of years, time does not really have any significance. The first capability life on Earth developed was instinct. You do as your great-great-great-great-grandfather/mother amoeba did, and it worked. As life became more complex, individual life had to develop new strategies to survive. In a

246 ASTROLOGY AND TIME

crisis, life has two possible reactions: fight or flight, to solve the problem or to avoid the challenge. As life became more complex, more things began to occur in the same time span. The next strategy life developed was emotional reaction. This happened around the time when dinosaurs became extinct and warm-blooded mammals took over Earth. Even in our language, to have feelings is associated with being warm-blooded. Feelings gave animals the capability to react on an individual level when something scary or inviting popped up.

But as life became even more complex, feelings did not save the day. Thus, life started to develop mind, the ability to think and consider a situation before you acted. Mind freed humans from being slaves to emotions and instincts, but at the same time it made it possible to lose contact with instincts and emotions. In that respect, it was—and is—a two-edged sword. This happened around the time when Cro-Magnon man took over the planet and the Neanderthals said goodbye and thank you for the company.

So the list for the first sixteen million years of development looks like this:

1. Instinct: cell memory and not connected to free will.

2. Emotions: personal inner reactions; individual adjusting to a situation.

3. Thinking: giving choices; the ability to postpone action and choose the road less traveled.

Today, more and more things happen at the same time. We often meet more people and get more information in one day than people got throughout a whole life in the Middle Ages. Time has started to move so fast that our minds have problems keeping up with the pace. The stress of our days comes from the fact that most people face situations that they cannot solve (fight), but they have no way to avoid the same dilemmas (flight).

In other words, the time has come for the development of a new faculty.

This faculty is connected to what we call intuition and awareness. Just as the industrial revolution freed our bodies from the really hard work of physical labor and created machines that could perform the labor faster and better than the human body, the computers are there to free our minds from the mechanical processes of the consciousness. Whereas machines were and are an externalization of our body, the computer is an externalization of our mind. In this respect, the Internet is an outward manifestation of our collective consciousness.

The development of this new faculty is like a fourth step on a staircase. If you do not have a good foundation on the first three steps, the fourth will be unsteady and undependable. The first three steps are, as mentioned, instinct, emotions, and thinking. Our thinking needs a good foundation in the emotions. If not, our thinking can be either very cold and inhuman, or just based on repressed emotion and not at all as logical as we would like to believe.

Emotions that run wild without having a foundation in good instincts will take us to places we never wanted to go in the first place. An example might be a woman who always marries psychopathic men. She gets emotionally attracted to these men because her father was the same sort. Her cell memory and instinctual reactions are very self-destructive, and she has to do some work through the mind to become aware of this so that she can guide her emotions with consciousness. Through this process, she will (hopefully) be able to rearrange her instinctual and emotional patterns.

Much of the work that is done in the self-development business these days is the reparation of these three first steps.

These steps can also be associated with the elements. We could say that the arrival of life in itself was the very first step. This emerging of life can be connected to the element of fire, and maybe especially to Aries, which is the starting point of the zodiac. The development of instincts can be connected to the element of earth, and maybe especially to Taurus, the builder and preserver of life. The second step of developing emotions is connected to the element of water, and it might also be linked with Cancer and the capability of feeling connection and love. The third step was about the development of mind and rational decision. It is connected to the element of air, and it may be especially linked with Gemini and the ability to learn new things and see different options.

The next step, which is intuition, is connected to the element of fire, and it might be seen as especially connected to the sign of Leo. It is an interesting thought that as we move into the Age of Aquarius and the collective experience and understanding of humanity as one being, we need to develop our individual connection to a greater source, and the faculty that makes this possible is the faculty of intuition.

But then, what is intuition? Is it the sixth or seventh sense, is it female intuition, or is it the ability to know without knowing? There can be many ways of getting closer to an understanding of this concept, but it has to be a constant ability that can be learned and used all the time. Thinking does not function very well if you have to sit and hope for the mind to work, and then say hooray when some thoughts pop into your head. A developed intuition is with you always, in the same way that instincts, emotions, and mind are always present as a possibility.

The mind solves problems by seeing the available data and basing an opinion on this external information. It has to have the data, and when the data starts to become overwhelming, the mind gets overloaded and we have a breakdown. Today, our minds have too small processors and too little RAM (random access memory) to sift through all the information coming at us.

That fact that the world is changing faster and faster gives the mind another new problem. The mind seems to base its decision on previous experience: what worked yesterday should work today. But as the world changes, as seen by generation gaps and other things, yesterday's solution is not only unusable today but is tomorrow's catastrophe.

Wisdom and knowledge become separated when your understanding of a situation is based on your own outdated experiences. This is the reason that the number of stupid old people is growing rapidly. All their life experience doesn't make them better equipped to understand and govern the world. Quite the opposite: they are worse than beginners because they try to solve tomorrow's problems with yesterday's solutions. Mere knowledge becomes out of date very quickly, but wisdom has no expiration date.

Intuition is closely connected to the concept of awareness. In my understanding, intuition is the ability of an entity to be in contact with both itself and the whole at the same time. The development of the personal identity is a necessary foundation for this step into awareness. When you have a clear and solid connection with yourself as an individual point of focused energy, you have a point of reference from which you can experience the condition of the whole. The decisions and movements you take then will not be based either on the past or on the mind. Instead, they will be based on the relationship between you and the whole, as it exists in the moment you move or make a decision. What is right today and in one situation might be wrong five minutes later or in another similar situation. By "wrong," I mean that it would not be the correct thing to do because it would not fulfill your intentions or needs. The development of this faculty is in fact necessary if we are going to survive as a race. The only thing you have to do to develop this reality is to develop your capacity of awareness in every moment, awareness of yourself, and awareness of the condition of the smaller and lesser units that you are a part of. To do this is necessary if you as an individual want to avoid the enormous amount of stress that is created by the increasing complexity in our society.

This ends this book. I hope that you have had a pleasant journey and that you might have received some new ideas about how astrology can help you to listen to the music of your soul and the spheres. I will let Alice Bailey have the last word, with a quote about the importance of astrology in our day. This comes from her book *Esoteric Astrology*, which, by the way, describes a very different esoteric or spiritual astrology from what you have been reading in this book.

> Astrology is *essentially* the purest presentation of occult truth in the world at this time, because it is the science which deals with those conditioning and governing energies and forces which play through and upon the whole field of space and all that is found within that field.[1]

---

1. *Esoteric Astrology*, Twelfth printing 1979. Copyright 1951 by Lucis Trust. Lucis Publishing Company New York. Lucis Press LTD. London. Manufactured in the USA. By Fort Orange Press Inc, Albany N.Y.

To Write to the Author

If you wish to contact the author or would like more information about this book, please write to the author in care of Llewellyn Worldwide and we will forward your request. Both the author and publisher appreciate hearing from you and learning of your enjoyment of this book and how it has helped you. Llewellyn Worldwide cannot guarantee that every letter written to the author can be answered, but all will be forwarded. Please write to:

Per Henrik Gullfoss
℅ Llewellyn Worldwide
2143 Wooddale Drive, Dept. 978-0-7387-1258-1
Woodbury, MN 55125-2989, U.S.A.

Please enclose a self-addressed stamped envelope for reply,
or $1.00 to cover costs. If outside U.S.A., enclose
international postal reply coupon.

Many of Llewellyn's authors have websites with additional information and resources. For more information, please visit our website at http://www.llewellyn.com